WHAT IS A
JEWISH JOKE?

WHAT IS A JEWISH JOKE?

An Excursion into Jewish Humor

Henry Eilbirt

JASON ARONSON INC.
Northvale, New Jersey
London

First Softcover Printing 1993

Copyright © 1981 by Henry Eilbirt

10 9 8 7 6 5 4 3 2 1

Library of Congress Cataloging-in-Publication Data

Eilbirt, Henry, 1914—
    What is a Jewish joke? : an excursion into Jewish humor / Henry Eilbirt
        p. cm.
    Includes bibliographical references and index.
    ISBN 0-87668-669-2 (hb)
    ISBN 0-87668-217-4 (pb)
    1. Jewish wit and humor. I. Title.
PN6231.J5E37 1991
818'.5402—dc20   90-22585

Manufactured in the United States of America. Jason Aronson Inc. offers books and cassettes. For information and catalog write to Jason Aronson Inc., 230 Livingston Street, Northvale, New Jersey 07647.

To my father

whose pleasure from hearing and telling a joke
became part of my inheritance

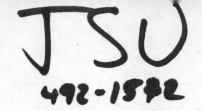

Contents

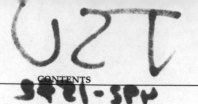

2

The Jewish Joke

3

This Is Your Life

4

If You Cut Me, Will I Not Bleed?

Epilogue

And in Conclusion   285

Preface

Is another Jewish jokebook really necessary? There are already a number of good collections of such jokes, those by Spalding, Novak and Waldoks, Wilde, Mindess, Learsi and, perhaps above all, Nathan Ausubel. Still another volume should, therefore, have something new to say.

The book into which you are about to dip starts with the assumption that many, if not most, real Jewish jokes are related to the conditions of Jewish life, Jewish experience, Jewish history, and the way in which these matters are perceived. Each of the many jokes here has been connected with some phase of Jewish existence.

You will, therefore, find that the arrangement of topics is different, very different from that of all other jokebooks.

I have tried to keep the style of this book as informal as possible because it is not intended as some kind of academic text. The jokes are printed in an obvious format so that the reader can pick out whichever jests he or she chooses to examine and read. Or, the reader may prefer to read the explanations and the jokes in order to understand better why and where such a joke might originate. Take your choice.

The book is an outcome of my own experience, for I have

been a teller of jests for many decades. I am indebted to my friend, Jerome Greenblatt, who suggested several years ago that I put together a platform lecture on the subject for a Jewish organization which he then headed. For the first time I realized that such an address really needed a structure and I began to think seriously about the nature of Jewish humor.

I am also grateful to my sister-in-law, Ruth Meir, who first made me aware of an International Conference on Jewish Humor. A presentation followed.

At a subsequent conference during which I had the opportunity of again giving a talk on the subject, Professor Sarah Blacher Cohen of the University of the State of New York at Albany suggested that I write a book on the subject.

It is this chain of unplanned causes that led me to the unexpected result of preparing a work of this kind.

I want also to acknowledge the encouragement I received from Arthur Kurzweil, vice-president of Jason Aronson, as well as the editorial help provided by Ilene McGrath and Gloria Jordan. My deepest gratitude must necessarily go to my wife, Jeannette, my most faithful audience and most severe critic, for bearing with my repetition of stories over the years and for the many suggestions she made while the book was in preparation.

And now the time has come for you to enjoy and benefit from an excursion into Jewish humor.

Before I Start Talking

Sam Goldwyn is supposed to have said: "Before I start talking, I want to say something."

So, before I start talking about Jewish jokes, I want to say something about jokes in general.

What is there to talk about? you may ask. Jokes speak for themselves.

True. But if you were to attend an international conference on humor, you would hear professors from all over the world reading scholarly articles—examining, dissecting, researching, analyzing. An old Russian proverb says that nothing is more serious than a joke. There may be more here than meets the eye—or the ear. Perhaps a closer look is in order.

Most people think you're not supposed to analyze humor. As someone has said, "A joke that is analyzed is no longer a joke." The essayist E. B. White has remarked that "humor can be dissected like a hog but it will die in the process." It has also been said that "trying to define humor is one of the definitions of humor."

And yet, Aristotle noted, "A jest that will not bear serious examination is false wit."

But it can't hurt to philosophize a little, speculate a little, psychoanalyze a little. We'll read a few jokes—laugh at some, disagree on others. Let's look at some jokes and, more important, look behind and inside them.

1

Meet the Joke

What's So Funny?

First of all—what *is* a joke? It's something to laugh at, you might say. But if you don't laugh, is it still a joke? Well, somebody else might laugh. Exactly.

There is a study in which some thousands of people were asked to rate several dozen jokes. For every single joke, some people said "very funny" while others said "not at all funny." Every joke had at least 500 people thinking it was hilarious and at least 1,000 saying it was the pits. Obviously, no joke pleases everybody.

The dictionary tells us that a joke is "something said or done to provoke laughter or amusement." So, it appears that it's the intention that counts. And yet some jokes are accidental. We've all had the experience of saying something and suddenly realizing that it's funny. And sometimes something is said that doesn't seem funny to you but is hilarious to others.

For example, Isaac Asimov tells a story about a man pushing a horse up the stairs of a boarding house.

"What are you doing?" screams the landlady.
"I'm going to put this horse into the bathtub on the second floor. Then, when all these wiseguys who never laugh at my jokes and tell me that 'they've heard them all before' go in there, they'll come rushing out to tell me there's a horse in the bathtub. And then I'll smile and tell them I've heard that story before."

Not a terribly funny story, but the reaction of Asimov's father to the telling is funnier. "Isaac," he said, "you're making a fool out of yourself. You're a city boy and you have no idea of how much a horse weighs. You can't push it into a bathtub if it doesn't want to go."

Obviously, the seriousness with which the father listened to the joke is funnier than the story itself.

An even better example is Sam Levenson's supposedly true story about being taken to the museum, together with his brothers. Naturally, they stopped to look closely at the pictures that interested them. Soon their father exclaimed: "Hurry up! Don't dawdle by every picture. If you're going to stop and look at everything, you won't see anything."

But the crowning glory of unintentional humor is probably found in the papers students write for their teachers. Thus, one English teacher reported:

Socrates died from an overdose of wedlock.
Floods can be prevented by putting dames in the water.
The death of Francis Macomber was a turning point in his life.
The difference between a king and a president is that a king is the son of his father and a president isn't.
A virgin forest is a place where the hand of man has never set foot.

True, these are all from schoolchildren, and they *are* just learning. The following, however, were written by adults reporting accidents to their insurance companies.

I thought my window was down, but found it was up when I put my hand through it.

A pedestrian hit me and went under my car.

This guy was all over the place. I had to swerve a number of times before I hit him.

I was on the way to the doctor's with rear-end trouble when my universal joint gave way, causing me to have an accident.

It's interesting that the dictionary definition uses the phrase, "to tell a joke" rather than "to *see* a joke." Physical humor, then, what clowns or mimes do, are not jokes in the usual sense. They might better be called "pranks." Jokes have what can be called "oralness": they are told and they are heard. They can, of course, be read as well. They will be in this book. But when we read them, we are really listening to them in our heads. As a well-known playwright has noted: "In reading, a voice comes to you and whispers. . . ."

Catching On

We've established the importance of joke *telling*. But we also know that you can tell someone a joke that you think is hilarious and get a blank stare. There are jokes and there are *jokes*. It's true that not everything we laugh at is a joke and not all jokes are funny enough to get a laugh. Furthermore, the same joke won't get the same laugh everywhere and every time, even if told by the same person.

There are even different kinds of laughs. Did you ever hear a comic do a routine about laughter types—the hearty *ho, ho, ho*; the people who throw back their heads with a hysterical *ha, ha, ha*; the person who just titters *hee, hee, hee*; the one who gives you only a fragmentary smile; and finally old stoneface; the person who either doesn't think you are funny, or can't laugh for some physical reason, or doesn't get the point.

In fact, the question of who laughs is itself the subject of jokes. The story is told about a Polish, English (or any other "stupid" aristocrat) who laughs three times any time he is told a story: first when the joke is told, again when it is expalined to him, and finally when he "gets" it!

There have always been people who miss the point of a story. A French doctor who wrote about humor in the sixteenth century noted, "Sometimes laughter does not come suddenly because we are slow to understand an obscure, difficult, complex, or ambiguous situation." Probably he was just being polite. Some people just can't catch on!

But why should anybody have to "catch on"? The answer is, because the story teller has *left a gap!* The listener has to make the jump to see the connection. If he or she does, the joke makes sense and the listener laughs or smiles. Here is an example of *gap*:

> The scene is set during the days of chivalry. A knight comes tearing up to an inn, on a horse covered with sweat and foaming at the mouth. The knight runs into the inn and shouts: "Mine host, mine host, I have immediate need of a new mount. I carry great news to the king and must perforce ride at once to his court. What animal is here?"
>
> The innkeeper shakes his head unhappily and answers, "My lord, we have no such animal as you require."
>
> At this moment, a huge dog ambles into the inn. The knight looks at the animal and turns to the innkeeper, saying, "Saddle me yon hound and I will ride him to court!"
>
> To this, the innkeeper responds: "My lord, he is old and short of wind. I would not send a knight out on a dog like this."

This joke will mean nothing to you if you don't know the original "I wouldn't send a dog out on a night like this." But if you do know it and grasp the inversion on which the jest is built, you may smile—or even laugh.

Let's call this the *get-it effect*.

Not all jokes have a gap. Take the following Old-World Jewish story for example.

> Consider the Jewish man, whose wife is constantly berating and insulting him. One Friday evening he watches her as she says the prayers while lighting the Sabbath candles. He is so

struck by the tenderness and devotion of her piety, that he asks, "Why don't you ever bless me as tenderly as you are blessing those candles?"

She instantly replies, "When you burn like the candles, I will bless you too!"

Here the unexpected twist of her suggesting that her husband burn like the candles is straightforward. There is no real gap. Even the above-mentioned Polish nobleman might laugh at this the first time with understanding.

A joke that carries a get-it effect may be considered more subtle. The teller is expecting you to participate and to be delighted not only by the joke, but also by the fact that you get the point. The next time you hear (or read) a joke with the get-it effect, see if you aren't satisfied really by having "jumped the gap."

Two people may have different perceptions of a punch line of a particular story. For example, Freud was fond of the following, which occurs in one of the books of the German writer, Heinrich Heine.

> Heine derisively describes a "lottery agent and curer of corns" who boasts: "As true as I pray that the Lord may grant me all good things, I sat next to Solomon Rothschild, who treated me just as if I were his equal, quite *famillionaire*."

First of all, it's obvious that if the statement stopped after the word *equal*, this would hardly be a joke. Unless we know the man and realize he is boasting, the words are pretty matter of fact. What really generates our amusement is the creation of the new word: *famillionaire*. When I read this, I concluded that this man is saying that he regards himself as a member of a millionaire family, similar to that of Rothschild, which is, of course, the silliest kind of boasting.

But look at how Freud interprets the statement: "Rothschild treated me quite as his equal, in a very familiar way; *that is, as far as this can be done by a millionaire* [italics mine]." Now how in the world he gets that interpretation, I fail to see. Maybe *you* can. The point is that a joke that has a gap calling for a get-it reaction may turn out to be seen in different ways by different people.

Another aspect of jokes is that some seem to last forever—some even going back to the ancient Greeks—while others have a sort of life cycle. Examples of the latter are political satire, which goes out of date very quickly, and any topical humor, jokes about current celebrities or events. One of Freud's translators notes a joke about the abdication of Edward VIII—*a case of Gone with the Windsor*. This is a word play which combined the event with the famous movie. Would it mean anything to a contemporary audience? I doubt it would get anything but a quizzical look. When was the last time you heard a traveling salesman joke? Once a staple of male talk, they're disappearing, "going out of style."

Big Jokes and Little Jokes

Although you may never have thought about it, jokes come in different shapes and sizes. There are, in fact, all sorts of classifications but for our purpose here we will consider two basic types, based on size or length.

First are the *little jokes*—one-liners, insults, zingers, wisecracks, putdowns, as well as epigrams and puns. Let's call these *jokebits*. Perhaps the most famous jokebit is Henny Youngman's "Take my wife . . . please!" Or this silly insult "May the bird of paradise fly you to Hawaii . . . and drop you in a volcano."

One-liners are not necessarily limited to one sentence. Thus:

Don't put your trust in money. Put your money in trust.

Alternatively, there is comedian Fred Allen's great pun:

Hanging is too good for a man who makes puns. He should be drawn and quoted.

Nor are all one-liners insults or putdowns. Some can be quite serious, even though they have a humorous face. When Adlai Stevenson observed, "An Independent is someone who wants to take the politics out of politics," he was expressing a serious notion in a funny casing. A meaningful idea in funny clothes is an *epigram*. Here's another one:

> Human life is divided into two halves: during the first, we look forward to the second; and during the second, we look back to the first.

Obviously, these are not hilarious rib-ticklers. But they are clever ways of saying something that could be said in a more boring manner and at greater length. Such comments are what we usually refer to as witty. And wit is certainly a form of humor.

Folk sayings are similar to epigrams but lack authors. They arise from the common sense of the people. For example, Proverbs 24:17 cautions us:

> Rejoice not at thine enemy's fall.

Eastern European Jews, with plenty of enmity to face, converted this saying into:

> When your enemy falls, you must not gloat—but you don't have to pick him up either.

Not all "little jokes" are one-liners. Some are in dialog form.

> *Student:* Rabbi, why did God make man before woman?
> *Rabbi:* Because he didn't want any advice on how to make man!

One can see that this could also have been in the form of a one-liner, beginning "God made man before woman because. . . ."

Repartee and retorts are examples of "duolog," too.

A: That young woman certainly is polished.
B: Right. And everything she says casts a reflection on some-one.

This, of course, is a pun on the words *reflection* and *polished.* While puns make some people groan, others are very fond of them. English essayist Charles Lamb once noted: "I never knew an enemy of puns who was not an ill-natured man. A pun is a noble thing. . . . May my last breath be drawn through a pipe and exhaled as a pun."

A contrary view was expressed by novelist George Meredith in his book on comedy: "The sense of the comic is much blunted by the habits of punning."

Some puns are also one-liners:

TV is called a medium because it's rarely well-done.

Others may be a sort of compound one-liner, such as the following sign on a music store window:

GONE CHOPIN; BACH IN A MINUET. DON'T TRY HANDEL; IT'S BAROQUE.

And as you will see, some puns are regular jokes.

Historical personalities are often masters of the devastating one-liner. Winston Churchill was famous for his wit. For example:

Churchill was once talking to another member of Parliament when Clement Attlee, the leader of the opposition Labour Party, walked in. His colleague observed, "There goes a modest man."

Churchill immediately responded, "And no man has more to be modest about."

Now what is the main difference between "little jokes" and "big jokes"? The answer is that little jokes *have no story line!* The punch line shows up immediately, before any kind of drama can be developed. Before the listeners or readers have a chance to prepare themselves—boom, the joke is over.

Where does the monolog fit in, the kind that stand-up comics use? Many of them are just a series of one-liners strung together like beads. Here's Woody Allen at work:

> I was breast-fed through falsies. My parents worshipped old-world values—God and carpeting. We were too poor to own a dog; so my parents went to a damaged pet store and bought me an ant. My neighborhood was so tough that the kids stole hubcaps—from moving cars. They broke my violin—and left it embedded in my body.

Some monologists alternate one-liners with longer jokes. Some of the more clever routines, such as Lily Tomlin's telephone operator or Bob Newhart's telephone bit, are really suppressed dialog. All though the monolog you can guess what the other party is saying. The form is monolog, but the reality is dialog.

If these wisecracks, epigrams, and duologs are the joke-bits, then, what are the big jokes? These are the jokes proper, the j.p. We'll call them *japes*.

In summary, jokebits have no story line; they are all punch line. Japes have both a story line and a punch line.

How Jokes Work

Now that you've seen the outside of the package and know jokebits from japes, it's time to look "inside the joke."

But first, let me say something about the *performance* involved in telling a joke. Keep in mind that a joke is a sort of mini-comedy, a short play. The performance is so important that one psychoanalyst who wrote about humor noted, "We shuld not speak of the teller of Jewish [or any kind of] stories but of their actors." Gesture, tone, facial expression, body movements—all convey meaning which the bare words cannot. The teller's role cannot be overestimated.

The telling of a joke involves three parties. First is the narrator, who tells the story. Second are the internal actors, the "cast" of the mini-comedy. Finally, there's an audience, who may be only one person.

The boss in this grouping is obviously the narrator, who is not only the main actor (the story teller) but at the same time the director of the internal dialog. Thus *the narrator is the controller of the whole joke-telling apparatus*. Obviously, the internal actors are his puppets. What the narrator can't control is the audience. Even professionals lose their composure, as in the case of one who was "bombing" on stage and, therefore, remarked "These jokes have always gone over before; it must be this audience." Woody Allen reportedly has said that, from the audience's point of view, he's right only about 75 percent of the time about what he thinks is funny! As we saw earlier, not everyone appreciates any given joke and yet there will almost certainly be someone to laugh at it.

It is also said that Jewish audiences can be very tough: when you tell them a story, you often get the comment: "That old chestnut I've heard before and told much better!" This attitude is illustrated in the following Old World Jewish joke, an example of the longer joke, or jape.

A man is sitting in a railroad car compartment and an older man enters, wearing a skullcap. He sits down, greets the other man, sighs, puts his head back, and closes his eyes. No sooner does the train start when the older man begins a strange sequence of actions. First he mumbles something to himself, then his face breaks out into a broad smile, and then he puts up his hand, palm out, in an obvious stop motion.

After he has done this five or six times, his companion, who has been getting more and more curious, finally asks him, "Friend, what is this strange business with the mumbling, smiling, and hand motion?"

The old gentlemen replies: "Oy, young man, this is going to be a long trip for me. So what should I do to make it more tolerable? So, when I mumble, that's because I'm telling myself a joke. When I smile, it's because it's funny. And when I hold up my hand, it's to remind myself that I've heard it before!"

So much for the triple cast of characters. Let's now get inside the joke. If your doctor wants to look inside your head, what does he do? He sends you to a CAT-scanning machine. We will look at these jokes through an imaginary "joke CAT-scanning machine."

First keep in mind that all japes are mini-plays and have a "plot." Things happen. The conversation suggests some sequence of occurrence. A good story teller will be building tension, with the audience waiting. As James Humes puts it, "A humorous story is like a balloon; you pump it up with details and then puncture it with a punch line."

But if the audience is not expecting a joke, then isn't the element of tension missing? My guess is that we always have enough tension that can stand relief. Or maybe we're just conditioned to laugh or smile at the unexpected and incongruous. What *is* clear is that the laugh explosion does release energy and break tension. Why does this happen?

The answer must be somewhere in the plot idea! Consider something as simple as Henny Youngman's famous one-liner, "Take my wife . . . please!" If you hadn't heard it before, and especially if you didn't know that Youngman is a comic, then you would expect a normal sequel. When Youngman said, "take my wife," you would expect, "My wife did so and so yesterday" or "Such and such happened to her." But the single word—*please*—puts a wholly different picture before you, what has been called "a sudden alteration in view." The direction of talk has undergone a sharp reversal. *Something doesn't fit!* A usual pattern of perception has been distorted.

So, the combination of incongruity and surprise is what makes us laugh, or at least smile. The two parts, the prelude (*take my wife*) and the punch line (*please*), have a connection which you can fill in, even though they normally do not go together!

Does there have to be a connection? For instance, if I say

to you, "Tomorrow is Wednesday and my computer is broken," you may think it incongruous and surprising and you may think me a little odd, but you probably would not laugh at it. (You might think I am going off my rocker, and you might laugh *at* me, but you wouldn't see it as a joke.)

Most of the time, then, there is a connection between the "front" of the joke and the punch line. But there doesn't have to be. What do you think of this?

> On March 16, 1882, Mr. J. C. Dubbs awoke in the middle of the night and saw his brother Amos, who had been dead for fourteen years, sitting at the foot of his bed flicking [plucking] chickens. Dubbs asked his brother what he was doing there; and his brother said not to worry, he was dead and only in town for the weekend.

Now, if you had no other information, you might conclude these sentences came from the ravings of a certified lunatic. In fact, they were written by Woody Allen!

Obviously, there is no logical connection between being dead and flicking chickens. And yet when a talented comedy writer puts it together, it *is* funny; in an asylum, it might not be. Clearly, then, the conditions under which you perceive the incongruity do matter.

Incongruity therefore depends on being out of line *under certain conditions*. What's incongruous in one time and one place may get only a blank stare in another time and place. Especially place. What would be funny to an Indian or African may not mean enough to be incongruous to Americans. The Navaho Yellowman stories get a lot of laughter in that environment, but we would be unable to understand how anyone could think them funny. Similarly, the formal Japanese comic (the *Rakugoka*) would almost certainly leave us stone cold.

When there is very little surprise or very little incongruity, you normally don't get much of a joke. Yet this is sometimes the case with epigrams or anecdotes. They are wry or witty, but they don't have a "real" punch line, and most don't have a story line. The moral is that there is no foolproof yardstick for incongruous or surprising. You just know it when you see or hear it.

Let's consider another example. When Mark Twain observed, "Let me talk of scoundrels," we have a very matter-of-fact sentence. But then he adds, "Let me talk about Congress." Now where did that come from? Finally, he punctures the balloon he has built up with the remark, "But, ladies and gentlemen, I repeat myself." Here again incongruity and surprise, with the listener or reader suddenly seeing a connection!

Mark Twain's sardonic remark is really a jokebit, an almost-one-liner. Let's see how this same idea works in a real jape. Here is a joke currently being told in Israel.

> *Aleph:* Do you know that the Messiah cannot come at this time?
> *Beit:* Why not?
> *Aleph:* Don't you remember? He will carry no sword, head no army, but come simply, riding on a donkey.
> *Beit:* But that doesn't explain why he can't come now.
> [*Up to here, simple conversation. Now watch.*]
> *Aleph:* You really don't see what I'm getting at. Where will the Messiah find a donkey? Don't you know that all the donkeys are sitting in the Knesset [Israeli Parliament]?!!

To repeat, *the basic mechanism which makes a joke work is the incongruity between the "front" part and the finale, the "punch line," which is unexpected, surprising, not appropriate to what has gone before even though it may appear to have some connection to the prelude.* Note that both incongruity and surprise are needed. O. Henry was noted for his surprise endings in his short stories, but these are not out of line or incongruous with what has occurred before in the story. Similarly, detective novels necessarily have surprise endings, but these too normally follow reasonably what has gone before. In both cases, the surprise is appropriate.

Remember, though, that incongruity and surprise are not always funny. As you saw earlier, they are sometimes a sign of "nutty" (today is Wednesday and my computer is broken). Or, they can be puzzling. If you opened your refrigerator and found your bowling ball there, would you think it funny? You

might, but you would more likely be astonished, and maybe
even annoyed. Similarly, if you were surprised to find a discrepancy between your checkbook and your bank statement,
you would most likely be uncomfortable and annoyed. No joke
there. And if at your annual physical your doctor found incongruity between your feeling well and your test results, you
would see this surprise as disagreeable and maybe dangerous.

Clearly, the surprise/incongruity must not contain disagreeable or bewildering aspects if it is to be amusing. It's been
said that humor is like guerilla warfare: Its success depends on
traveling light [short and snappy punch lines], striking unex-
pectedly [surprise], and getting away fast [don't, repeat, don't
try to explain the point of the joke; it rarely if ever works].

Now, here's a test to see how incongruity and surprise
work. I will use a story about the Jews of Chelm, a Polish city
whose inhabitants are known as specialists in foolishness.
There are whole books retailing these jokes; some probably
never saw the inside of Chelm.

> The cobbler of Chelm has just discovered that his wife has
> been unfaithful; he actually caught her in the act with a friend
> of his. As you might expect, he is beside himself. So he does
> something you rarely meet in Jewish humor, he grabs a knife
> and kills them both—in full view of witnesses!
>
> Well, the whole thing is a scandal. The town's rabbi calls
> a meeting of the council, but the whole town attends. The wit-
> nesses are heard and an open poll of the council decides on the
> death penalty. (Don't ask how a town council has the authority
> to impose a death sentence. There is an old Yiddish saying that
> about a story one doesn't ask questions.)
>
> The rabbi informs the cobbler: "Mordecai, we have no
> choice. You did it; you were seen doing it; you don't even deny
> it. Tomorrow morning we will have to hang you." There is a
> general murmur of assent in the assembly.

Your suspense should have been built up by this point.
Now stop and ask yourself what happens next. Do you have
any idea? Take a minute or two and work out an ending before
you read on. OK?

Before the murmur of assent has died down, Joseph, the town dissenter, calls out from the back of the room. "Rabbi, you're forgetting something. Mordecai is our one and only cobbler. If we hang him, who will mend our shoes?" Again there is murmured agreement in the hall.

The rabbi thinks. He consults with council members while lively conversations are going on throughout the audience, and then he holds up his hand for silence.

"Friends and neighbors," he says, "we have arrived at a better solution. True, we have only one cobbler, but we have two tailors. We'll hang one of them instead!"

Did you guess the ending?

The Jocular Vein—Mechanisms in Humor

Well, now you've met the dramatis personae—the actors involved in delivering a joke—and you understand the importance of the story *teller*. Moreover, you also recognize the *basic* mechanisms that "operate" jokes. Now let's take a look at some other mechanisms you'll find in the construction of jests.

In general, jokes can be divided according to their content into two main categories: *word play* and *observations and reflections about human behavior*.

You've already seen word play in puns. That's just fooling around with words. Remember Fred Allen's "drawn and quoted," which plays with "drawn and quartered." So the pun always has two faces: the words used, and the words to which they refer.

A lady in California gets a letter from her son in Wyoming informing her that he and his brothers have just purchased a cattle ranch and they're having arguments about what to name it. They will abide by her decision. She promptly responds, suggesting the name Prism Ranch.

Within days, her son calls. "Are you okay, Mom?"

"Of course," she answers.

"So why in the world would you suggest that we call our spread the Prism Ranch?"

"It should be obvious," she replies, "it's where the sun's rays meet."

The word *prism* becomes a source of *double entendre,* or double meaning, a very common mechanism. The term *double entendre* has been used mainly for jokes about sex, but there is no reason it should be limited to those.

Another word play mechanism uses *inversion,* taking something well-known and twisting it. An example is one of Oscar Wilde's epigrams: *"Work is the curse of the drinking classes!"* What Wilde did was to reverse a common saying that suggested that drunkenness was characteristic of the working man: Drink is the curse of the working classes.

But word play is not always just fun. It can deal with quite serious matters. Sigmund Freud was a profound student of jokes. One of his stories will illustrate the point.

A man has called a doctor to examine his wife, who appears to be ill. The doctor completes the examination and comes out of the bedroom with a long face. "I don't like the way she looks," he tells the husband.

The husband immediately answers, "I haven't liked the way she's looked for a long time!"

Of course, this story is also an observation on human behavior, but the joke rests on the word play.

You can see that the mechanism of word play depends on the fact that a given word or phrase may have more than one meaning or may be close to a word or phrase with a second meaning. And if you can confuse the two, you can also create a joke.

Some jokes will fall into both the word play and human behavior categories. Here is another of Oscar Wilde's epigrams: *Nothing succeeds like excess.* Clearly, this is an observation on human behavior, but the wit turns on substituting the word *excess* for the more familiar *success* in a common proverb.

There are also jokes that are called *noodle* stories, because they illustrate stupidity. Stupidity, of course, is a type of human behavior, but these are so extreme that they are totally unbelievable. Every culture has them, but here is one from Jewish lore, which takes place in Chelm, the famous city of fools.

> Two citizens of Chelm are talking. One looks at the sky and suddenly asks, "Which do you think is more important, the sun or the moon?"
> "The sun, obviously," is the response.
> "You're wrong."
> "How can I be wrong?"
> "Don't you understand that the moon is more important? After all, the sun shines during the daytime when we don't need it!"

Here is a more modern version of this kind of thinking. Again, two people are talking.

> *Mr. A.:* I'm going to be an astronaut. I want to be the first man to fly to the sun and land on it.
> *Mr. B.:* That's impossible. You'll be burned to a cinder by the heat of the sun.
> *Mr. A.:* No I won't. I plan to fly at night.

Some noodle stories can sound even more "reasonable."

> You see a man running up and down 42nd Street in New York flapping his hands wildly. Curious, you stop him and ask him what he's doing.
> "This is very important work," he tells you. "It keeps the elephants off the street."
> "What are you talking about?" you ask. "There are no elephants in New York."
> He responds, "See, it works!"

Sometimes, such noodle stories reach the highest levels.

> A research specialist in insect behavior has trained a flea to jump when he snaps his fingers. Now he decides on another

experiment. He cuts off the two front legs of the flea and snaps his fingers.

The flea jumps.

He cuts off the two hind legs and snaps his fingers. The flea still jumps, though feebly.

Now he cuts off the remaining two legs. The flea does not jump. So he enters in his notebook the following observation:

"When a flea that has been conditioned to jump at the snap of one's fingers has all its legs removed, it also loses its hearing."

What makes these japes amusing is the *drawing of illogical conclusions from a set of facts*. The incredible stupidity is really an inadequacy in human thinking.

A relative of the noodle story is the story that depends on *anachronism*. To explain anachronism, let's look at old riddles. A man finds a coin dated 482 B.C. What's wrong with that? Right! How could they have known at that time that they were B.C.? So the story is out of sync, as far as time goes. That's anachronism.

Here's another illustration.

Christopher Columbus arrives in the New World on October 12 and wants to cash a check. He is unable to do so, because it's a holiday and the banks are closed. What holiday? Columbus Day, of course.

This next one is somewhat more subtle.

Mary and Joseph are on their way to Jerusalem, pregnant Mary riding the donkey and Joseph walking alongside. Suddenly, Joseph stumbles and twists his ankle. "Jesus Christ," he moans, "that hurts."

Mary looks at him and muses, "Jesus Christ? That'll be a nice name for the baby, if it's a boy."

A related group of "unbelievables" are *tall tales*. These also are found in many countries and cultures. Perhaps you remember Baron Munchausen and his incredible voyages and adventures. For example:

The baron has made a trip to the North Pole. Having arrived there, he begins to sing, but it is so cold that the notes freeze in the air. Several days later a thaw begins and all the songs can now be heard.

If you believe that, you'll believe anything.

An interesting group of tall tales deals with animals. Aesop's fables, many of which are amusing, are usually anecdotes of this sort. More recently, we have the "shaggy dog" story, which gives animals human characteristics. For example:

A man comes into a bar with a dog (a lot of these stories happen in bars, probably because you have to be drunk to tell them or to appreciate them). The dog climbs up on a bar stool next to the man. The man orders a martini and the dog immediately adds: "I'll have one, too—extra dry, straight up, no olive."

The bartender, eyes goggling, turns to the man and says: "That dog is wonderful. Imagine being able to speak and drink just like a person."

"Oh, he's not *that* wonderful," the man responds. "Ever since he began drinking, I've had to drive the car home every time we go out."

Strangely enough, shaggy dog stories aren't only about dogs.

A grasshopper comes into a bar, hops up on a stool, and looks at the bartender.

"I'll have a whiskey and soda," says the insect.

The bartender, who can't believe his eyes and ears, finally stammers, "Do you know that we have a drink named after you?"

The grasshopper looks incredulous. "You mean you have a drink named Irving?"

(You didn't know that there's a drink called a grasshopper? So now you know!)

So tall tales and shaggy dog stories use as their mechanism

the wildly improbable or impossible. They do not illustrate human behavior, nor are they merely word play.

Closely related to the noodle story is *nonsense talk*. One pure form of this is *double-talk*. Sometimes, it can be done as straight talk, as when a comedian, in an imaginary presidential speech, observed, "Where would this country be without this great land of ours?" The only response to that is—huh?

But for real double-talk in action, listen to this.

A professor who has been lecturing to his class for about half an hour sees glazed looks in the eyes of his students. So he tells them: "You take the loose section of the steefil and you snerb it, being careful not to overheat the trufenfoil. Next, extract and wamf it gently for a time and a half. Tursin it twice and quickly place it into the blinger. Remember, you must taffinate the whole instrument in the twetchel. Any questions?"

Well, one student certainly has been listening, because he raises his hand and asks: "Sir, can you please explain what a twetchel is?"

Would you score this one Professor 1, Class 0, or Student 1, Professor 0?

Another cousin of the noodle story is the story whose mechanism is the *exposure of the ignorance or stupidity* of one or more actors in the story. But here it's *credible ignorance*.

Such jokes do not depend on the impossible. Their punch line or thrust rests on what sometimes really happens; someone's ignorance turns out to be funny. Here are some examples.

A man comes into a bank, gets on line, reaches the teller's cage, and presents a check.

"You have to endorse the back," the teller says.

"What's 'at mean?" asks the man.

"Sign your name on the back."

"I ain't writin' my name on no paper. All I want is my money."

"Well, I can't give it to you unless you sign."

Back and forth—sign, no, you must, I won't. Finally, the clerk, exasperated, suggests: "Do you see that man over there at the desk, who is looking at us? He's the manager. Go talk to him."

The check holder approaches the manager, who looks at him, motions for him to come closer, and says very quietly, "Sign the damn check or I'll kick your ass right out of the bank."

The man immediately walks back to the teller, signs the check, and pushes it through the window. The teller, curious at the speed with which this has happened, asks, "What happened when you talked to the manager?"

"Oh," comes the reply, "he explained it to me."

Here's another one.

A couple has recently become rich and they are dying to get into the right set despite their lack of education and social veneer. Well, they are finally invited to a fashionable party, and Mrs. Parvenu is sitting and listening to the talk, her husband standing behind her.

The talk turns to Russian music. Someone speaks of Moussorgsky and how Rimsky-Korsakov helped him with his music. Another person refers to Glinka as the great master of them all. And a third remarks "Yes, and what about Tchaikovsky?"

At this point, Mrs. Parvenu breaks in: "Oh, I saw him on the number 6 bus to Brighton Beach only this morning."

There is a moment of silence and then the guffaws break out. The husband turns red but says nothing. Soon afterward, they leave the party. No sooner is Mr. Parvenu outside, when he explodes: "Stupid, don't you know anything? How many times have I told you that the number 6 bus doesn't go to Brighton Beach?"

A double dose of ignorance is really something to laugh about.

Closely related to this is the mechanism of *error*, the joke that depends on inaccurate use of words. The term *malapropism* has come to mean an inaccurate use of words. Eighteenth-century playwright Sheridan actually created a character, Mrs. Malaprop, in one of his plays, who continually uses words incorrectly. In recent times, no one was better at this than the late Sam Goldwyn. There are stories galore attributed to him.

A writer brought Goldwyn a script. Goldwyn read it and become enthusiastic. "Nice work, young man! I like it and I think we can produce it. I have only one objection. I don't like your title, *The Optimist*. How many people will want to go see a movie about an eye doctor?"

A similar form of humor comes from *misunderstanding*. An example is found in this Old World Jewish joke, which also has appeared in other forms.

It was traditional to invite a guest to the Sabbath meal. In one such case, the householder notices that the guest put a silver spoon into his pocket soon after arriving. An hour later, another spoon.

So the householder inquires, "Why are *my* spoons in *your* pockets?"

The guest replies: "I wasn't feeling well and went to the doctor yesterday. He gave me medicine and told me to take a teaspoon every hour."

You might call the theme stupidity, but it rests on a misunderstanding, apparently not deliberate.

An even clearer example can be seen in the following.

Two men meet at a bar and become friendly. As their friendship ripens and they become slightly tanked, one says to the other: "Shay, I live in a beautiful housh right around the corner from here. Why donshu come along and I'll show you around."

They arrive at the house, which is large and rather impressive. The owner shows his newfound friend a living room full of beautiful antiques, a comfortably appointed den, a lavishly furnished dining room.

"C'mon," he says, "lemme show you the bedroomsh."

At the third bedroom, the owner opens the door and there are on the bed are a man and woman engaged in the obvious.

"Oh," says Mr. Owner, "meet the wife."

He closes the door and says, "C'mon, buddy, lesh go down to the kitchen. I'll make shome sandwiches for the two of ush."

The newfound friend is consumed with curiosity. As they

enter the spacious kitchen, he can't hold it in any longer. "Say, Mac," he asks, "what about that fellow up there in the bedroom?"

"Oh, him," responds Mr. Owner, "let him make his own sandwiches."

Misunderstandings can also arise from what I call *errors of reference*. Person A is talking about matter X while Person B understands it to be about matter Y. Look at how simple this is in the next example.

Jones: "Did you hear what happened last night? Jack Williams got drunk and shot his dog!"

Smith: "Was he mad?" [I would take this to mean, "Had the dog gone mad."]

Jones: "Well, he wasn't pleased!" [But Jones has interpreted the word *mad* differently and the whole thing gets twisted and funny.]

Here's a misunderstanding that is also word play.

A Catholic couple has just been married. As it happens, the young woman has a secret which lies heavily on her mind. Finally, she can hold it no longer.

"Patrick," she says to her new husband, "I have a confession to make. As you know, I came from a very poor family, and when I was younger the only way I could help support the family was to become a prostitute."

"My God," exclaims the new husband, "our marriage must be dissolved."

"Can you not find it in your heart to forgive me? After all, it was a matter of necessity and I was a prostitute for only a short time."

"Oh," replies the husband, "Did you say *prostitute*? I'm sorry, I thought you said *Protestant*."

But is the misunderstanding in these jokes deliberate or accidental? Of course it's deliberate on the part of the narrator. The internal actor may or may not be presented as realizing that he or she is in error. But it's clear that ignorance and misunderstanding are closely related. In one case, the person is just not knowledgeable about what is going on; in the other, the person seems not to understand a particular piece of information or has not been paying attention. It is sometimes difficult to distinguish between the two, however.

Another mechanism is *paradox*. A paradox is a contradiction—something in which one part contradicts another. Here is a beautiful example of contradiction built into the joke itself, an Old World Jewish joke.

> Two men meet at a railroad station.
> "Where are you going, Moishe?" says one to the other.
> "I'm going to Lemberg, Avrom."
> "I don't understand you, Moishe. Why are you like that?"
> "Like what? What are you talking about?"
> "I know, I know. You tell me Lemberg, because you want me to think you're really going to Cracow. But I know you have a ticket to Lemberg. So why do you have to lie about it? If you're going to Lemberg, why don't you just say so?"

Jewish humor is rich in paradox. Here's one more example to show you how it works.

> A marriage broker (a favorite subject of many Old World Jewish jokes) brings a young man to meet a prospective bride. As they sit in the parlor, the agent is "selling" the product.
> "Look at that closet," he notes, "with all the beautiful things displayed in it. I told you, these folks are real class, and the money shows."
> After a thoughtful moment, the cautious young man observes: "You know, I wonder, maybe they borrowed all these things when they heard we were coming."
> "What are you talking about?" the broker reassures him. "Everyone in this town knows them. And who in the world would ever lend them anything?"

One of the neatest bits of paradox is in the following story.

A man gets a flat tire right in front of an insane asylum. As he is changing the tire, he is carefully observed by one of the inmates standing with his face in the bars.

And now tragedy. As the tire fixer raises the wheel cover containing the nuts with which to secure the cover, his hand slips, the nuts roll out, and all but one of them roll right into a sewer.

"Good God!" he exclaims, "what do I do now?"

The man behind the bars call to him: "Hey, why don't you take off the other hubcap, take two nuts from there, and add them to the one you've still got? That way you'll get the cover to stick until you can get to a service station."

"Thank you," says the driver, and then he turns and stares in astonishment at the other man. "That was pretty smart. What are you doing in that asylum?"

The reply comes back: "I may be crazy but I'm not stupid."

And now a jokebit that will be impossible for you to misunderstand.

Two army officers are sitting at an outdoor cafe, drinking coffee (or whiskey). They are deeply engrossed in their conversation.

At this point, a detachment of soldiers marches by. One of the officers looks up, sees the marching men, and stands up. "Good Lord," he says to the other officer, "those are my men. I am their leader. I must follow them!"

That's paradox!

So much for the family of mechanisms that depend on word play, unbelievable happenings, ignorance, stupidity, error, misunderstanding, and nonsense. While many of these deal with human behavior, the main idea is that the people in them do or say bizarre things.

Now let's look at a different kind of mechanism, one in which the joke is intended to *puncture superiority*, what S. J. Perelman called "the deflation of pomposity." Suppose your boss forgot to turn off his intercom and you heard him pleading with his wife. Even though that isn't a joke, it would be funny to you if your boss always acted high and mighty.

Here is a sci-fi joke along the same idea.

A planeload of people is in embarkation. An obviously metallic voice comes through a loud speaker as follows: "Ladies and gentlemen, Intraworld Airlines is please to welcome you aboard the first trans-Atlantic flight that will be controlled entirely by computer. Since there is no crew in this plane, all possibility of human error has been eliminated. Everything will be done by the very latest technology. Every contingency has been considered and dealt with by our computer, so that nothing can go wrong . . . go wrong . . . go wrong. . . ."

If you were to hear this, you would be laughing—provided the doors of the plane were still open and you could disembark. Here's another one:

A certain professor of business was very sarcastic, always making fun of students and even of businessmen. One day he is talking about marketing research, and to illustrate he brings in a toothbrush contraption—a toothbrush attached to one of those criss-cross things that pull out and then snap back and that in turn is attached to a suction cup.

"Let me tell you what this company did," he explains. "They put this damn-fool thing on the market without doing any market research!" Then he pulls himself up to his full domineering height and says very loudly: "And how many of these fool things do you think were sold last year?"

From the rear of the class, a quiet voice pipes up: "Just one, sir!"

Sometimes this puncturing incorporates a related mechanism, the *introduction of common sense.*

An older gentleman is talking to his son, who is a graduate student in science. "Listen," the man says. "After all the money I spent on your education, can you explain Einstein's theory of relativity to me?"

"Well, Dad, it isn't easy," the son replies. "But I'll try. What he wanted to prove is that there is a time–space continuum and that mass is not as constant as had previously been believed. It changes as its velocity approaches the speed of light. Of course, it gets more complicated and mathematical, but I'm trying to give you the basic ideas."

The father thinks for a moment and then comments: "That's relativity? And from this he makes a living?"

Another example of common sense:

Two men are talking about their car experiences. One says to the other: "I had a bad accident about three months ago when my brakes failed. What do *you* do when your brakes fail?"

And the other man answers, "Hit something cheap!"

That makes sense, doesn't it?

A different type of mechanism involves a *shift to an unintended reference*. The following story was told about Winston Churchill.

At one political rally, Churchill was heckled by someone in the audience, as follows: "I presume we may expect you to be subservient to the powerful interests who control your performance in office."

Churchill immediately retorted, "I'll thank you to keep my wife out of this discussion."

Churchill of course was not making an error here; he simply turned an attack into a witty counterattack.

Still another mechanism is *disguise, or the substitution of one event or condition for another*

A man comes home from a day's work and is greeted by his wife with: "You know, dear, I have a problem with the car."

"What sort of problem?"

"Well, there's water in the carburetor."

He is astonished. "Water in the carburetor? How do you know that? Since when did you become an auto mechanic?"

"Oh, dear," she responded, "I know because the car is in the pool!"

Now there is a case where a major event is hidden by something minor and the major point comes out as the punch line! It is also possible to reverse this order and move *from major events or conditions to minor ones.* As in the next joke:

A lady meets a friend she hasn't seen for a month or so. Naturally, the friend asks her how things are going and immediately gets a long face.

"If you have time to listen, I'll tell you."

The friend urges her to go ahead and talk. "After all, what are friends for?"

"You won't believe the troubles I've had since I saw you last. I don't know what's going to become of me! To begin with, my husband Arthur had a heart attack two weeks ago and is hovering between life and death. Last week my son, Bill, announced that he is leaving his wife and children and is going to live with a man. Three days ago my daughter Jane was in an automobile accident; she has a bad concussion and may lose a leg. *And tomorrow, the painters are coming!!*"

A related mechanism is the *addition of the irrelevant detail.*

A young man takes his mother to see a movie about the French Revolution. Trials are being held, heads are being lopped off by the guillotine, beautiful women are crying.

The mother watches intently as a count and countess are being dragged out of their house by a mob. She leans over to her son and murmurs, "What a lovely home!"

Woody Allen is a master of this mechanism and his quips are wonderful illustrations. Who else would put together the following two ideas: "I don't know if I believe in an afterlife . . . but I'm taking a change of underwear."

In fact, any sharp *contrast* serves humor well. A man jogging while dressed in a sweat shirt and tennis shorts and wearing a top hat would make anyone smile. It's the same in jokes. Listen to this.

Cohen is complaining to Bernstein. "Good God, what a year I'm having. In May I just broke even. In June we had a two-week strike and I lost a lot of orders. July was terrible, and. . . ."

Bernstein interrupts. "By you, that's trouble. By me, that's nothing! My wife has been ill for months. I just found out that my son is a homosexual and my daughter ran away with some penniless painter. That's what I call trouble. What could be worse than that?"

"What could be worse? August!"

A simple question put, supposedly, to Isaac Asimov shows contrast in a painfully funny way. After one of his lectures, a lady walked up to him and asked, "Are you a Ph.D. or a real doctor?" Funny? In a way.

Similarly, *comparison* can serve as a joke mechanism, if there is something incongruous and surprising in it.

A businessman comes to his wife. "Dear," he tells her, "you know I've always been open and above board with you. My partner, John, has gotten himself a mistress. We take exactly the same out of the business. Now he's running some of her "expenses" through the business. I should even things out. I need a mistress, too."

His wife thinks for a minute. "That seems fair," she agrees. "All right, I'll pick one out for you."

So she gets him a nice young girl and, presumably everything is going along, as they say, swimmingly.

One evening our man takes his wife out to dinner. As they are being shown to their seats, Mr. Husband looks around and then whispers to his wife: "Margaret, first chance you get, look to your left. There's my partner, John, with his bedmate."

Margaret steals a glance, turns back to her husband, and remarks, matter-of-factly, "You know, dear, ours is nicer!"

Let us now turn to *irony*. Here, one says one thing but means something else. Often, but not always, bitterness or sadness underlies irony. Look at the following story, for example.

The scene is a Jewish ghetto in a medieval city. According to a city ordinance, the community must bury its dead within the walls. However, the space available has gradually diminished to the point where there are almost no plots left.

The community applies for more land but the only land available is outside the ghetto. The application is denied. The Jews appeal, explaining their situation. Now the city fathers dawdle and dawdle, giving no answer at all.

Finally, the rabbi writes a letter in which he notes, "Since the city will not give us a clear response to our request for land for burial, perhaps they will grant us a permit to cease dying."

(In a play format, this story has a slightly different ending. The council is informed that the Jews couldn't wait for an answer and one of them took the liberty of dying.)

This is humor, a joke, but it is wry, bitter, gallows humor, the wit of extreme frustration.

Irony is not always sad, however. Look at the following jape.

Two men are leaning on a bar. One has a glass of whiskey and is chatting with the bartender. The second is ordering shots, one after another—one, two, three, four, five, six. At the end of the sixth, he turns, starts for the door, and falls flat on his face.

At this point, the bartender says to the first man, "That's what I like to see—a man who knows when he's had enough."

(Is the bartender stupid in his use of the word *enough*? Maybe. More likely, however, he is using the word *enough* to mean too much.)

Now consider the following one-liner.

A young adolescent is telling his younger brother: "You always exaggerate. I told you a million times—don't exaggerate!"

The mechanism here, of course, is *exaggeration*, also called *hyperbole*. A joke such as the above is also ironic, because the

youngster's advice is contradicted by what he himself does—
a sort of secondary meaning for irony.

Sometimes exaggeration reaches absurdity, as with the girl
who is so thin that she fell through a flute and never struck a
note. Many stand-up comics have developed routines full of
such exaggerations.

One of the commonest and most important mechanisms
in jokes is *establishing inferiority* or *going one up*. All putdowns,
such as Winston Churchill's earlier remarks about Attlee, fall
into this category. So do many husband/wife stories. Here is
an example:

> A man is waiting outside the five-and-dime store (it's an
> old joke) for his wife, who is inside buying something. He looks
> at the scale in front of the store and, having nothing better to
> do, decides to weigh himself. Out comes the ticket, giving his
> weight on one side and a personality description on the other.
> "You are firm, resolute, decisive, kind, and attractive."
>
> Just then his wife comes out, grabs the ticket, reads it, and
> observes, "They got your weight wrong, too!"

There is nothing especially new about this device. Back in
ancient Rome, Cicero wrote about putting someone else down.
Why should an orator use humor? ". . . Because it overthrows
the adversary, or hampers him, or makes light of him, or dis-
courages or refutes him."

Of course the putdown can be very funny. Here's a story
that has been told about many celebrities. This version is an
exchange between nineteenth-century British prime ministers
Disraeli and Gladstone, who were members of opposing parties
and disliked each other intensely.

> At one point during a debate, Gladstone became so angry
> at Disraeli that he shouted: "Sir, you are contemptible! I say you
> will end up either on the gallows or in a hospital for the treatment
> of venereal disease!"
>
> Disraeli immediately replied, "That, my worthy friend, de-
> pends on whether I embrace your principles or your mistress."

Any number of jokes depend on *outwitting* someone, either by putting down an opponent, as in the joke above, or by beating the system. For example:

> A man has just been acquitted of having burglarized an establishment and stolen a sum of money, a charge to which he has, of course, pleaded innocent. Freed of the charge, the defendant turns to the judge and asks, "Does that mean that I can keep the money?"

Here is another instance:

> A man has just been convicted of a capital crime in a country where the death sentence is permitted. He has been tried by a military tribunal. Now the presiding officer addresses him: "It is my duty to impose sentence upon you. This panel has decided to permit you to choose whatever death you wish, that is, whatever means you would prefer. Tell us, then, what is your choice.
> The man does not think very long. "Sir, I choose death by old age!"

Keep in mind that any given joke can have more than one mechanism at work. Here is an example of a paradox putdown.

> A comic is having fun with his audience. "I have a test for you men. Let's divide the group. All the men who are henpecked, go to the right; those who aren't, go to the left."
> All but one man move to the right. One meek little fellow walks to the left. The comic regards him with mock awe. "Say, my friend, as you can see, you're all alone on that line. How come you chose that one?"
> Back comes the answer: "My wife told me to."

And finally, one of the most powerful mechanisms of all is *shock!* (If you feel the next few pages will be too shocking for you, you may want to skip them.)

Do you remember the Challenger disaster, where several astronauts and a schoolteacher were blown up? Well, a student of humor informs us that, "In the world of professional comedy, the reaction was immediate. A speaker at an international humor conference told his audience that some comedians began formulating shuttle jokes while the horror of the tragedy was still fresh in the media." And so we got, for instance:

> Where did the Challenger crew spend their vacation?
> All over Florida.

Yes, someone must have thought it was funny.

Shock is prominent, of course, in the areas of erotica and scatologica—that is "dirty jokes." The late Lenny Bruce is famous for having opened up these matters systematically in his stand-up routines. Many didn't like him because they found him shocking.

So-called sick humor seems to be a fairly modern phenomenon, but dirty jokes have always been common. What was once the preserve of boys and men now is relished by both sexes—a tribute to the progress of equality.

Stand-up comics will tell you that these routines usually draw the strongest laughs. In one study, college students were asked to repeat jokes that they had heard during the week. Nearly half of the stories dealt with sex and/or excrement.

As you would expect, some stories of this type are crude, some are clever; all deal with what used to be proscribed, forbidden topics. That is precisely what their mechanism is. They *open up repressed feelings*. The same may also be true of sick humor. The same phenomenon is at work in political satire in countries where there is no free speech. It is a way of working around feelings or statements which cannot be openly expressed. We will also see it later when we discuss anti-Semitism.

For illustrations, let's first look at sexual japes and then at one dealing with "elimination."

> A man comes home from work. His wife is not in the kitchen. He hears a sound in the bedroom, walks in, and finds his wife unclad and a man getting ready to join her in bed. His wife screams: "Alex, he's a burglar and he wants to rape me. Quick, do something."

The burglar sees the husband, whips out a revolver and a piece of chalk. He draws a large circle on the floor. "Step inside of that circle," he commands the husband. "If I find you outside, I'll kill you both."

The husband obeys and the burglar has his way with the wife. Taking the jewelry he has collected, the intruder leaves.

Now the woman is hysterical. "You stood there like a big ape the whole time he was on top of me. Why didn't you do something?"

"I did, I did," the husband answers. "At one point, when he wasn't looking, I stepped outside the circle."

This response may appear to bring this joke very close to being a noodle story, but isn't it really the incongruous and inappropriate claim to courage that is being satirized here? And isn't the shock of rape being minimized by making it seem funny?

As we have already seen, a joke will often fall into more than one class. A sexual joke may also be a tall tale and more specifically a shaggy dog story. Look at this silly story, for example.

A woman is traveling through Africa and decides to go alone into the jungle to see if she can get some pictures of animals. Sure enough, she is captured by a male gorilla. He forces her to engage in sex over several days and then he wanders off. (Yes, I know this can't happen, but remember it's a story.) Finally, she is rescued by a hunting party.

A few days after arriving back home, she is visited by one of her oldest friends, who finds her depressed, moody, sallow, and teary-eyed.

"Your vacation seems to have done you no good at all," her friend notes.

The woman breaks down into tears and gives her friend the full details of her trip, including everything that happened with the gorilla.

"Oh, my God," the friend bursts out, "what a dreadful thing to have happen! No wonder you look ill and depressed."

"Of course," the woman sobs. "By now, that damned gorilla should have called—or at least written!"

As this shows, the sexual joke is capable of all sorts of imaginings. And so is the tall tale.

Sexual stories are hardly recent. Freud has a comprehensive treatment of them based on Old World jokes. He even has a polite word play example:

> A rich old fellow is, as they would say nowadays, "coming on to" a lovely young actress. Not only is she young, but she is, in Freud's terms, "respectable." So she tells the old man, in the antique phrase of an earlier day, "You are very nice, sir, but I want you to know that my heart is already given to another."
>
> To which the old fellow replies, "I never aspired as high as that."

The perfect retort, and elegantly put as well.
Now try these, in the area of scatology.

> An old gentleman is taking a stroll in a largely uninhabited district. Suddenly he is gripped by the need to defecate. He looks around, sees no one, does what he needs to.
>
> Suddenly a patrol car with two police officers rounds the corner and pulls up alongside him. Frightened, the old man quickly removes his hat and places it over the evidence.
>
> "What are you doin' there?" one policeman shouts at him. And both get out and approach him.
>
> Thinking fast, he replies: "I just saw a very rare bird here and I threw my hat over it. I want to get it to the museum of natural history. If you'll watch it, I'll get over there and have the specialist in rare birds come back with me. I'm sure they'll pay a nice sum for the bird. I'll split it with you fellows."
>
> The cops look at each other and one says: "Go ahead. Don't be too long. We'll watch your bird."
>
> Of course, the old man hurries away, glad to be rid of the problem. After a couple of minutes, one cop turns to the other and says: "Mike, this is dumb. Why should we let the old geezer get the money for bringin' in the bird. Tell you what. I'll pick up the hat and you grab the bird and we'll just run it over to the museum ourselves and get the reward."
>
> "Okay," says Mike. "Let's do it, Jimmie."
>
> Jim raises the hat and Mike grabs. Then Mike shouts: "Holy

Mother Mary! I got the damn thing but I think I broke every bone in its body!''

There is another type of joke, which does not depict sexual activity or bodily functions, but uses only the words which were so strongly forbidden until they became commonplace in the Sixties.

> An old bum is sitting on a bench in Bryant Park (behind the famous library in New York City) eating crackers. Pigeons are alighting all around him and even on his shoulders to share the crumbs. He is screaming at them, "Fuck off, you goddam birds, fuck off."
>
> At this point, a nun comes walking by. Thunderstruck, she approaches the bum. "How can you speak like that?" she admonishes. "Don't you see there are mothers and children all over the park? You must stop using such unacceptable language immediately!"
>
> "Well," he responds, "them damn birds are shittin' all over me and tryin' to take the food right out of my mouth. I just want them to get the hell out of here. Whadya ya want me to do? Just sit here?"
>
> To which the nun replies: "All you have to do when you want them to move is to say, 'Shoo, shoo, shoo.' They'll fuck off."

If you're laughing, remember, it's only the words, not any act that's amusing you.

These, then, are some of the basic mechanisms in the jokular vein. Regardless of the mechanism, notice that surprise and/or incongruity always show up. Time to move on.

Do Jokes Teach or . . . ?

Many people who write about humor tell us that jokes are aimed at teaching us to be better human beings, that is, they have a *didactic*, or educational, purpose. It has been said that "Comedy teaches us . . . to be honest, to interrogate ourselves and correct our pretentiousness."

Let's think about what this means.

First, think of Aesop's fables, Do you remember the one about the fox and the crow.? The crow has the cheese and the fox needs a meal, so he flatters the crow by praising the beauty of her singing. Thus encouraged, the crow begins to perform, promptly dropping the cheese. The moral is obvious. If you have some money saved up, don't let a con artist tell you how marvelously smart you are to invest with him or her.

So anecdotes of this kind, fables and parables (not always funny and almost always without a punch line), are intended to feed us some sense of right and wrong, or good and evil, or even smart and dumb.

There is another sense in which some could argue that jokes are educational. Take the story about Mrs. Parvenu claiming to have seen Tchaikovsky on the bus. We all enjoyed her stupidity (as well as her husband's), but in our making fun of her, some would say that we are trying to point her toward improvement; in this case, maybe she should take some courses and learn about music before opening her mouth.

In ancient Greece, Democritus, known as the Laughing Philosopher, was considered mad by many of his contemporaries. But Hippocrates (the one for whom the doctor's oath was named) said that he was really exceptionally wise, because his laughter came from his observation of human folly and stupidity. And a Roman writer observed, "It is better to keep your mouth closed and be considered a wise man than to open it and prove that you are a fool." So we must suppose that when someone makes fun of our foolishness, it may act as a stimulus for us to correct the behavior.

I don't fully agree with this concept of education via jokes because I think an important ingredient here is the *pleasure of malice*. In truth, almost all of us enjoy putting someone else down, and we enjoy hearing about it. Recall Winston Churchill's remark about Clement Attlee: "No man has more to be modest about." Was he trying to teach Attlee something? Hardly. He was just being mean, catty, and malicious.

Repartee is full of this kind of thing.

Lady Astor once said to Mr. Churchill, "If you were my husband, I would feed you poison."

To which Churchill gallantly replied: "Madam, if I were your husband, I would swallow it!"

Do you really suppose anybody is educating anyone here?

There are books full of insults, and every stand-up comic develops them for his "trade." It is said that Milton Berle, upon being hissed in a club where he was performing, immediately shot back with: "There are only two animals that hiss, geese and snakes. Which are you?"

Here's another:

When the famous New York politician Alfred E. Smith was running for the governorship and addressing a street crowd, some heckler yelled out: "Tell us everything you know, Al. It'll only take a minute."

Smith immediately retorted: "Let me explain what we both know. It won't take any longer."

Is this education? Or is it plain malice?

Similarly, political satire intends to needle, demean, and undermine rather than to educate. Thus, political satirist Mark Russell observes about Republicans that they define integration as mixing Episcopalians and Presbyterians. Making this clear to them *might* cause changes in their attitude. More likely, it will cause laughter and applause in the audience.

Russell also noted about candidates running for the presidential primary in both parties that if they turn out to be the nominees there isn't enough caffeine in the country to keep voters awake during the campaign.

And someone has told the following story about an interview with a president.

"Mr. President," asked the reporter, "it appears to some of us that you are frequently uninformed about our current problems. Would you care to comment on that?"

The President answered: "What current problems?"

Here satire is on the border of sarcasm, which is sometimes funny and always cruel. There is little difference between satire and sarcasm. According to the dictionary, sarcasm is the use of bitter, caustic, or stinging remarks expressing contempt with intent to wound, while satire is holding up human or individual folly to ridicule or derision. Normally, we think of sarcasm as having more bite. The root of the word comes from tearing of flesh!

Here's a perfect example of funny sarcasm, a sort of long little joke. It comes from Tom Wolfe's novel *The Bonfire of the Vanities*. He is talking about a fictional district attorney in the Bronx.

> Weiss never went near a courtroom. He didn't have time. There were only so many hours in the day for him to stay in touch with Channels 2, 4, 5, 7, and 11 and the New York *Daily News*, the *Post*, the *City Light*, and the *Times*.

Funny, but nasty too.

Mark Twain was a master of sarcasm as well as other forms of humor. In his description of his travel in Europe, *The Innocents Abroad*, he tells of his great desire to be shaved by a French barber. He gets his wish, in, of all places, a wig-making establishment! The experience is less than satisfactory and he concludes:

> He dried my features with a towel, and was going to comb my hair; but I asked to be excused. I said with withering irony [note] that it was sufficient to be skinned—I declined to be scalped.

Robert Benchley, in contrast, is relatively mild in talking about his difficulties with opening a package.

> It may be a perfectly dandy wrapper, air-tight, water-tight and germ proof, but if the buyer has to send it to a garage to get it off, something is wrong somewhere.

The first has a lot of bite; the second pokes fun but doesn't draw blood.

Are the following comments sarcasm or satire? About Tammy Bakker: "She's currently in seclusion in Palm Springs, where she has entered the Institute for Mascara Abuse!" About the city of Chico, California: "Where Velveeta will be found in the gourmet section of the supermarket." It's not always easy to tell the difference, and maybe it's not too important.

This type of humor is not confined to the United States. In Moscow, one of the standard jokes, I'm told, is this one:

> What's the tallest building in the city?
> Answer: KGB headquarters! From there you can see Siberia, even from the basement.

Humor and jokes, then, are not intended to be kind. Comedy actor Tony Randall has put it clearly: "We laugh because it's happening to someone else, not to us." In fact, there is an old Jewish story in which a woman has a stupid son who is always doing things to make people laugh at him. His mother says, "Sure, I would laugh, too, if the fool weren't my own."

Humorist Jean Shepard has a story about a clown who can't make it big anywhere, until the night a sandbag accidentally falls on him. It can't be very pleasant to the clown, but the audience is delighted and so it goes into his act. No wonder Al Capp called humor "man's inhumanity to man."

So other people's being down is important in humor. We are frequently amused by someone else's troubles, especially if we know that they are not really too dreadful. We laugh when someone, such as a clown, slips on a banana peel. In this case, we know, or think, that "it's not serious." But of course not all humor is of that character.

Much of *ethnic* humor is malicious. Often its purpose is to make fun of the people of a particular group. Interestingly enough, in one study the most educated people and the ones who described themselves as intelligent enjoyed jokes about minorities the most.

Earlier in this century comedians used to poke fun at stock figures of Jews, Scots, Greeks, Italians, Swedes, and others.

Most of the stereotypes created were not intended to be flattering. Look at how the following jest beats up a whole group of ethnics.

A ship is wrecked and only three survivors are cast ashore, two men and a woman. And now the ethnic malice:

If they are French, they form a ménage à trois.
If they are Italian, one man will do away with the other.
If they are English, the two men will do away with the woman.
If they are German, they will agree to spend six months studying the resources of the island and put out an appropriate report.
If they are American, they will immediately begin discussions as to whether to build two homes or just one, and what the right price should be.
And if they are Russian, they will try to contact Moscow to find out what Communist doctrine calls for in such a contingency.

The following is Larry Wilde's version of a joke that has different regional variations.

Why is Sunday morning the best time to ride the Los Angeles freeways? Because . . .

the Catholics are in church.
the Protestants are still asleep.
the Jews are in Palm Springs.
the Indians are restricted to the reservation.
the Chinese are stuffing fortune cookies.
the Blacks are stealing hubcaps.
and the Mexicans can't get their cars started.

Nasty stuff!
Finally, applying ethnic humor to heaven and hell.

In heaven,	In hell,
the chefs are French.	the chefs are English.
the police are English.	the police are German.
the lovers are Italian.	the lovers are Swiss.
the mechanics are German.	the mechanics are French.
the administration is Swiss.	the administration is Italian.

All these jokes are "wholesale" applications of ethnic humor. In every case, the needle is being applied to what is held to be a national stereotype. Larry Wilde's explanation is that we "laugh at the images that the gag created. It conjures up certain recognizable ethnic characteristics. Though these traits are not *true*, they *are* familiar and we laugh even though we know that the barbed jest has no basis in truth."

That may well be. Nevertheless, a lot of us really believe that there is at least a tiny bit of accuracy in the joke. In these "wholesale" national stereotypings, all the nationalities come off poorly at some point.

In short, jokes can be very cruel and people enjoy that. It may be, in some cases, that the ridicule will cause some individual or group to look for improvement—but this is highly unlikely.

So What's It All About?

Now that we've had a good look at the mechanisms, let's consider the content of jokes. Generally, it can be divided into four main themes.

The first is hostility and aggression. As we have seen, jokes are vehicles for needling or insulting others. Some "experts" in this field would say that most or maybe all humor is aggressive. Whether it is Lenny Bruce, or Don Rickles insulting the audience, or Churchill putting down some antagonist, or a Jewish rabbi asking the town council whether they will pass an ordinance forbidding Jews from dying—all are expressing hostility in some form.

A second group contains jokes that rest on some form of human weakness—stupidity, ignorance, or even a physical or mental disability. The Chelm noodle stories make us laugh because of the stupidity of the actors. Also remember the fellow in the bank to whom the bank manager "explained" the need for his signature by threatening to kick him out. Think of jokes about stutterers or about people who don't speak or think well. There may be some subdued hostility here, but the main situation is more one of relief because there-but-for-the-grace-of-God-go-I, who am really superior.

Third is a somewhat related theme: absurdity. When Woody Allen tells you that he's uncertain about the hereafter but will take a change of underwear, you know he isn't being stupid and he isn't hostile. It isn't just the narrator who can make absurd statements, either. Remember the scientist who concluded that fleas lose their hearing when they have their legs cut?

The fourth theme is cleverness or wit. In this category are Oscar Wilde's epigrams, and the folk saying about not gloating over your enemy's downfall but not picking him up either, and Disraeli's response to Gladstone (whether I end up on the gallows or in a hospital will depend on whether I embrace your principles or your mistress). This Disraeli example illustrates that sometimes a joke will exhibit more than one theme—in this case, both wit and hostility.

You can see that these themes may show up in either word play, observation about human behavior, or "total unbelievables," those that cannot possibly have occurred.

The Superiority Factor

As the story about Disraeli and Gladstone shows, one of the common mechanisms of jokes is that of putdown, of establishing inferiority. Of course, if you establish inferiority, you automatically establish superiority. If Gladstone gets put down, Disraeli goes one up. If the lady in the weight story puts her husband down, she's telling us that she's the boss in this duo, at least in this joke.

This idea is a crucial one because, in a sense, every joke

has the common foundation of this *superiority factor*. Someone is up and someone is down. This factor is obvious in pranks. You laugh when the circus clown trips and falls on his nose; it's not your nose. When someone gets a hot foot, the sudden jump of the victim is hilarious, but not to the recipient. A psychiatrist has argued that when a child gets control of his or her own body movements and then observes that playmates can't do so, their mistakes will seem funny to the child. Again the expression of superiority.

The same factor is at work even when you laugh at yourself. It is probably easier to take a joke about yourself when you yourself say it. Laughing at oneself never hurts as much as someone else's ridicule. Here's one example of self-joking.

> A speaker, standing up to address the audience, delivered the following one-liner: "I won't keep you long. It will only seem that way!"

No doubt, he doesn't really mean that he's a boring speaker and that his five-minute speech will seem like an hour's oration. What he is probably saying is: "Look! I'm so clever (i.e., superior) that I can fool around with you and tell you that I'm going to bore you, but you and I don't believe that! Only some simple yokel (the implied fool, maybe somewhere in the audience) would believe that."

If you look back at the jokes you have been reading here, you'll easily be able to find the superiority factor. It's obvious in the story of the old man who needs to defecate, in the Winston Churchill jokes, in the Tchaikovsky story, and on and on. In fact, when the joke leaves a gap, remember the get-it effect: *you* even feel superior jumping to the hidden part in the punch line!

There is a famous joke that illustrates a combined self-putdown and putdown of another person. It has been attributed to George Bernard Shaw.

> The actress Ellen Terry was so dazzled by Shaw's brilliance that she propositioned him. "You are so brilliant and I am so

beautiful," she is said to have written him, "that we should produce a child. Can you imagine anyone so brilliant *and* so good-looking?"

Shaw promptly replied: "A wonderful idea. I am, however, moved to decline for an obvious reason. Suppose our product were to inherit my looks and your brains!"

If we look closely at the superiority factor, we can see two models, so to speak—internal and external. How do these differ? The internal one is self-evident. Any putdown is an example. Remember the Churchill/Lady Astor story: If I were your husband I would take the poison you offered. What happened here was one internal actor went one up on some other internal actor in the drama. There is a winner and a loser, a victor and a victim. That's what internal superiority is all about.

The external form is seen in the story about the cobbler of Chelm, the convicted murderer for whom the council finds a tailor substitute. What's going on here? Well, the Chelm *naronim* (Yiddish for fools) certainly don't emerge on top. Rather, it is the *narrator*, who is so clever and tells about those dummies, and it is the *audience*, who is smart enough to understand their stupidity, that are the superior ones. So, in the external form, no actor *within* the joke emerges as superior, but the narrator and the audience certainly do!

Epigrams also illustrate this. There is no victim, but the superiority factor is still there. When Oscar Wilde told you that nothing succeeds like excess, who was superior? Oscar, of course. He has given us a brilliant and concise way of making a serious social observation about human beings. But you too are smart. You got the point, didn't you?

Why Do We Laugh?

Humorist Peter DeVries has said, "Nobody knows why we laugh . . . what we laugh at lends itself somewhat more gracefully to analysis."

Why *do* we laugh? Because something is funny? But what

makes it funny? You already know that the main mechanisms are surprise and incongruity. But are these always funny?

A telegram at 2 a.m. telling you that your uncle has died may be a surprise, but it's not likely to make you laugh. Similarly, not all discrepancies are funny: remember the discrepancy between your checkbook and your bank statement. Obviously, then, *the surprise and the incongruity must give pleasure and not be a cause for worry or sorrow.*

What makes us laugh must have something to do with how we look at things. Sure, babies smile and young children laugh. A four-month old baby may become hysterical with laughter when someone wiggles a sounding toy in front of his or her face. Most adults would find nothing laughable in that.

So it would seem that laughter is innate but, for most of us, what we laugh at is learned. Child psychologists will tell you that very young children laugh at nonsense sounds. During their development they begin to pick up ideas as to what is funny, and they will laugh at jokes that meet the test—surprise, incongruity, pleasure, non-threat. Their reaction will also be influenced to some extent by where they live, their education, their class, and other factors.

The fact is that we become conditioned to laugh at jokes. When you go to see a comedy, if you're in the right mood, have the right attitude, something said will start you off and the writer and actors "have" you. The same thing happens when stand-up comics perform in comedy clubs. Most people start laughing as soon as the comic says something, regardless of whether or not it's funny. Why? Because they *came* to laugh, and by God, they will, no matter *what* is said.

Of course, this may not happen if the audience members are in a poor receiving mood or if the performer doesn't get them started "laughingly." That's why the first few minutes may be crucial to the success of a comedy act.

An audience can even be conditioned to laugh before the comic starts. The great Jack Benny used to come out on stage, look at his audience, put his right hand under his chin and the left hand under the right elbow, and say "Well!" in a certain way, and the audience would double up with laughter. Why?

He had conditioned them over a period of time to expect this to be the beginning of funny talk.

There is another way of looking at this. In the course of our maturing, we all have to learn to inhibit our feelings, suppress what we would like to say, do what has to be done rather than what we would prefer to do at any particular moment—in short, to be sensible and realistic and learn to live with other people. Psychoanalysts will tell you that this process exacts a certain price, a certain amount of tension. Humor and jokes enable us momentarily to escape from those pressures, to enjoy something that may be silly, inane, unreasonable—*funny*. It permits a moment of pure pleasure without restraint. In a way, it makes us children again, youngsters who have not yet acquired all the inhibitions that living will demand. (There *are* some people who are always tight-lipped, who won't laugh, or who tighten up when certain topics are broached or certain words are used. These are the exception.)

This casting off of inhibitions is what carnivals are all about—an attempt to go crazy for a short period. In Jewish life, the Purim festival is that type of celebration. At this time, Jews are permitted, even advised, to let go, have fun. The Greeks had their Dionysian festivals; the Romans, Saturnalia. The medieval church attempted to suppress the Feast of Fools, but the theology faculty of the University of Paris argued that: "folly, which is second nature to man and seems to be inborn, may at least once a year have free outlet."

So you can see why Bergson said that comedy "consists in the eruption of vitality through deadening social constraints." With all the pressure of everyday living, we sometimes just have to say, "Hey, that's ridiculous!"

And sometimes we laugh to keep from crying. When things really seem impossible to handle, we will sometimes make a joke of it. Doing that makes our difficulty bearable.

Finally, joke telling is an important social ritual. Friends get together and tell each other stories, many of which they would never tell to outsiders. It's an "inside" thing that confirms and builds the friendship and makes the participants feel closer—as though they are sharing a secret.

So Let Me Ask You Something

What have we learned so far? First, jokes offer us pleasure; they permit us to get away from the restraints imposed on us by our upbringing and our daily lives. Freud told us that civilization is too difficult to be borne without palliatives. And jokes *are* palliative.

Second, jokes give us feelings of self-elevation. Consider this quip: "The Indian scalps his enemy, the paleface skins his friends." The ordinary white person may laugh or smile at this, but how do you think it would make an Indian feel? Such jests can foster feelings of greater self-esteem. Told within a group, the stories will build a feeling of solidarity, a notion of "among ourselves, we know that. . . ."

Third, jokes enable us to deal with serious problems that we have great difficulty handling. For example, in reality, poverty in Jewish life in Eastern Europe was almost intolerably oppressive. See how the following Old World Jewish joke deals with it.

> A man comes to his rabbi and tells him: "Rabbi, we are so poor and have so little. Our home is terrible, a one-room hut where my wife and I and our four children are crowded so tightly that a sneeze would blow someone out of the house. What shall I do?"
>
> The rabbi thinks for a moment and then asks, "Do you have a goat?"
>
> "Of course," is the reply, "we need the milk."
>
> The rabbi continues: "How about some chickens?"
>
> "Yes, we have a few. We need the eggs, and sometimes, for a holiday, we'll have the *shochet* (the ritual slaughterer) kill the chicken."
>
> "All right, my friend. Now what you must do is bring them into your house and come back and talk to me next week."
>
> The man is astounded, but if the rabbi says to do it, there must be some good reason. So off he goes home to carry out the advice. Seven days later, he is back in tears. "Rabbi, what did you do to me? Our conditions were dreadful before. Now they are impossible!"

"Now, my son, listen to me. Go home and put the goat and the chickens out again, then come right back and talk to me."

An hour later, the man returns. "Rabbi," he says, "may the Lord's blessings be upon you always. What a wise man you are! I can't believe how much room there is in the house now."

To be sure, it's unlikely that anyone ever went through such an experience. The point is that some Jew invented a story that would make Jews laugh at their poverty and give them some relief from it.

Note that while this story reflects a deep-seated problem, it is hardly a real tragedy. The humor of real tragedies is so-called black humor. Do you recall the bad taste of the Challenger explosion "joke" earlier? And yet some psychologists argue that this type of joke is a way of dealing with a tragedy too difficult to be borne without relief. Maybe laughing is useful for dealing with something so repulsive. Shakespeare, too, introduced comic relief into his tragedies to lighten the burden on the audience.

Nevertheless, there *is* a big "but" here. When the speaker told the story about the astronauts, he added that, in his research, he interviewed someone who had known one of the astronauts. This man did not find the stories amusing. He concluded that "joking about tragedy may be comfortable primarily for people not touched personally by the situation."

Moreover, he tells us that these jokes were told mostly by children to adults. "Typically, the tellers smiled as they told the jokes and could barely contain their own laughter in anticipation of adult responses." In one case, a youngster was asked whether "jokes of this type upset him." He laughed and replied: "No. I think they're cool"—the ultimate accolade!—or is this an early example of the pleasure of malice?

How about this one:

A man is standing out on a ledge, poised to jump. Inside the room there is much hand wringing, pleas to come back, to think it over. Suddenly a man rushes breathlessly into the room, proceeds to the window, and addresses the prospective jumper: "Have you really decided to jump, Andrew?"

"Yes, I'm going to do it in a minute, Sidney."

There is a pause and then Sidney asks, "In that case, may I have your new car?"

This joke, told by a comic, may have been an attempt to mitigate the feeling of tension. There are probably some people who might enjoy that joke—maybe because it is some one else's tragedy, or maybe because of a touch of sadism. Maybe there's more of that in our makeup than any of us would like to admit.

This leads to a fourth point. Jokes permit us to express hostility without suffering consequences. Many rip, tear, hurt. The Churchill wisecracks and other needling express hostility. When someone says that when Columbus landed on the American shore one Indian turned to another and remarked, "Well, there goes the neighborhood," that person is taking advantage of a time and person transfer to satirize the bigotry associated with contemporary housing problems. If I punch you with my fist, everyone expects you to be angry and respond in kind, if possible. But if I hit you with words, you are supposed to laugh. The verbal cruelty is permissible. If the recipient gets "sore," he or she is told, "It's only a joke; can't you take it?"

Fifth, jokes *may* get us to correct faults. The idea is that if I make fun of something you do, you may stop doing it. My own guess is that this works in personal ridicule but, in general, I don't think it operates very often through jokes per se.

Finally, jokes have one other purpose. They permit the teller to emerge center stage. They satisfy the ma-look-at-me craving. In short, they make exhibitionism legitimate. We all like the limelight, whether we admit it or not.

So where do jokes come from? The answer is simple: Who knows? Well, that's not exactly right either. The truth is that some come from people we could name, but more of them come from Anonymous. Much jokelore is folklore that has been traveling around for centuries. Folklorists will tell you that some, in different variations, go back at least to the Greeks—

and for all we know, they may have gotten them from the Egyptians, who, in turn, got them . . .

On the other hand, many jokes are "created" by writers (or speakers) of comedy, or by professional gag writers who work for comedians or political figures, or even by ordinary people who submit them to newspapers and magazines.

Actually, it's difficult to tell which jokes are old and which are newly created. Some people say that there are no new jokes, only old ones that have been forgotten. Furthermore, some newly invented jokes pass into the folklore after a while, and, on the other hand, sometimes old jokes that have been floating around are picked up and adapted or transformed by the skillful writer.

Charles Neider, writing about Mark Twain, talks about his closeness to "native speech" and links him to the oral traditions on which he drew, mostly from our Western frontier. Who can be sure where the jokelore ends and Mark Twain's jokes begin? Irving Howe says much the same thing about Sholem Aleichem, the Jewish writer and humorist. Probably you know that when Sholem Aleichem settled in the United States, Mark Twain came to call. Mark Twain began by saying that he was so pleased to meet at last the man who was known as the Jewish Mark Twain. Sholem Aleichem bowed and said that he was equally pleased to meet at last the "American Sholem Aleichem."

2

The Jewish Joke

Jews in Jokes

Now that you have gotten a grip on what jokes are all about, it's time to take a look at the "logic" behind Jewish jokes themselves.

We have all heard of ethnic humor, American humor, Russian humor, English humor, and Scottish humor; there are black jokes and Indian jokes. My guess is that what I am going to say about the Jewish joke would hold true for many of these, too. And students of folklore will tell you that what may appear to be a joke of a certain ethnic group frequently finds parallels in the tales of one or more other groups.

At some point in history, the outside world began to stereotype Jews in humor. This classifying of Jews as different no doubt arose primarily because of the religious difference and, more important, because of the hatred generated by the Church.

Type Cast—Jewish Stereotypes

First, what do we mean by a Jewish joke? A joke about Jewish people? Well, read this one:

> On the train between New York and Chicago, a middle-aged man is sitting in the dining car. A young man enters, looks around, walks up to the seated fellow and inquires, "What time is it?"
>
> The middle-aged man looks at the questioner and doesn't respond. The latter asks more loudly, "Beg your pardon, sir, can you tell me what time it is?"
>
> Still no answer.
>
> Now the young fellow bends over close to the other man's ear and repeats his question very loudly. The older man shakes his head. "It's not necessary to yell, young man," he observes.
>
> "Well, I thought you might be hard of hearing, sir."
>
> "No, it's not dot. You see, if I tell you vot time it is, you'll esk if you could sit don here vit me. Den vun void vill lead to anodder, vee'll get ah leedle friendly. So I'll invite you to my house fahr ah dinner. You'll mit my beaudiful dudder, and before you know it, I'll hev ah merich proposal on my hends. So I vant you should know right now. I dun't vant a son-in-law vot doesn't even own ah vatch!"

Now, what is it that makes this joke Jewish? Why can't it be Norwegian, African, Wasp? It certainly could be!

What makes this story Jewish is that I, the narrator, chose to put Jews into my telling! How? Obviously, by the use of speech that marks one of them as a Jew.

The point, then, is this: A great many so-called Jewish jokes depend entirely on the narrator. They become "Jewish" if the joke teller insists on making them so!

Humor from Jewish Life?

Before we go on to the question of what can really be called Jewish jokes, a few words about the Jewish "accent" used in the story above.

Obviously, the use of "dialect" or "accent" was tied to reality, the reality of Jewish immigration to the English-speaking world. Most immigrants have difficulty mastering the language of a new environment. Both Jewish and non-Jewish comedians have exploited this to mock the results for Jews as well as other ethnic groups. The boundary between nasty derision and mockery on one side and gentle irony on the other is not easy to draw. As a result, many immigrants, realizing that people are making fun of them, find dialect offensive.

Think for a moment about what telling "accent" jokes means, especially in terms of the relation between the teller and the listeners. One of two things is going to happen. Either the teller will reassure the listeners, establish a sort of solidarity with them, reassure them that "we're on the same team"; or else the teller will confirm some reason why the listeners should hold the butt of the joke in low esteem.

It should be no surprise, therefore, to learn that a Jewish story teller delivering dialect jokes to a completely Jewish audience is generally welcome. However, when even a great story teller like the late Myron Cohen begins to offer these stories to *general* audiences, some Jews become uncertain. Finally, when *non*-Jews tell such stories, Jews often become uneasy, feeling for the needle of mockery in the texture of the delivery.

Nevertheless, there are two conditions under which it seems okay to use the accent: (1) when it merely identifies without mockery, as in the joke above, and (2) when the story depends on it as a necessary part. How can that happen? Here's an example.

A young Jewish man has just graduated from college with a degree in business. He wants to make it in the field of marketing and has been told to start his career in selling. He manages to get a job with a company that makes and sells dictating machines. Because he is clearly Jewish, his sales manager assigns him to work in the New York garment district, which at one time was predominantly Jewish.

Fresh from his sales training and full of enthusiasm, the new salesman, Richard, goes to a large building on Broadway where garment firms are concentrated to begin his calls. He decides to start on the top floor, where he finds the impressive loft of Lefkowitz & Lefkowitz.

He manages to ingratiate himself with the secretary-receptionist at the front desk and she tells him to go into the manufacturing area and look for Mr. Lefkowitz, whom she describes fully—short, stout, wearing a gray vest, and smoking a large cigar.

Now the following dialog takes place.

"May I speak with you for a few minutes, Mr. Lefkowitz?"

"Vot are you, ah salesmon? I don't vant notting; I don't need notting; I von't buy notting. So don't bodder."

"Sir, I'm not here to sell anything today. All I want is your permission to leave this machine for demonstration. If the machine itself can't convince you of its usefulness, no sale, no obligation. All I can tell you is that it will make life much easier because you can sit down and dictate when *you* have the time while your secretary is doing something else."

"Pleess, I'm not interested; fahget it."

"Sir, why don't you let me leave the machine here for a week? I'll teach your secretary how to use it. *There's absolutely no charge for that.*"

Lefkowitz stops at this point. "You mean, dere's not even ah deposit; I don't hev to sign notting?"

"That's right!"

"In dot case, leave it. But remember, I'm not promising notting!"

Richard leaves the machine, giving the secretary detailed instructions in how to use it. A week later he returns, is welcomed back by the secretary and sent right in to see Lefkowitz. The latter no sooner catches sight of him when he exclaims: "Aw, young fella, dot's some mahsheen. Yesser. It's vunderful! I talked into it late in die efternoon ven I got die time and it did die job. In fect, I listened to it myself to get de idea how it voiks. Sure, I'm gonna buy it. But maybe you could do me ah faver. Maybe it's possible to get ah mahsheen dot don't hev such ah strung eksent."

Now you may laugh at the final absurdity of this story, but you see it deals with a real problem—the embarrassment felt by immigrants who realize that their speech is not that of the general population. In such a joke, dialect is proper. However, if you use dialect simply to ridicule somebody, you should expect resentment. Even the gentle irony of the story above might be resented by some.

There is also an interesting reversal of this kind of story.

In a courtroom, the clerk calls, "Mr. Finkelstein!"

A man, clearly a Chasid, long beard, wearing the traditional black gabardine coat and the *shtreimel* (flat fur hat), steps up. The judge, obviously experienced, leans over and quietly tells the clerk, "Call Levy."

In walks an older man and takes a position next to the clerk. The judge says to Levy, "Ask him whether he is willing to give evidence here today."

Levy immediately starts his interpreting duty: "*Der richter vil ich zol eich fregen.* . . . (The judge wants me to ask you . . .).

But at this point Finkelstein interrupts. In a perfect British accent, he states: "I beg your pardon. I hold a degree from Oxford University and there is certainly no need here for an interpreter. I am quite prepared to do what is necessary in this court of law."

At this point, Levy turns to the judge and says, "Your honor, *er vil ihr zolt vissen* (he wants you to know . . .).

So, once again we learn not to judge the book by its cover.

Now, getting back to the joke about the two men on the train, if it could be told about other nationalities as well, then what *is* an authentic Jewish story? There seem to be three fundamental requirements, any one of which would permit us to regard a joke as really Jewish.

First, *it may stem from the conditions of Jewish life or from the experience of the Jewish people.*

Even this requirement has some flexibility. For example, probably the most pervasive element in the Jewish experience, a major cement holding Jews together and dominating their life, has been religion. Further, the holiest day in Judaism is Yom Kippur, the Day of Atonement. Now read this:

One Yom Kippur a rabbi has a slight sore throat and doesn't feel up to taking part in the long prayer session. He calls his assistant and tells him, hoarsely, to carry on without him. After taking a nap, the rabbi feels better but decides that he doesn't want to go to synagogue. It occurs to him that it would be a good day to play a round of golf. Obviously, he doesn't expect any of his friends and especially his co-religionists to be there, so he plays the round solo. As luck would have it, on the short third hole, he scores a hole in one!

Up in Heaven, both God and Satan have been watching. Satan turns to God and says: "Is that the way your so-called justice works? Here is one of *your children* who has transgressed on this holiest of days and you punish him by permitting him a hole in one?"

To which God responds: "Not so fast, my evil friend. A hole in one is a great thing to human golfers, something they're proud of and like to brag about. Now tell me, whom is he going to tell about it?"

A truly Jewish joke, right? So imagine my surprise when I found the same story in a joke book, but about a priest who had given up golf for Lent!

The fact is that many ethnic jokes have the wonderful characteristic of *transferability*. That's why professionals in this field can take material from one situation and develop stories for different circumstances.

When more than one ethnic group is considered to have the same characteristic, the jokes can obviously be transferred. Thus, a Scottish joke:

A Scotsman gets on a London bus with a suitcase. He sits down and puts the suitcase down on the seat next to him. "How much is the fare?" he asks.

"It's five pence for you and two for the case," is the conductor's reply.

"What? I'll nae pay a penny for the suitcase," is his horrified answer.

"Well then," says the conductor, "if you don't, I'll just throw the case right out."

Evidently, the Scot doesn't believe him, because he offers the five pence and stubbornly sits down. The conductor picks up the suitcase and hurls it right out the door, and into the Thames River.

Now the Scot, jumping up and down and screaming, shouts: "You English bastard, what hae ye done? You've gone and drowned my grandson."

What is a Scottish joke doing in the middle of a discussion of Jewish jokes? Precisely the same joke is told about a Jew on the Lower East Side of New York! So don't be surprised if you hear a joke told about one ethnic group which you had heard told about a different group. Tellers can switch the people and locale, *if the situation fits,* that is, if the internal actors have similarities.

A second requirement of a Jewish joke is that *the joke or the punch line may depend on the use of a Jewish language, especially Yiddish.* Since Hebrew has been the sacred language, folk humor and jokelore have tended largely to use Yiddish. Other languages used by Jews might also contain many jokes, but not so much is known about those. It is, however, true that there is a whole group of jokes in Yiddish that depend on quotes from the Torah or the Talmud. Usually these are puns or involve situations with double meanings related to phrases from the Torah or the Talmud.

Can a Yiddish joke be translated? It can, but some Yiddish jokes depend on very special idioms that are difficult to translate.

Finally, *Jewish jokes may show real or supposed Jewish characteristics or stereotypes.*

Of the three types of Jewish jokes, the simplest concerns the Yiddish idiom. Remember that the great bulk of humor has come in the Yiddish mode. Many of these jokes are word play. Often, they are hard to translate. Here is a simple example.

Two old Jews are sitting on a porch in a small Miami Beach hotel reading their newspapers. One turns to the other and says, "It sez here dot Lizobbet Taylor is gettin' married ahgen, die sevent time awreddy."

His friend, the cynic, responds: "Hoo, ha! I tell you it von't lest even ah yihr."

The first gentleman looks up and says, "Azah yohr ahf mir."

The literal translation of the punch line is, "Such a year for me." But this leaves out the flavor of a Yiddish idiomatic expression which is commonly used as a "wishing phrase," to wish some one well, but can be reversed to wish someone ill (*azah yohr ahf dir*), a negative pejorative.

Similarly, a bilingual joke:

Some years ago it was rumored that the Budd Company, Hupp Motors, and John Deere were about to merge to form a conglomerate. The new name was to be Hupp, Deere, & Budd.

Now it turns out that the three names parallel a Yiddish phrase—*Hub dir in bud*, which translates literally as "I have you in the bath," but idiomatically, and sarcastically, means "I'm paying you no mind at all." Thus, a worker who has just been bawled out by a supervisor might mutter under his breath, *"Ich hub ihm in bud,"*—"Who gives a damn about his yelling?"

An Israeli writer has observed, "All the wrinkles of sorrow and of laughter to be found on Jewish faces are engraved on Yiddish words, sentences, and intonations." I suppose understanding Yiddish, then, is half the fun of Jewish jests.

Unfortunately, since jokes of this type require a fairly good knowledge of Yiddish and Yiddish idioms, we will put them aside. The rest of this book will deal primarily with the other two classes mentioned above. Let's turn first to stereotypes.

How's Business?

In the first few centuries after the Diaspora, Jews were still both cultivators of soil and artisans. But during the Middle Ages various governments forced them off the land. Furthermore, the guilds required Christian oaths of people who joined, so the Jews were unable to continue in crafts. As a result, they were increasingly pushed into commerce and money lending which was basically a new field for Jews. Probably not all were greatly successful, but enough of them were so that an image was created of the Jew as a business- or money-man.

The stereotype of the Jew as business entrepreneur was well established in Old World Jewish humor. The following example is translated from one of the best collections of European Yiddish stories, Olsvanger's *Royte Pomerantzen* (red oranges).

> A large passenger ship is on its way to America. Among its many passengers are a Jew and a Chinese man. Suddenly a huge hurricane hits the ship. The ship is in big trouble, apparently overloaded, so the decision is reached to throw out several barrels full of apples. But this doesn't help at all.
>
> Next it's decided that someone has to go overboard to lighten up further. The Chinese man is chosen. But that doesn't help either. Next, the Jew goes overboard. Then, by some miracle, this quiets the storm.
>
> Shortly thereafter, the ship encounters a whale and the crew decides to capture it. The whale is loaded onto the main deck and opened up and—guess what?—there is the Jew, selling apples to the Chinese man.

It's not terribly funny, granted, but then some anecdotes are not hilarious. And there's no question that this story is totally unrealistic and rather inane. For one thing, the Chinese are just as good merchants as the Jews. Nevertheless, the point is that it shows the Jew as entrepreneur, as trader, in Jewish jokelore.

The attitude toward business is also seen in the following old story.

> Again, there is a ship caught in a huge storm. Matters are so serious that it looks as though the ship will sink.
>
> One Jewish passenger is really carrying on. "Good God, please help, the ship is sinking. Save us, save us!" On and on and on.
>
> Another Jew is sitting calmly, smoking his pipe, reading a book. The anxious man turns to him: "How can you be so calm when such a terrible tragedy is about to happen?"

The calm Jew responds: "Why are you carrying on so? Is it your ship?"

We can't be certain whether the next joke is illustrative of what Gentiles think about Jews as businessmen—or it is a self-evaluation by some Jewish wit.

A Jewish recruit in the Russian Army is not doing too well in his military training. He doesn't seem to be able to master what's required of him. Finally, an officer calls him aside and tells him, "Isaac, buy yourself a cannon and go into business for yourself."

Freud has a version in which the officer is "kindly disposed." In other versions, he is exasperated. In one version, the recruit who has been doing badly suddenly becomes marvelous, accomplishing no end of unusual feats. When HQ wants an explanation of why Private Levy is doing so well, the answer comes back that since he went into business for himself he has achieved unheard-of deeds. I suppose the way it is told depends on who tells it to whom. The joke can be an indication that the Jew doesn't fit in, showing what intellectuals call his *marginality*, or it can be a so-called indicator of the Jew's ability as an entrepreneur released from the controls of bureaucracy. Take your choice.

In Eastern Europe the Jews were permitted, during certain times, to own and operate taverns. Here's a story about their money lending activities.

Two tavern owners are discussing business. One asks the other, "Tell me, do you sell whiskey on credit?"

"Sometimes," is the answer, "and when I do, I charge double. How about you?"

"Also rarely. But when I sell on credit, I charge the customer less than when I sell for cash."

"What kind of sense does that make?"

"Don't you see? Then, if they never pay me, I lose less."

Sheer stupidity, along the same line as the fellow who loses money on every item sold but believes he makes it up on the volume.

There's a negative aspect to the money lending image, and I don't know whether it was generated by Jews or non-Jews. It's the element of unethical or sharp behavior. The following is from an Old World jokebook, which means that it was told among Jews.

A Jewish vintner in a small town has been doing a good business with both non-Jews and local Chasidim for many years. His wines apparently have developed a reputation—maybe because he is the only winemaker in the whole area, or maybe there is something about the local water he uses.

He is now old and ill and the time has come for him to leave this world, so he is putting his affairs into order. He calls his three sons together and instructs them thus:

"My children, my time to depart is fast approaching. It is good to know that you will carry on this business after I am gone. But I must leave you with one important idea which may not be clear to you even though you have worked in the winery for years. Remember, my children, that it is also possible to make wine out of grapes!"

This joke is not very funny, but it does indicate that the folks in Eastern Europe knew something about sharp practices.

Now a final Old World story, an interesting anecdote involving business and religion.

The Jew is commanded to devote Saturday to prayer, rest, and reflection about the Torah. Also, there was at one time a Jewish parallel to circuit riding preachers, men who traveled, gave a sermon in a given town or city, and then moved on. Such a *magid* comes to a city. He is well-known for his piety as well as for the strength of his delivery from the podium. He meets with the major householders and asks about what's going on among the Jews in the city.

They tell him about one man who is a nonbeliever and who keeps his shop open for business on Saturdays. The *magid* is outraged. "Wait until I deliver my sermon," he says. "I will let him have it with all the force at my command."

The reputation of the man is so great that even the non-believer turns out for the sermon. During the speech, the *magid* comes to the question of keeping the Sabbath holy and laces into those who don't do so, really giving it to them.

The day after the sermon, as is the custom, the *magid* and several major householders walk around the Jewish quarters collecting contributions. (This is how these fellows made their living.) One of the householders says to the *magid:* "You know, we ought to ask Shmuel, the nonbeliever, for money. After all, he was at your sermon. Let's see what will happen."

To everyone's surprise, the nonbeliever is most courteous and, wonder of wonders, he contributes 25 rubles! Of course, the story travels all over the area.

Shortly thereafter, a second *magid* comes to town, also a well-known speaker. Having heard about what happened, the second *magid* delivers a sermon in which he downplays the profaning of the Sabbath, saying that if it is a question of making a living, the difference between hunger and sufficiency, it is probably permissible according to some of the Talmudic precepts. He figures if *magid* number one could get 25 rubles for his fiery condemnation, he should do even better with a more permissive speech.

The next morning, he too begins his trip soliciting contributions. He stops in at the nonbeliever's home and is received courteously, and the nonbeliever contributes one ruble!

The *magid* is stunned. "What's this? You gave the other *magid* 25 rubles and for me only one? Why the difference?"

The nonbeliever responds: "It's not difficult to understand. Your predecessor gave us a tongue-lashing about the holiness of the Sabbath, so all my competitors who are pious fools, kept their businesses closed, and all the customers came to me. Therefore, the 25 rubles was an appropriate contribution. But you've spoiled my business, because now all my competitors will stay open on the Sabbath too. Even one ruble is too much for you."

Not all Jews were businessmen: In the latter part of the nineteenth century there were already enough Jewish workingmen to form a Jewish trade union movement in Eastern

Europe. But there seem to be no jokes about this development.

Immigration to the Western countries did not change the stereotype of the Jewish businessman. He remains a stock figure in Jewish humor. Usually, he is depicted as a successful individual entrepreneur.

New York City has been the largest Jewish center in the United States, and in the early period of Jewish immigration the Lower East Side was the district there where Jews congregated. Jacob Riis has described and photographed how dreadful Jewish existence was in those days. It truly wasn't a very funny situation, but humor did seep out of it. Thus—

> A Jewish couple have a little dry goods store on the Lower East Side. They work hard, six days a week, from early morning until late at night. For years now they have heard about a great "dry goods store, optown," called Macy's. Finally, one day they decide to close their store early and go uptown to see Macy's. They take along something to eat and a large shopping bag and they're off.
>
> At Macy's they are absolutely enchanted with the store. Eyes and mouths open, they wander around, looking at the displays, the flow of people, the sound of cash registers ringing. Finally, the man walks over to a gentleman with a carnation in his buttonhole, obviously an official, and asks him, "Meester, could you tell me—who owns dis store?"
>
> The floorwalker tells them: "This is a corporation. The president is Mr. Straus."
>
> The man asks, "Tell me, vould be possible to talk to dot Mr. Straus?"
>
> For some reason, the floorwalker decides to go along with the two elderly folks and says: "As it happens, Mr. Straus is here today. You'll find him on the top floor. Take the elevator."
>
> The couple appear at the secretary's desk. Graciously, she rings the president and tells him: "There are two nice elderly Jewish people out here who want just a few minutes of your time. Will you see them?"
>
> Surprised that his secretary would let things go this far, but intrigued, Mr. Straus agrees.
>
> "Mr. Straus," says the old gentleman, putting his bag

down next to the chair in which he has seated himself, "vee are also in de dry goods business. I gotta tell you, you got here some fine store."

Beaming, his wife adds, "Obsolutely; it's beaudiful."

"Thank you," says Mr. Straus. "Is there anything I can do for you?"

"Yeh," the old man answers, "could you tell me maybe vot it vould cost to buy dis store right now, say, fahr kesh."

Mr. Straus, amused, decides to play along. "Right now, for cash, I'd say about half a million would do it."

The old gentleman pulls up his bag, opens it, and starts counting money. Straus, eyes popping, watches and listens as the old man counts: "Here's one hundert tousand, end now here you got two hundert tousand, end now vee got tree hundert tousand, and dere's four hundert tousand, fifty, sixty, seventy, eighty"—suddenly he turns to his wife and says, "Sarah, oy vay, dee beg's empty."

His wife looks at him, shakes her head, and says: "Abram, vot did you do? You took de wrong beg!"

The mechanism at work here, of course, is exaggeration. But the point is being made about the success of small businessmen who worked hard and knew their business. Here's another successful businessman.

A Jewish man who has been a storekeeper in a small city for many years is being given a testimonial by the local Chamber of Commerce. He is interviewed by the reporter for the local newspaper, who wants to know to what he attributes his success as a businessman.

"Very simple," answers the retailer. "If I buy something for a dollar and sell it for two dollars, I'm happy; just so long as I make my one percent."

The mechanism here is credible ignorance. And notice that the joke says that ignorance of arithmetic doesn't necessarily get in the way of those bound for success. In jokes, at least.

One of the classics of this genre predates the current "Channel" construction, which will probably generate its own jokes.

The British have decided to build a tunnel between Calais and Dover. Bids are called for and begin to come in—£1,000,000, £1,500,000, £2,000,000, and so on, all in the seven-figure range except for a £400,000 bid from Shapiro and Shapiro.

Confronted by such a vast difference, the government feels compelled at least to confer with the Shapiros. It turns out that this is a father and son firm, and the elder Shapiro is invited to meet with the Home Secretary to discuss matters.

Shapiro turns out to be a short, round man with a cigar and a ready smile. He puts away the cigar and proceeds to listen to the secretary.

"Mr. Shapiro, we must inform you that your bid was the most attractive received by this government. However, since it *was* considerably lower than all the others, we wish to assure ourselves of your ability to carry out this engineering project in the event that the government should decide to award the contract to your firm. Will you be good enough to explain how it is that your figures are so much lower than others and to inform us as to how you would prepare to carry out the work entailed."

Shapiro smiles, folds his hands in front of himself, and begins: "Well, Mr. Secretary, you're got to understand that Shoppiro and Shoppiro (vestige of an East European accent) is not like odder firms. We are a very down-to-earth organization which cuts costs to the bone. I believe you already know that everything we do is done by the principals, that is, by myself and my son. We do not have the administrative structure, the in-between levels of management, the overhead which your odder firms carry. In fact, let me oxplain to you something important.

"Our plan is otter simplicity. My son will start digging at the French side wit a large shovel and I will start digging at Dover—also wit a very large shovel. When we meet somewhere near the middle of the Chennel, we will have completed your tunnel.

"And if by some mischence, we do not meet, you will have two tunnels for the same price!"

The "small" business entrepreneur par excellence! But results are not always so rosy. At least not for the Jewish merchant in the next story. He is telling an acquaintance:

"You ask about my business, so I'll tell you. My small wholesale jobbing place has always made a good living for the family. You know my boy, Sammy—a very smart fella. So, from my little business I was able to send him to a good college and then on to get an M.B.A. from Wharton in Philadelphia.

"So he comes home about a year ago and says, 'Dad, now that I have my M.B.A., I want to come into the business.'

"Well, that's just what I always wanted, so I don't say no. So Sam spends a few weeks poking around and then he comes to me with a long face.

" 'What's the matter, son?' I ask him.

" 'Dad,' he says, 'I don't understand it. How do you run a business? You have no accounting controls, no cost accounting system. You don't have any product line analysis, and you've never worked out any scientific routing for your salesmen so they can maximize their effort. Even if you have just six men, you should do that.'

" 'Okay, Sam,' I tell him, 'go ahead, show me what you can do.'

"Well, he's now been running the business for a year and I'm real proud of him. It's true that, for the first time since I opened up, we lost money last year—half a million dollars. But let me tell you, I know where every penny went!"

The joke works through irony and an inverted puncturing of presumed superiority. Remember that in jokes it is often fun to make fun of the educated and the presumably superior. Try the next one.

A Jewish man owns a little cleaning, dyeing, and tailoring shop. He works hard (always the emphasis in the small, individual business) and slowly amasses a considerable amount of money, what immigrant Jews used to call *kishkeh gelt*, money saved at "gut" (in Yiddish, *kishkeh*) expense by denying yourself and saving, saving, saving.

A friend whom he has not seen for some time comes to see him. "How are you doing, Izzy?" his friend wants to know.

"God be praised, I make a decent living and save a little too," is the answer. "To tell you the truth, I've already put aside $25,000 for my old age." (This story dates back to a period when such an amount meant something.)

"Really?" is his friend's comment. "And what do you do with the money?"

"What does one do with money? I keep it in the bank, where it's collecting interest."

"From 2 percent interest (remember, it's not today) you can't get much," his friend explains. "Why don't you call a broker and invest in the stock market. That way you'll make real money and you'll be able to retire, with God's help, in a really comfortable way. Wait a minute. I just heard about a good stock, Golden Egg Farms; they just put out shares. They say they're making new ways to improve eggs and to increase production."

Well, no sooner said than done. The tailor invests his 25 grand in this golden opportunity. Several months later, his friend calls him up in a state of excitement. "Izzy, you remember I told you about the Golden Egg Farms Incorporated?"

"Of course," says Izzy. "I invested my bundle in that company."

There is a long silence and then the friend says: "Oy vay, Izzy, I wanted to warn you. I just heard the company just went broke."

Again there is a long silence, and then Izzy observes, "Well, I always say—easy come, easy go!"

Irony— a characteristic of Jewish humor. Maybe no one you know would react that way, but to people who have had to practice resignation for a long time, it's a different story.

There is also a negative aspect to immigrant business jokes, just as there was in the Old World humor.

Two partners who are in the busines of producing women's dresses are leaving their office for lunch. As they get into the elevator of the building, one suddenly says to the other, "Oh, Max, I forgot to close the safe."

And the second replies: "So what are you worried about? I'm here with you."

Here is another example, an old one.

Two Jews meet in Miami Beach. "Hello, Einhorn," says one. "How are you feeling? Everything okay? Or are you down here for your health?"

"Not exactly. You see, Finkelstein, by me in the shop there was a big fire. So when I collected the insurance, I thought I would come down for a little rest, before I open again. But, Finkelstein, what are you doing here right in the middle of your busy season?"

"Well, it happened like by you. Except by us we had a big flood. While the insurance company is arranging to pay off, I thought I would come down for a while."

At this point, Einhorn looks at him quizzically and asks, "Listen, how to make a fire we all know, but how do you make a flood?"

You may wonder why the people in these jokes can't be non-Jewish businessmen. Of course, they can be. But I for one have always heard the stories told this way, and, of course, there is a germ of reality here. But for those who might feel that Jewish businessmen are more dishonest than others, all they need do is read the business sections of the newspapers for a month, not to mention all the great scandals of history, like the South Sea Bubble, the Credit Mobilier scandal of the Grant administration, the Teapot Dome scandal. And Daniel Defoe, who wrote *Robinson Crusoe,* also wrote a book called *The Compleat Tradesman*—talk about a picture of sharp business practice!

In any case, there is a point to be made. For Jews, there are few jokes about working in a big organization. Business has been an important occupation for generations, but it is predominantly small scale. The jokes deal with what happens in little businesses where the principal does most of the work. When we say "my business" in such a case, we mean just that!

I Can Get It for You Wholesale

We have seen how Jews, driven from many occupations, were practically forced to get into small, family-owned business endeavors. Of course, there were the Rothschilds. How many Rothschilds were there among Jews? Or among non-Jews, for that matter? Moreover, as every student of economics knows, money is what your teacher called a "portable store of value," meaning that you can carry it with you wherever you go. And someone who is habitually being chased, would be expected to put a high value on it.

So it is no great surprise that Jewish people should hold money in high esteem. The end result is that jokesters start kidding them about it. The Jewish stereotype of being money grubbing becomes established.

Some of these stories go far back. For instance (this one should go back several hundred years):

> A caliph had a Jewish jester. The caliph asks his jester to prepare a list of foolish things done by everyone at the court. The jester does so and brings in the list.
>
> "Is my name on your list?" the caliph asks.
>
> "It is," the jester responds.
>
> The caliph's eyebrows go up. "You dare to say that I, the caliph, have done or said something stupid? What are you talking about?"
>
> "Did you not put a large sum of money in the hands of a Turk last week in order that he might bring you jewelry from his travels?"
>
> "Is that foolish? The Turk is an honest man. He will come back with what I want. He will prove you wrong. And what will you say then?"
>
> "If he does," the jester answered, "your name will come off the list I have here. And his will go on!"

Of course, this jest exhibits money consciousness, but also a certain kind of common sense about these things as well as a hint of sharp practice.

Consider the eagerness to get one's hands on money which the following jape shows us:

> Two friends meet. They have not seen each other for some time. Abe says: "What's the matter, Morris, you look *eppes* down in the mouth. Something wrong?"
>
> "I feel all right. It's just the way things are going. Or better—not going."

"Business is bad, huh?"

"No, it's not that. Three months ago my tante Raizele died and left me $25,000. Last month my uncle Berl passed away and left me $30,000."

"Listen, Morris, they were old people. What's so bad if they died and left you their money?"

" What's bad," he wants to know. "This month, nothin'."

There is also the following, a more recent story:

A Protestant minister goes to a barber shop to get a haircut. The barber finishes and the minister gets his billfold out to pay up.

"Oh, no," the barber tells him. "I no take money from a man of God."

An hour later the minister is back with a handsome Bible, which he presents to the barber as a gift.

The next day a Catholic priest gets a haircut in this shop and, similarly, the barber refuses payment: "I no take money from a man of God." The priest returns with a fine crucifix, which he presents as a gift to the barber.

Next a rabbi (what else?) enters to get his haircut, and the whole process gets repeated. Again, "I no accept money from a man of God."

The rabbi leaves and soon returns—with another rabbi!

Do I have to tell you that this is not intended to be flattering?

Old World Yiddish stories often deal with money consciousness as downright stinginess.

A middleman who deals in grain leaves for the big city. He tells his wife that an important deal is in the works. If it works out, he tells her, he will send a telegram.

Well, God helps, as they say, and he makes a neat profit. And he's off to the telegraph office. "Made nice profit love to you and the children home tomorrow, Moishe," he writes on the telegram pad.

He gets up and approaches the clerk, then stops and thinks. "Why do I have to tell her I made a nice profit. I already told her I would send a telegram only if I made a profit."

So he crosses out those words and starts toward the clerk again. "Wait a minute, *yuld* (fool)," he says to himself, "you have to telegraph her that you love her and the children? Doesn't she know that already? Cross it out!"

Out it comes. He takes one step and stands and looks at the paper. "Why am I telling her that I'm coming home tomorrow? If the deal is finished, when would she expect me to come home, Yom Kippur?"

All that's left now is his name. He asks himself: "Why do I need my name here? Who else would send my Sarah a telegram?"

Now he looks at the paper and says to himself, "Of course, it's all so obvious—see, you saved 50 kopecks!"

Stories about tight-fisted people will be found in both Old World and early immigrant humor, but they have largely disappeared in more recent Jewish American jokes. Why is that?

Let's look at the money question from another point of view. A lack of money enforces a strict discipline in spending. As was mentioned earlier, poverty was like an epidemic in Eastern Europe, and Jews reacted accordingly. If someone's cash were chronically short, the person would make do with whatever he or she could. As in the following:

A *melamed* (Hebrew school teacher) is running his class. This particular *melamed* not only teaches Hebrew, he likes to bring in natural science. One day he is telling the students about trees, birds, flowers, and also animals. Now, he calls on little Yankel and asks him, "Why do we need sheep?"

No answer. The child seems dumbfounded.

"Yankele," the teacher persists, "what do they take off a sheep?"

The kid comes to life. "Oh, yeah, wool," he answers.

"And of what use is wool?"

Yankel offers a look of bewilderment. The teacher loses patience. "C'mon, stupid, what do they make out of the wool?"

Still no answer. "Dummy, what is your jacket made of?"

"Oh, yeah," Yankel replies, "my father's old pants."

There were no doubt American Jewish immigrant youngsters who would have responded the same way. Here too, most
of the new arrivals had to face poverty, a condition where every
penny counted. Of course, other immigrants have probably
faced the same situation; it is the Jews who have incorporated
it into their humor.

So we should not be surprised to learn that Jewish buyers
were very cautious about spending. For one thing, they tried
not to buy at retail; the Jewish myth about this is that only non-
Jews do this. The fact is, however, that other ethnic groups are
also considered to be shrewdly careful about spending money.
Jokes about Scotsmen and Dutchmen often make the same
point.

Still, jokes abound about the behavior of the Jewish consumer. This one comes from Sam Levenson.

> Levenson's mother, so his story goes, went out to buy a
> tie for him. "This is a nice one," she told her Sammy, not asking
> for his opinion. To the retailer: "How much does it cost?"
> "Fifty cents," the retailer said.
> "Okay."
> To Levenson, such behavior was unheard of. He could
> scarcely wait until he got home before asking his mother: "Ma,
> you paid him 50 cents, without any bargaining? How come?"
> After all, Levenson knew that such price haggling was an article
> of faith with his mom.
> "Why I did it? I'll tell you. I hate that man because he once
> cheated me. Now I've repaid him."
> Levenson stared at her, mouth open. And she continued:
> "Now he'll eat his heart out. Because I paid him what he wanted,
> he'll be sure he should have asked for a dollar. He won't sleep
> tonight."

As you may know, the one-price system in retailing is a
relatively new idea introduced by the department stores. Before
that, and in most places today, it was and is expected that a
sale will be the result of negotiation, as satirized in the following
story, apparently about the Lower East Side earlier in this century.

A man comes into a clothing store, apparently interested in buying a suit. The storekeeper shows him several and he settles on one. The obvious next question is, "How much?"

"Here we are a one-price outfit," the storekeeper tells him. "So, I won't ask fifty dollars, not forty dollars, just thirty dollars buys you the suit."

"I believe you," the customer responds, "and I respect the way you're doing business. So I won't offer you ten dollars, I won't say twenty dollars, but twenty-five seems just right to me."

"You got it!" is the response.

We are also indebted to Levenson for another story illustrating money consciousness and bargaining sharpness among Jews.

His mother goes to the fruit and vegetable store. "What do you ask for these cucumbers?" she wants to know.

"Two for a nickel."

"So how much for one?"

"Three cents."

"Two for a nickel and one is three cents. Awright. I'll take the other one."

One of the funniest illustrations of this penchant for getting a "bargain" is the following.

A lady comes into a clothing store. She wants to buy a warm coat "dot also looks goot." After several tryons, she finds one she approves of and of course asks about the price.

"That coat is gonna cost you a hundert end fifty dollars," the dealer tells her.

"Are you crazy? You think money grows by me on trees? Ah hundert fifty dollars is ompossible. Give ah better price or I em going elsevare," she announces.

"I already cut die price," he tells her. "If you vant, I'll show you my bill. I gotta make ah few dollars, no?"

After much haggling back and forth, the lady finally says: "I em tellink you right now. I'll be beck vit die same coat and it vill cost less money, so you're losing ah customer."

"I don't think it could heppen, but good luck to you, missus," is his response.

Well, two days later, the same lady walks into the store with a package under her arm.

"Remember vot I told you?" she asks the retailer.

"Yeh," he responds warily, eyes on the package.

"Noo; here it is." And with that, she opens the package and takes out the coat! The two look exactly alike.

"And how motch did you pay for it?" the storekeeper wants to know.

"You vahnna siddon?" she responds. "Just ninedy-nine fifty. How do you like dot?"

"I kent bahleeve it," says the dealer. "I'll show de bill, you'll see it costs me more. Lemme look on de coat."

Well, he examines the outside, the collar, the cuffs—all seem identical; he opens it up, looks at the lining and then at the label. "Uh, huh," he exclaims, "now I understend. Look vot it says here on de label. You see, dis vun is made from reprocessed vool. End here look on mine. See—voigin vool. Dot's de difference."

The lady looks at him with a cool smile.

"Listen, Mister," she says, "if I could safe fifty dollars, vot do I care vot die sheep is doing?"

It's true that reprocessed wool may not yet have been used in those days and the story is probably anachronistic. But it does illustrate something and it's funny.

To show you that groups other than Jews think carefully about their money in their humor, here's a Bulgarian story.

Gabrovo is a Bulgarian city famous for its House of Humor and Satire. A resident of the city gets off the train and sees a cabman. "How much do you charge to go to the city center?" he asks.

"Only two leva; get in already."

"No, thanks," is the response. "I only asked to find out how much I'm saving by walking."

There is another aspect to the wise and careful consumer, and it doesn't really have to do with money. Jewish jokes have developed the notion that Jewish customers are picky. For example:

> A lady comes into a Jewish delicatessen and says to the counterman, "Let's see the corned beef."
>
> He shows it to her, and she says, "All right, I'll take some. Cut, cut."
>
> The counterman starts to cut. After the first five slices, he says to her, "Enough?"
>
> "Cut, cut," she answers.
>
> He cuts another half dozen slices and repeats his question.
>
> "Cut, cut," she commands.
>
> He continues cutting and she continues urging until he is about halfway through the beef. "Okay, lady," he tells her, "you got here a couple pounds already. Should I stop now?"
>
> "Yeh. Stop there," she says. "Now you're in the middle of the corned beef, right from there I'll take a quarter pound."

Picky-picky.

> Similarly, a Jewish woman comes to an East Side herring dealer. These were frequently sold right out of barrels on the sidewalk. The lady asks for a herring. The man digs into the barrel and comes up with one.
>
> "No," she says. "I don't like that one."
>
> Well, as you have guessed, he is pulling them out, with her hanging over the barrel, and she is turning them down, one after another. Finally, as they near the bottom, she says: "Ooh, that one looks good. No, the one to the left of it. Right."
>
> The dealer digs way in and brings up the herring. She looks at it and says: "You know, it looked better in the barrel. You know what? I think I won't buy a herring today."

And so the Jewish-American joke celebrates the presence of the Jewish woman in the marketplace. But haven't these jokes been mostly about older, first-generation people? Interestingly, this money consciousness and search-for-bargains stereotype have not disappeared in more recent Jewish humor, as is shown in the following jokes.

Levine goes to Miami Beach for a vacation and picks up a gorgeous girl. He propositions her. "Natalie, stay with me. I'll buy you a mink coat!"

"I already have one, so who needs you!"

"Okay, how about I get you a convertible?"

"Yeah? And what do I do with the Cadillac in my garage at home?"

"How about if I buy you a big diamond ring?"

"I've already got more jewelry than I know what to do with. But let me ask you something. I would consider going back with you if you put 25 grand in my bank first."

"Sorry," says Levine, "that's the only thing I can't get wholesale."

And in a similar vein:

In an affluent home, with excellent furnishings, a well-dressed, middle-aged man is pacing the living room. He looks at his watch. "Barbara," he calls out, "aren't you through dressing yet?"

"Just a few minutes more," comes a voice from another room. "Sheldon," the voice continues, "shall I wear the dress with the sequins or the one I just bought?"

"Put on the new one," says Sheldon to Barbara.

A moment later, the voice comes back: "Sheldon, should I wear the pearls or the jade necklace?"

"The pearls will go better with the new dress," Sheldon advises.

Again the voice is heard: "Sheldon, should I wear the fur stole or the plaid, you know, the one we bought in Scotland?"

Impatiently, Sheldon shouts: "For crying out loud, put on the plaid and let's go. If you don't get a move on, we'll miss the Early Bird Special at the restaurant!"

Old habits die hard. Everyone loves a bargain as well as that most tempting of all slogans, "I can get it for you wholesale!" My wife has an interesting astrological symbol. She was born under the sign "discount."

If You Got It, Flaunt It

Humor is not kind. Sometimes it is kinder than other times, but making fun of people is one of the staples in the joke business. By now you should be convinced you that we laugh *at* people as well as *with* them.

We have been looking at stereotypes in the area of business and money. One of the stereotypes that really intends to poke fun at Jews deals with the so-called love of showing off their possessions. These are shown as primarily Jews in the Western world, since the Eastern European had little to show off.

Now there are countless Gentiles who do exactly the same thing, and furthermore not all Jews behave this way. But the stereotype is there, a convenient way of poking fun at the wealthy Jew who wants to let the world know about it.

Let's see what this looks like in humor. Milton Berle tells this typical story.

A man is sitting and drinking at a bar. A tall creature comes in the door and stands looking around. It is nearly eight feet tall, very thin, gaunt face, thin chin, thin pointed nose, thin pointed ears, thin spiky spines on the head, standing straight up, staring eyes, almost no lips—you get the picture. *And*, it's all in green: the clothes are green, the face is green, the hair is greenish, and around the neck a variety of green gems—emeralds, jade, green diamonds.

The drinker at the bar closes his eyes, opens them; the stranger is still there. The bartender has stopped pouring and is standing goggle-eyed, mouth open.

Undaunted, the drinker gets up from the bar stool, saunters over to the man-creature, and asks, "Is everything all right, Mac?"

Very slowly, as if it hurts, the stranger answers, "E v - e r y t h i n g i s a l l r i g h t . "

"Where ya from?" asks our questioner.

"I c o m e f r o m a f a r a w a y p l a n e t."

"Zat so," our questioner observes. "And tell me. Where ya come from, does everyone look and wear green like you?"

"Y e s ."

"And does everyone wear all that jewelry?" is the next question.

"O n l y   t h e   J e w s ," is the response.

Well, you may laugh. It *is* a funny joke. But you should be aware that this story has a distinctly anti-Semitic undertone. Or take the following jape.

Three Jewish ladies are engaged in their habitual coffee klatsh, gabbing away. One of them asks: "Do either of you know any outfit that cleans diamonds and does a good job? I can't seem to get it done by myself."

"Oh, yes," one of her friends replies. "I use a jeweler in my neighborhood who does an excellent job. I'll call you tonight and give you the address and phone number."

At this point, the third one gets into the conversation. "I really don't know what you girls are after," she notes. "All I can tell you is that when my diamonds get dirty, I just throw them away!"

So there you have it—disposable diamonds. If you've got it, flaunt it. While you're laughing, ask yourself, "Am I laughing at the joke, or is my bias showing?"

Here's another question. Is the last joke really a Jewish joke? The fact is that, aside from the stereotype, it could be told of people from any group. Nevertheless, it's always told about Jewish women. Similarly:

Two middle-aged Jewish ladies are sitting in the lobby of a resort hotel. One leans forward and says to the other: "If I could trouble you, could you please tell me the time? You see, my diamond watch is by Harry Winston to get fixed."

And the second answers: "It's no trouble at all. I'll be glad to tell you." She raises her forearm conspicuously. "It's just exactly five rubies after nine emeralds."

To conclude, here is another jest with a unique wrinkle.

A man and a woman are in a jewelry store which sells very fine stuff. The jeweler asks, "What are you interested in seeing, sir, madame?"

The man says: "I want to buy my wife a matched set—earrings, a pendant, and a ring. Money is no object. What would you suggest?"

"I'm sure we can find something that will satisfy you. Would you prefer diamonds, rubies, sapphires, emeralds? We have fine material in all of those," is the answer.

The husband turns to the wife and asks, "So, Bertha, what would you like?"

"Irving," she replies, "I really don't care. All I want is something so when my best friend, Molly, sees it, she'll take one look and drop dead!"

Malice in wonderland! This is friendship?

Now we've seen both stereotypes—the mainly Eastern European and immigrant "Jewish tightwad," and the Jewish Americans who want to dazzle you with what they own. More about this later.

We Are Smart, Aren't We?

Another prevalent stereotype about Jews is that they are smart. Non-Jews often assert this and Jews are generally willing to concede it. True, a large number of Jews have won Nobel and other prizes. But does that mean that all Jews are brilliant?

Anyhow, folklore alleges this to be so, and it certainly shows up in Jewish humor. What's interesting is that it takes several different forms.

For example, the renowned great reasoning ability of Talmudic scholars appears in humorous stories. Often such jests concern the wisdom of the rabbi or scholar as in the following:

A countryman comes to a rabbi and requests of him: "Rabbi, please, I know next to nothing about Talmud. Can you teach me what it is and how to reason like you great students of the Talmud do? Then I may be able to teach myself."

The rabbi sighs: "I don't think that's possible. It takes years of study to explore the Talmud and to learn the methods of reasoning used by Talmudic students."

"But surely, Rabbi, you can give me a beginning so I can decide whether I am able to go further," the countryman persists.

"All right," the rabbi relents. "Let me do it in the form of an example. Listen. Two robbers enter a house through the chimney. One has a sooty face and the other's face is clean. Now tell me, which one will wash his face?"

"I think it will be the one whose face is dirty."

"You see," the rabbi tells him, "your reasoning is flawed. Don't you see why?"

The countryman puts his face in his hands. He is obviously thinking very hard. But he shrugs his shoulders, "No, I don't!"

The rabbi goes further. "Dirty Face will look at Clean Face and see it as clean. And . . . ." He leaves his statement unfinished.

"Oh," the countryman says, "and Clean Face will look at Dirty Face and see that it is dirty. I see. So I guess the fellow with the clean face will look to wash his face. Right, Rabbi? Now I begin to see what the Talmud is!"

"Better," says the rabbi. "That's better, but you still don't understand Talmudic reasoning."

"But Rabbi, what other possibility is there?" asks the countryman.

The Rabbi responds: "You see, in Talmudic reasoning we always start by asking the right question. In this story, you should begin by saying to me, 'Rabbi, how is it possible for two men to come down the same chimney and for only one to have a dirty face?' "

This story establishes the rabbinic superiority, in intellectual terms. But this reasoning skill is not limited to men of the cloth. Look at what happens in the following Old World story.

Benjamin is seated in a railroad car on his way back to his home in the town of Maronezh, in Hungary. (Many European jokes take place in railroad cars.) He is reading his newspaper, when a well-dressed young man —Homburg hat, attaché case, pince-nez glasses—enters the compartment. He nods briefly and proceeds to open his case, pull out some reading matter, and bury his nose in it.

Soon the conductor appears. Benjamin surrenders his ticket and hears the young man say: "I do not have a ticket. I would like to purchase one to Maronezh."

Benjamin is consumed with curiosity. Who can this man be? After all, Maronezh is a small town. The local *poretz* (nobleman) is currently away for the season, so there is no major Gentile social life which would draw such a man to the town. The peasants, forget it—what could he have to do with them?

So, he must be going to see some Jewish person or family. But whom? Wait a minute, just before I left, two weeks ago, Rubenstein, the flour merchant, went bankrupt. This must be a creditor. No, look how composed he is.

Maybe he is an accountant coming to look over Rubenstein's books. I can't believe that! Rubenstein would burn his books before letting anyone see them.

So who? A doctor going to see a patient? No. What would a doctor be doing with an attaché case, and without a black bag, yet. Rule that out. A lawyer to try a case? Impossible. The court is not in Maronezh. We go to Bogavoy to try cases.

Wait a minute. Didn't I hear that Levin is marrying off a daughter? Oho, that must be it. So let's think . . . The oldest daughter, Sarah? She's too old for this fellow. The second daughter, Malka? She's ugly—with these modern children I can't believe that an impressive young man like this would be looking to marry such an unwholesome looking girl, *nebich* (the all-purpose word of pity in Yiddish).

So that leaves the youngest daughter, Naomi. Right. She's a good-looking girl and well educated. It fits.

What else did I hear? They said Levin had struck it right, that the girl was marrying into a very good Budapest family and that the young man was a lawyer. If I remember correctly, they also said that the family is a well-known rabbinic one. What was the name? Of course, Cohen.

So, a Doctor Juris from Budapest. Wait a minute, who am I kidding? A lawyer named Cohen! C'mon. Those anti-Semites in Budapest would never let a man named Cohen practice law in their courts. So, Benjamin, what do you conclude? Right. He must have changed his name.

But I'll bet he stayed close to the Jewish surname. They always do. So what name would he use? Cohen, Cohen, Cohen. I've got it. I'll bet he changed it to Kovach.

At this point, Benjamin leans forward and says: "Dr. Kovach, I want to congratulate you on your forthcoming marriage to Naomi Levin. May I wish you long life and much happiness together!"

"Thank you," replied the young man. "But, but, just a minute. How did you know who I am and that I'm marrying Naomi Levin?"

Benjamin waved his hand and responded, "Oh, that—it's obvious."

With the word "obvious," he is, of course, trying to establish superiority. Can all Jews do this kind of reasoning? Of course not. And what's more, many other people can. There are Jesuit-trained Catholics who are just as proficient at this type of reasoning as any Talmudic scholar. But the jokes credit Jews.

And now let me offer you a theory. Do you remember the Chelm stories? The townspeople who decided to hang the tailor instead of the one cobbler in town, and the fellow who thought the moon was more important than the sun? These "noodle stories" are common in many cultures, but in Jewish life they perform an additional function. They may have developed in part to make fun of the Talmudic reasoning illustrated above. If you want logic and reasoning, they seem to say, we'll show you some beautiful, left-handed sort of reasoning which looks right from the point of view of a certain sort of logic but which is really nonsense. Here's an example.

A fire breaks out one night in the city. Naturally, there is great commotion, people running to and fro with water buckets. The fire is finally put out, and now the weary townspeople are addressed by the rabbi, to wit: "Friends, do you realize that you have just witnessed a miracle for which we should be thankful?"

There are all kinds of expressions of surprise. "Miracle? What kind of miracle? Thankful? The whole town almost went up in flames and he wants us to be thankful? What is he talking about?"

"Let be quiet!" the rabbi shouts, and when the crowd quiets down, he continues: "Don't you see what happened? Think how bright the flames were. If the *Reboineh Shel Oilem* (Master of the Universe) had not made the flames to be so bright, how would we have been able to see how to put out the fire on such a dark night?"

It's logical, isn't it? Inverted, maybe, but it is a logical conclusion drawn from an established fact. That's what makes some jokes—the bizarre conclusion drawn from a reasonable premise.

Another kind of mental ability that appears in Jewish stories is mental agility, quick thinking. For example:

A little Jewish man is going up in an airplane for the first time and he is scared to death, a real member of the white knuckle brigade. He is, in fact, holding on for dear life with one hand and munching on a chocolate bar (to give him strength) with the other.

He has an inside seat and now a big fellow with a wide-brimmed Stetson-type hat boards the plane and checks his seat number, which turns out to be the outside seat next to our Jewish friend. He smiles, says "Howdy" to the Jew, and sits down. He pulls his hat over his eyes and is almost instantly asleep.

Well, the plane has no sooner started and is still on the runway when our poor, frightened little Jew *oopses* without benefit of bag—all over the Texan's lap. Now he's really frightened. What will the big man say or do when he wakes up?

After about two minutes, as the plane rises, the Texan stirs, opens his eyes, and looks down at his lap. His eyes open wide and he turns to the man next to him.

And at this point the Jew leans over and asks, "Now you feel better?"

Quick thinking, wouldn't you say? A special case of mental agility is in the category of outwitting, discussed earlier in the book.

In a Russian city, a Jew, with long sidecurls and the traditional gabardine and skullcap, is taking a walk on a path near the river. He passes a policeman, nods, and accidentally stumbles over a root, tumbles over, and plops into the river.

"Help me! Help! I can't swim," he screams.

The policeman stands there grinning.

"Please, please, I can't swim. Help me get out of here!"

Now the policeman is laughing uproariously.

Weakly, with his last breath, the Jew yells: "Down with the Czar! Down with the Czar!"

Immediately the policeman jumps in and drags him out. "How dare you speak like that about the Czar. You're going right to jail. We'll teach you to talk revolution!"

In the next section we'll consider another aspect of smart.

Commonsensical

Related to the stereotypical business acumen, thinking ability, and mental agility, is the commonsensical character of some Jewish jokes. Jews were well aware that they had to keep both feet squarely on the ground in order to survive, and some humor celebrates this characteristic. There are even Chelm stories that pay tribute to it.

Since, like all Jews, the Jews of Chelm have many difficulties, they have a great deal to worry about. There is a lot of "oy" saying (the traditional word when difficulties arise), usually accompanied by a sigh, hand wringing, and exclamations of "what are we going to do now?"

At one of the town council meetings, Berel, a householder, proposes that something be done about all this worrying that goes on in Chelm. What to do?

"Let us hire Yussel, the chimney sweep, and arrange for him to do all the worrying for all of us. That will leave us free to do the things that are required without always worrying. And for this we will pay him five rubles a week."

A murmur of agreement. (Up to this point, a typical Chelmer noodle story.) But now Chaim speaks up: "Jews of the council. Let me pose a question for you. If Yussel is paid five rubles a week, what will he have to worry about?"

A neat commonsense reversal, wouldn't you say?

The Chasidim, the segment of Ashkenazi Jews mentioned earlier, came to believe very strongly in the wisdom of their rabbis. As a result, they show up in Jewish humor as extolling these sainted men beyond all expectations.

Two Chasidim are in dispute regarding the relative merits and abilities of their respective rabbis. Each is arguing what a wonder worker his particular rabbi is.

"My rabbi," says one, "a real miracle worker. Once he brings home an unexpected guest for the Sabbath. His wife is appalled. On the side, she whispers to him, 'I have only one little fish; it will surely be insufficient for all of us.'

"To which the rabbi answers, with a wave of his hand, 'Look again.' And behold! Two fishes."

The second Chasid responds: "That's all very well. But do you want to hear a real miracle? Our rabbi is playing a new card game with his wife. Well, his wife puts down four aces and says, 'I think I win.' But my rabbi says, 'Just a minute.' And he puts down five kings. That's a miracle!"

"Now wait a minute," exclaims the first Chasid, grabbing him by the coat. "I know that game. It's called poker. You can't have five kings."

"Is that right? Well, I'll tell you what. If you will give up one fish, I'll give up one king."

So, underneath the miracle bragging is a dose of good common sense.

That particular joke sounds very suspicious. It's phrased in Chasidic terms, but poker playing by a rabbi? It's a good story, but it sounds like an invention of an American gag writer. Here's one that's more authentic.

Velvel has apparently died and the burial committee of the *shtetl* has come to his home to arrange for the funeral. Suddenly, Velvel sits up. Naturally, there is excitement, commotion.

"We were sure you were dead," one of his friends exclaims.

"Really?" he wonders. "But I have to tell you, I knew the whole time that I was alive. You want to know why? Because I was hungry and my feet were cold."

"Hungry, cold feet. What are you talking about?" his friends want to know.

"You understand," Velvel shakes his index finger at them. "If I were in *Gan Aiden* (Paradise), I wouldn't be hungry. And if, on the other hand, I were in *Gehennim* (Hell), my feet wouldn't be cold!"

This type of common sense is characteristic not only of Old World stories. Here is a story about modern Israel.

An American is visiting Israel. Among the sights he goes to see is, of course, the Western Wall. Some Jews who go there to pray are in the habit of putting *kvitlach,* or paper slips, into the crevices in the wall. These are usually requests for some form of divine intervention, some prayer that the person would like to see actualized. The American sees a man putting such a *kvitel* in the wall. He walks up to him and asks, "Sir, do you speak English?"

"Ah little," is the reply.

"Good. Then would you be good enough to tell me what you are doing. What is the reason you are putting that piece of paper in the wall?"

"Vell," the Jew answers, "you see, ven vee hev, how you say, ah petition to Gott, vee put it here in die vull."

The American is astonished. "Really. Do you do it often?" he asks.

"Yeh," the Jew replies, "ullmost every veek."

"And does it really help?" the American wants to know.

"Duz it help? It's like tukking to die vull!"

For the record, talking to the wall is an old Yiddish idiom for what we would call getting nowhere. And so here you see the triumph of common sense over custom.

Here is a common sense story that has a more Old World, Yiddish flavor.

A Chasid comes to his rabbi. "Rabbi," he cries, in tears, "I can't make ends meet. Counsel me, tell me what I must do to provide for my family."

The rabbi looks at him with great compassion and advises: "Fishel, go home. We will both pray. You will see God will help you!"

The Chasid starts to the door and then turns.

"Fishel," the rabbi asks, "what is it you want to ask?"

"Rabbi," says the Chasid, "I believe you when you tell me that God will help me. But please, tell me, what should I do until He helps me!"

Common sense—even where faith is concerned! Another superb example of this is a Jewish-American jest:

A young woman is the first girl in her family to have gone to college, where she majored in art history. She has just returned home and is talking to her grandmother, an immigrant woman.

"So vot did you end up with in collitch, Pauline?"

"I specialized in art history," the young woman tells her.

"Ott history? I hoid accounting, law, medicine, teaching, noissing, but vot is ott history?" was the inevitable question. (This already illustrates the down-to-earth views of many Jewish parents in earlier generations.)

"I'll tell you what, Grandma. Tomorrow, I'll take you to the museum. There you can get a better idea of what I'm talking about than if I try to explain it here."

So the next day grandmother and granddaughter arrive at the museum. As it happens, the first turn they take presents them with a picture of the nativity. The young woman pauses and says: "Look at this picture, Grandma. It was painted about 300 years ago by a famous Italian painter. He was one of the leading innovators in what is called chiaroscuro. Look how interesting he makes the difference between light and dark, how he creates shadows. Look at the wonderful skin tones he gets. You see, he developed some new ways of doing faces. Isn't it wonderful, the color he gets into the sky? And into the halo around the Madonna's head?''

The old lady stares at the picture. ''Pauline,'' she asks after a pause, ''vot is dis place vere all dis is going on?''

''Oh, that,'' the young woman replies. ''You see, Mary has had to give birth to Jesus in a stable or a barn, which is where they are staying.''

''A stable?'' the old woman is astonished. ''Vy in a stable? Vy not a hospital or at least a house?''

''Well,'' the young woman says, a little out of her depth, ''you see, Grandma, there was no room for them at the inn, like a motel. And anyway they were too poor to afford a motel.''

''Oh,'' says the old lady. ''And tell me, vot kind of cloding is dot fahr de baby? It looks to me like day don't hev reggela tings, like a little suit or something?''

''Oh, you're right, Grandma. As I said, this is a poor family.''

''Now tell me,'' the grandmother digs further. ''Who and vere is de fodder of dis baby, de husband?''

At this point, Pauline launches into a long explanation of the birth of Jesus and the role of Joseph, ending with the statement that he has probably gone to make other arrangements.

The old lady is silent for a minute or two and then she says: ''You know, Pauline, I rilly don't understend vot's going on here. Look, a decent place to live or to hev de baby she ain't got. Reggela clothes she kennt offord. A husband you don't see. End de only ting in dot woman's mind is to hev her piktshe taken?''

Surprisingly, this common sense appears even in ancient Jewish literature, in the stories created around explanations of the Bible, what Hebrew scholars call the *aggadic* literature. For example:

A young Jewish boy is brought up in the king's household and the king becomes very fond of him. Now the young man has come of age, and the king says to him, ''As a token of my affection, and since you are now grown to be a man, ask whatever you want and you will get it.''

So the young man thinks. Should I ask for wealth—gems or gold? That would be good. Or maybe I should ask for land—

an estate. That, too, would be good. Or a palace, fine horses, noble apparel. All of these would be good. No! I will ask for his daughter in marriage, for then I will get all of these!!

Pretty sensible young man, isn't he?

You Got Some Nerve!

The stereotypes of smartness and common sense are friendly ones. Some of those on money consciousness and flaunting are rather hostile. We will now consider one that's somewhere in between, namely, *chutzpeh*. The classic definition of *chutzpeh* is, a young man who kills both of his parents and then comes before the court and pleads for leniency on the grounds that he is an orphan. English has adopted this word and you will find it in contemporary dictionaries.

The characteristic of *chutzpeh* showed up frequently in Old World jokes. It was a stereotype. In the West, however, it seems to have virtually disappeared as a source of humor. Why? I have a theory, but let's hold that.

A whole branch of Jewish humor that has delighted collectors for years are the Eastern European stories dealing with the *shnorrer*. This word describes more than a mere beggar (the Yiddish word for that is *betler*). *Shnorrers* had developed a technique which (1) called for them to visit their "patrons" rather than, say, beg on streets, (2) often had them develop a regular clientele on whose generosity they depended, and (3) played on the well-developed concept in Judaism of the need for the haves to aid the have-nots (*tzeduckeh*).

The client relation can be glimpsed, for example, in the musical, *Fiddler on the Roof*. In the opening "Tradition" scene, during the dancing, a man who turns out to be a *shnorrer* asks another man why he has reduced his "allowance." He is told that the donor has not been doing well. "So," the *shnorrer* protests, "if you're not doing well, I have to suffer?"

Regarding the *chutzpeh*, or gall, of *shnorrers*, our old friend Freud, who was a collector of these jokes, argued that *shnorrers* really viewed themselves as *entitled* to funds, feeling that they were doing the donor a favor in permitting him to discharge his obligation under the laws of Judaism. They developed *chutzpeh* to a fine art. For example:

> A *shnorrer* comes to Rothschild and is received by his secretary.
> "I need to see the Baron," he declares. "Please announce me."
> "With reference to what?" the secretary wishes to know.
> "It is a private, confidential matter which I will announce only to the Baron."
> Dialog ensues back and forth, the secretary pressing to learn what the man wants and the fellow insisting on seeing Rothschild only. Finally, the secretary decides to tell his boss what is going on.
> "Your Excellency, there is a Jew outside who is most insistent about seeing you regarding some private matter. Shall I show him in? He will not tell me what it is about."
> "Show him in."
> Once inside, the man begins: "Dear Baron Rothschild, let me explain. We are very poor. Food is scarce on our table, my wife is ill, and I need desperately some money to start a business so that we can better our lot. Can I count on you for some help?"
> Rothschild is outraged! "You had to see me in order to beg for money? You could have told all this to my secretary!"
> The *shnorrer* draws himself up haughtily. "Herr Rothschild," he says. "I don't tell you how to run your banking business, so don't tell me how to run my shnorring business!"

For obvious reasons, Rothschild figures frequently in these *shnorrer* stories. That is itself a sort of stereotype. Listen to this one.

> A man comes to the Rothschild office and tells the secretary that he has an important business proposition to discuss with the baron. He explains further that Rothschild stands to make half a million rubles. (The Rothschilds were in Germany and other countries in Western Europe, but the ruble was the currency used in the Yiddish jokes.)

The man is admitted to the baron's office, where Rothschild invites him to sit down and inquires about the deal.

"Not so fast," the stranger answers. "I want a finder's fee of 100 rubles before I even explain it to you."

Well, Rothschild decides to go along and produces a 100-ruble bill. "Now tell me what your deal is. As plainly and specifically and briefly as possible. I have other appointments this morning."

"Well," says the stranger. "Isn't it true that you are marrying off a daughter?"

"Yes," the baron replies. "But what has that to do with a deal?"

"It's like this. Rumor has it that her dowry will be a million rubles. I want you to know that I will take her for half that amount, thus saving you half a million rubles. How does that sound?"

Mercifully, we leave out Rothschild's response.

And now one of the greatest of all *shnorrer* stories, one that has often been reworked to other situations.

A *shnorrer* has come to a wealthy man for the obvious reason. "Herr Neumann, I am suffering from a dreadful internal disease. The doctor who has been treating me for nearly a year has finally told me that I cannot recover or at least improve if I do not go to a spa. But I am a poor man and do not have the funds to do so. Since I know you to be a generous man, I have come to you for help."

Apparently moved, the prospective donor looks at the man and says, "Well, how much would it cost for you to go to a spa?"

"Well, the ticket to Baden-Baden costs. . . ."

The other man interrupts: "Where is it written that you must go to Baden-Baden, the most expensive spa in all of Europe?"

The *shnorrer* looks at him and replies: "Herr Neumann, for my health *nothing* is too good!"

There are also many *chutzpeh* stories that have nothing to do with *shnorrers*. Here's one about a Jewish businessman.

This fellow has perfected a technique of borrowing from Bank A and then paying off the loan by making a similar loan from Bank B. Then he borrows again from Bank A to repay the loan to Bank B. Going back and forth in this way, the borrower seems to be managing very well.

A time comes when he owes money to Bank A and he doesn't pay. The owner of the bank asks him to come in and he does so. "Mr. Cohen, you have not paid up your loan. What's wrong?" the banker wants to know.

"Oh," the businessman replies, "I've gotten sick and tired of this running from your bank to Bank B and from theirs to yours. I feel like a messenger service. From now on, you fellows arrange it between yourselves that every few months you'll transfer the needed funds."

Here's another one of these amusing stories:

A Jew has to go from his shtetl to a larger city. And of course, this must be done by train. A week later, he returns home.

"How did everything go?" his wife wants to know. "Did you do what you had to do in the city?"

"Everything was all right," he tells her. "But I did have a couple of bad minutes on the train coming home."

"What happened?" is the natural question.

"Well, the conductor came by and looked at me in a peculiar way."

"Peculiar? How?"

"He looked at me as though I had no ticket."

"So what happened?"

"I looked right back at him—as if I had one!"

The following story, like so many Old World stories, also takes place in a train.

Reb Yudel, who has purchased a second-class ticket, goes right into a first-class compartment, which is empty. (That's only the first *chutzpeh*.) He's sitting there, smoking his pipe. Finally, just as the train pulls into the next station, the conductor arrives.

"Sir," he tells Reb Yudel, "you must leave this compartment. It has been reserved for the bishop."

Reb Yudel doesn't move a muscle. He looks up at the
conductor and, through the smoke of his pipe, remarks, "So
who said that I'm not the bishop?"

It wasn't only *shnorrers*, then, who exhibited this "ingra-
tiating" characteristic of *chutzpeh*. One of the most famous *chutz-
peniks* of them all was a man called Hershele Ostropolier. He
was the best-known of a number of wags whose stories fill
Yiddish jest books.

The Chasidic rabbi was always the major Jewish figure in
a *shtetl* or town, and many of them had a sort of court, like
royalty. Hershele was unsuccessful in most things until he
showed up at the court of one of these rabbis and became the
"court jester." The following stories illustrate the kind of fellow
he is supposed to have been.

Hershele goes into a bakery and orders a roll and butter.
The owner brings the roll. Hershele looks at it and says: "You
know, I've changed my mind. Here's the roll; bring me a bagel
instead."

The owner takes the roll and returns with a bagel, which
our hero proceeds to eat with great relish. After finishing, he
gets up and starts walking to the door.

"Just a minute!" the storekeeper calls, running after him.
"You haven't paid for the bagel."

"Why should I?" he answers. "I gave you the roll for the
bagel."

"But, but," the owner sputters, "you never paid for the
roll either!"

"Pay for the roll! What do you want from my life? Tell me,
did I eat the roll? No! So why should I pay for it?"

It sounds a little like Abbott and Costello to you. It makes
one wonder if they ever read about Hershele. Here is one more
Hershele story.

Hershele comes to the burial society. "I need money to
bury my wife—for a coffin, for shrouds."

With expressions of condolence, the officers of the society
provide him with funds. As is the custom, a committee is appointed to make a condolence call. When they arrive later in the
evening, they discover that the wife is in perfectly good health
and is preparing dinner.

"Hershele, what is this?" the committee head shouts at
him. "You lied to us! You took money under false pretenses.
How could you do such a thing?"

"My friends," Hershele answered, "she will surely die and
be buried by the society ultimately. Do you begrudge me a few
extra years of having her as my wife and companion?"

Why were such stories plentiful in Eastern Europe and
rare in the Western world? Probably because poverty breeds a
certain ingenuity in getting the basic needs. Eastern Jews no
doubt needed to use their wits to survive. *Chutzpeh* was useful.
Of course, the stories exaggerate a little, or maybe more than
a little, but they most likely had some basis in reality.

For those living and prospering in the West, this audacity
has become less important. Whatever *chutzpeh* there is has to
be transferred to nonfinancial fields. Perhaps we will find some
of it in other parts of the book.

Good God!

Sometimes *chutzpeh*, mental ability, or common sense cannot
prevail. So where does a Jew turn then?

One of Jews' most interesting, and desirable, characteristics is their desire and ability to converse with God. The type
of discussion Tevye has with the Almighty in *Fiddler on the Roof*
is sprinkled throughout the Sholom Aleichem stories that inspired the musical. They were originally written in Yiddish,
and they mirror Yiddish speech. In fact, Eastern European Jews
often used the word, *gotenyu*, a diminutive of "God," in their
ordinary speech. Doesn't that suggest a speaking relationship
between Jews and God? (Remember too that the Biblical patri-

archs, Abraham, Isaac, and Jacob, were in frequent conversation with the deity, as were Moses, Jonah, and Job, and presumably all the prophets.)

As you would expect, this aspect of Judaism shows up in Jewish jokes. Here is an example.

Mrs. Goldstein is taking care of her grandson for the weekend while her son and daughter-in-law take a short vacation. The Goldsteins live on New York's East Side. What does an elderly grandmother in that neighborhood do with a six-year-old? She takes him for a walk down to the East River docks "to look around."

As luck would have it, the little boy wanders too close to the edge and suddenly, plop, he's in and he's not coming up. Grandma Goldstein is in shock. What to do? She decides to go to the highest authority.

"God," she wails, "How could you do this to me? All my life, I have been a pious and devout Jewish woman; I have observed all the holidays; I lit the candles every Friday; I have brought up my children as close to the Law as possible. And this is how I am repaid? What will I tell Sidney and Lorraine when they come home Sunday night? Have you thought of that? Unless you help me I think I will have to join my little grandson, Stuart."

Apparently the Almighty is listening, because suddenly— there stands little Stuart, soaked, a little bedraggled, but alive, crying, "Grandma, Grandma."

Grandma opens her arms to the little boy and lifts her head again to Heaven. "Lord," she says, "you have justified my deepest belief in your goodness, in your mercy, in your love for us."

But suddenly her eyes narrow and her expression hardens. "Just a minute, God," she adds. "What kind of business is this? When Stuart went into the water, he had a hat!"

That's *chutzpeh!* It's also funny. Similarly:

Bachelor Marty Harwood (born Hershkowitz) has just retired after many years as a New York schoolteacher. He moves to Florida, where he buys a modest condominium. Now fortune intervenes. He suddenly gets word that an uncle has died in Cincinnati and, to everyone's surprise, has left a cool half a million dollars to his closest relative—one Morris Hershkowitz, also known as Marty Harwood.

Joy reigns. Marty collects his inheritance and suddenly he blossoms. His eyeglasses are the first to go, replaced by contact lenses. His teeth are all repaired and his smile reveals gorgeous new caps. A face lift follows; the nose gets a bobbing and a set of toupees are acquired. Next the clothes, yellow trousers with shirt and yellow shoes to match—just one of the new outfits in the Florida style.

Marty soon begins to squire young women, that is, women in their forties and fifties. What can I tell you—it's a picture of complete happiness.

And now the ultimate—Marty decides to get himself a brand new red convertible. On his first day out, on his way to a date—tragedy. There is a collision. The convertible is totaled and Marty is next seen at the Pearly Gates.

He is screaming. "This has to be a mistake! This has to be a mistake! I have to see God and talk it over with him."

So loud is the commotion that the Angel-in-Charge calls in for advice and receives word that the complainer is to be allowed to come in and state his case.

So Marty begins: "Good and just Lord of the Universe! How could you do this to me? After a lifetime of genteel poverty in which I barely made ends meet, I get a little relief and happiness and before I know it, only two months' pleasure, you have taken it all away. God, I must appeal this divine decision. I was not ready for the Angel of Death to take me. In the interests of fairness, I demand a review."

God shuffles some records in front of Him, then looks steadily at Marty. Finally, he asks, "What did you say your name was?"

"My name is Marty Harwood."

"Marty Harwood . . . Marty Harwood. . . . We have no record of a Marty Harwood." The Lord seems momentarily puzzled.

"Maybe you should look under Hershkowitz, Morris Hershkowitz; that was my original name."

"You are Morris Hershkowitz?! No wonder the Angel of Death took you. We didn't recognize you!"

The first joke puts God in a merciful light and the second in an apologetic frame. Obviously, God can behave differently in various conversations. As we see again:

> The brothers Mandelbaum are precise opposites. Abraham is pious, studious in the Torah, not materialistic, and . . . poor. Brother Hilary (né Hershel) is flippant, rakish, given to wine, women, and song, totally uninterested in Jewish law and tradition . . . and well-to-do.
>
> Abraham prays and studies ever harder, ever harder, trying to understand why his brother has such ample rewards and he gets so little. Finally he decides to go directly to the source and fountain of all knowledge. And so he begins to include in his prayers the question: "Oh, Lord of all creation, author of love, justice, and mercy, it is written in our books that the virtuous and pious shall be rewarded and the sinners who pay no attention to Your commandments shall receive their just due. So how do You explain that my rewards are so meager and my brother's so bountiful?"
>
> And, on a certain day, at the end of his praying, he hears a thundering voice: "You want to know why? It's because you *nudye* me!!"

For those who do not understand, the word *nudye* is a Yiddish term combining the ideas of boring and bothering. And so in this somewhat irreverent joke, God's mood is that of impatience.

To prove how close the relation is between Jews and God in this stereotype, here is one more jest.

> The Israeli prime minister is visiting the United States. While he is in the Oval Office discussing matters with the president and the secretary of state, his curiosity is piqued by a red telephone on a small desk in the corner. Finally, when the serious discussions are over, he asks, "Mr. President, maybe you will explain to me that red telephone over there?"
>
> "Certainly," the president replies. "That is the special hot line to the Kremlin."
>
> "Oh, that's the famous hot line. So can you tell me—how does it work?"

"Well," the president explains, "all we have to do is get the long-distance operator, give her the special number in the Kremlin, and we will be connected to a special line. Then we get through to the general secretary and it's done. Normally, it doesn't take too long."

"That's very interesting and important to the peace," the prime minister concludes.

"That's right. That's why it's there."

Some months later, the U.S. secretary of state is visiting with the Israeli prime minister in Jerusalem. As their discussion begins, the secretary notices a red telephone on the desk. Recalling the previous meeting in Washington, he inquires jokingly: "Do you also have a hot line to Moscow?"

The prime minister replies, "No, no. That's our hot line to God."

The secretary's eyebrows go up. "Really!" he says and adds sarcastically, "I suppose it works like our hot line to Moscow; you put in a long-distance call and. . . ."

"No, no," the Minister interrupts, "for us it's a local call."

I doubt if other jesters are so easily tempted to discuss matters with the Creator, but Jews . . . well, you just saw some samples.

It is fairly common knowledge that Jews look at their status as one of chosenness. Those who know Judaism understand that this election really means that Jews see themselves as chosen to bring the word of God to other nations. God did not offer them any particular privileges to match this burden—with the exception of promising their settlement in the land of Canaan. But this doesn't deter what I am sure are Jewish-American joke writers, as you will see in the following.

A Protestant minister has died and arrived at Heaven's gate. St. Peter, serving as the admissions officer, pulls his personal information file out of the heavenly computer.

"Reverend Simmons," he says, "I am impressed! So many good deeds; so many charitable actions; so much help and comfort to your fellow man rates you an A, even an A plus. We will measure you for your halo and your wings later. Meanwhile, we want you to have every heavenly comfort. We are supplying you with a Cadillac to show that your evaluation means something. And here it comes now. You may take it to your heavenly home at this address. You may be certain that your home will have every comfort."

The minister, who never owned a Cadillac, is naturally pleased. He gets into the car and begins driving through the heavenly streets. He has gone only a short distance, when he comes abreast of another automobile, a Mercedes. Inside, he notices a man wearing the garb of a priest. Somewhat disturbed, he turns back to the heavenly gate and questions St. Peter: "St. Peter," he asks, "on my way home on Heavenly Drive, I stopped at one of the heavenly traffic lights. To my surprise, I noticed a Mercedes next to my Cadillac, with a priest inside. Why should a priest merit a Mercedes when all I get is a Cadillac? Do you have a grade higher than A plus here?"

"Let me explain," St. Peter reassures him. "There is no higher grade than yours. However, your wife and children will ultimately join you here. Consider the priest. As a celibate, he has not had the pleasure of sexual experience and the joy of having children. We feel it necessary to make up for that difference in your respective lives. And so, by way of compensation, he receives the pleasure of a Mercedes."

"I see," the minister responds thoughtfully. "Well, I suppose there is justification there." And off he drives again.

Shortly, he stops at another heavenly light and, you guessed it—a rabbi, skullcap, a prayershawl over his shoulders—*in a Rolls-Royce!*

Now the minister is really irate. He drives back to St. Peter and demands: "Why should a rabbi have a Rolls while I have only a Cadillac? I could understand the priest's situation. But a rabbi? What deprivation entitles him to compensation?"

St. Peter looks at him with an air of surprise. "Listen," he says, "you are a nice man, but he's *mishpocheh* (family)."

Well, admit it, people who talk so easily with the Creator are entitled to the inside track, at least in humor.

Our Rabbi Is a Wise Man

You might be wondering why these Jewish people have a direct line to God. Shouldn't they be speaking to their rabbi? Well, in Judaism, the rabbi is a teacher, a leader of the community, a judge in matters of dispute, but he is not an intermediary between man and God as the priest or minister is in many Christian denominations.

Over centuries, the role of the rabbi became strongly established as the man of wisdom, so Jews developed great respect for these leaders. After the emergence of the Chasidic movement, described earlier, the devotion of Chasidim to their rabbis became legendary, going far beyond respect. Recall the stories about miracle workers? Naturally, then, we would expect to find jokes about the cleverness or astuteness of rabbis. Some samples:

In many places in the Old World, the rabbi's was not a full-time job. Often, for example, he was also a merchant. One such rabbi, who was a successful businessman, suddenly suffers a huge financial loss through a serious error in judgment. The rumor spreads around the town. Some of the townsfolk, whose regard for him is very high, get together and decide that they must go and console him on his losses.

So that evening a deputation goes to call on him. And lo and behold, what do they find? The rabbi is engrossed in his studies and welcomes them warmly without any sign of unhappiness or worry.

"Rebbe," one of the visitors asks, "we have heard of your loss. To tell the truth, we expected to find you in sorrow, since so much of your fortune has been wiped out. And yet you seem so calm and unmoved by it all. How do you account for your lack of agitation and concern?"

The rabbi responds: "Have I not heard you people boasting frequently about the quick mind of your rabbi? So, the worrying that might take someone else a month I accomplished in a half hour!"

The joke can be taken either as a tribute to the way Jews felt about their rabbis or as a bit of satire. Now this one:

It was common for writers in Eastern Europe to get their rabbis to write letters of recommendation. Such an aspiring author shows up at the rabbi's home with his manuscript.

"Rabbi," he begins. "I have just finished this work about our blessed Torah. Principally, it deals with the Book of Exodus, and I call it 'The Hand of Moses.' Will you please do me the great favor and honor to read it and give it your letter of approval?"

"I will read it tonight," the rabbi assures him. "Come back tomorrow and we will talk about it."

Well, the rabbi spends some time that evening examining the script and is appalled. It is dreadful, as far as he is concerned.

When the young man arrives the next morning, the rabbi bids him sit and then picks up the prospective book. "First of all," he observes, "you should change the name of this work."

"Fine," the young man replies. "What should I call it?"

"I would suggest you call it 'The Face of God.' "

"Isn't that a rather strange name?" the young man asks. "Meaning no disrespect, rabbi, why is that better than the original name?"

The rabbi looks at him. "Why 'The Face of God'? Because, young man, no one can look at it!"

A little roundabout, but sharp nevertheless.

Often the punch line sounds like an epigram, as in the following:

The *shammes* (sexton) addresses the rabbi: "Rebbe, I must tell you how surprised I was to see you talking to a woman in the market square this morning. Do I have to remind *you* that it is not right for the rabbi to talk to a woman in public?"

"Reb Yoineh," the rabbi answers, "tell me, which is worse—to talk to a woman and think of God, or to talk to God and think of a woman?"

It's true that this answer has nothing to do with the question, but it *is* clever or witty. Sharp answers are found in many jokes involving rabbis.

> A young student asks, "Rabbi, where does one find God?"
> The rabbi answers, "Wherever He is admitted!"

The youngster's search for a location is met by the rabbi's directing him toward an attitude. Instead of just saying, "God is not in any specific place," the rabbi has coined an epigram. One more:

> A young prospective rabbi is being examined for ordination (to become a rabbi). The examining rabbi asks a tough question: "On a Saturday, if a man were to cut his hand and be unable to stop the bleeding and come to you for help, what would you do?"
>
> The young man thinks. (Observant Jews may do no work on Saturday.) "Rebbe," he says, "let me go to the bookshelves, get the Talmud, and look it up in the proper section to get the answer. I think I know where to find it."
>
> "Forget it!" The rabbi throws up his hands. You need more study. In a case like this, by the time you found the answer to my question, the poor man might have bled to death!"

Again the common sense referred to earlier.

Despite all this respect, there is also some needling directed at rabbis. For example:

> The rabbi is asked to define the basic difference between righteousness and wickedness. His answer: "Both righteous men and wicked men will be found to commit sins. As long as the righteous man lives, he knows he is sinning, whereas as long as the wicked man sins, he knows he is living."

Or take the case of the man who is talking about his rabbi:

> "Oh, he's a great scholar, a deep thinker. You know, he will sit quietly, deep in thought, not saying a word. Such silence is difficult, wouldn't you agree? So I think he becomes tired out. So he goes and rests awhile, quietly. Then he again sits and thinks, silently. A deep thinker, a deep thinker. . . ."

And one of the most famous of all:

A rabbi is engrossed in study in his alcove. Just outside, his disciples are discussing him. He hears one say, "Our Rabbi Hillel, the kindest, most gentle of men, a pearl."

A second one agrees: "And a marvelous judge. People bring disputes to him from all over, because his opinions are so widely respected."

And from a third: "And a renowned scholar, known all over Poland and Lithuania!"

At this point the rabbi remarks, "What? Will you say nothing about my modesty?"

A trifle nasty, wouldn't you say?

Here is a story that is somewhat odd: In the old country as well as in the new, when prospective rabbis moved from one town or city to another, people asked questions about them before appointing them. Thus:

The community head of one city writes to the community head of another, asking him about their previous rabbi, who is being invited to take the podium in this new city. The answer that comes back describes him as an unusual man, a man like Shakespeare, like Moses, like an angel!

After the rabbi has been hired, he turns out to be a very poor performer. The community head gets in touch again with the other man and writes: "How could you have said about this rabbi that he was like Shakespeare, Moses, and an angel? We found him to be awful."

And the answer comes back: "Like Shakespeare, he knows no Hebrew. Like Moses, he stammers. And we thought he must be like an angel. He's certainly not a MENTSH!"

For the record, the word *mentsh* in Yiddish means a real person. What is suspicious about this joke is its mention of Shakespeare. If it is a European jest, it must have originated in Western Europe or been created late in the nineteenth century, by which time familiarity with Shakespeare might have been expected.

The following is a really uncomplimentary story about a rabbi. As you may know, it was customary for the people in a

town to invite strangers to their home for the Friday night
Sabbath meal. So:

> A prosperous householder sees a stranger in the shul at
> the Friday night service and, after a brief conversation, invites
> him to his home for the Sabbath repast. There is some study of
> the Talmud, some discussion of world affairs as they affect Jews.
> Then on Saturday, more meals, more shul, more study, more
> discussion.
>   On Saturday evening, after the Sabbath is concluded, the
> host comes to the guest with a bill for food and lodging!
>   "I've never heard of this before! When does a Jew charge
> another Jew for Sabbath hospitality?"
>   "Oh, in this town we do it all the time. If you don't believe
> me, let's go ask the rabbi."
>   So they go to the rabbi. He listens to the story and tells
> the guest: "Of course you must pay for the food and lodging.
> It's only the services that are free to all."
>   The guest returns to the host's home, secures his belong-
> ings, and presents the money for the bill to his host.
>   "Forget it!" the host tells him. "I don't really want the
> money!"
>   "What?" the guest exclaims. "You put me through this
> whole business and you don't even want the money. What kind
> of foolishness is this?"
>   "I must beg your pardon for any worry I have caused you,"
> the host replies. "I only wanted to show you what a fool our
> rabbi is."

That's going pretty far just to run down the rabbi, but this
was a joke that circulated among Jews in Eastern Europe. And
in the New World, the rabbi's wisdom remains a subject of
jesting. On the complimentary side:

> A poor woman comes to her rabbi with a *shileh* (tradition-
> ally, a question having to do with some aspect of Judaic law).
> "Rabbi, we have very little money. Today I went to the meat
> market and bought some beef for the children and me to eat,
> but when I got home and looked at it, I realized it didn't look
> like beef. I think it looks like ham."

The rabbi looks at the meat and it is obviously ham; he also realizes that the woman has no more money to make a substitute purchase. He turns to the woman. "My dear woman. It may look like ham, but it's kosher flanken!"

We might argue whether this is wisdom or compassion. My guess is that an Orthodox rabbi might be outraged by it. A logical question is, why didn't the woman complain to the retailer?

A common group of New World stories deal with the trio of the priest, the minister, and the rabbi, and, as Jews tell it, the rabbi has the edge. Sometimes just the Jew and either the priest or minister operate in these jokes. One sample should be enough:

An atheist becomes aware that he will soon die. He asks a priest, a Protestant minister, and a rabbi to visit him.

"I have a last request of each of you which I know you are honor bound to respect. I want to go to the Hereafter, in which I do not believe, well supplied with funds (he's obviously needling them). And in any case, I have no heirs.

"Each of you will receive $25,000 before you leave. I want you to appear at my funeral, and each of you is to place the money in the coffin. Can I rely on you to honor this last request?"

Despite their reservations, the three agree to do so. And so the day comes when the funeral is to take place and the three men are there.

The priest looks at the other two and says: "You know, I just cannot bring myself to put such a sum into a coffin when the needs of our parish are so great. I think the Lord will forgive me if I do not honor that request but use the sum for a better purpose."

"Oh, I can't agree with that," the minister says. "However, I will put the matter before God. After all, this man has gone to his just reward. So I will throw the money into the air. Whatever God wants to take will ascend to Heaven with him. Whatever falls back to earth we can use here. At least this takes the matter out of my hands and places it where it rightfully belongs."

The rabbi looks at his two colleagues and shakes his head: "I must say I am astonished at your behavior. Each of us gave our word to a dying man. How can we go back on it now or use obvious stratagems to get around that? Do what you want, of course, but as for me—I have here in my hand a check for $25,000 which goes into the coffin."

Triumphs like this occur in many jokes, especially in Jewish-American humor. It's a stereotype. The next one has a slightly different twist.

At an inter-religious conference, there is nothing scheduled one evening, so a priest suggests to a rabbi and minister with whom he is acquainted, "Let's play cards in my room after dinner."

A friendly poker game ensues, money on the table, kidding and joshing, and a good deal of laughter. What our clergymen do not know is that the city has a strict anti-gambling ordinance.

Sure enough, someone in the hotel reports that there is a lot of noise coming from their room. When the police arrive, to the consternation and embarrassment of the clergymen, they are handed summonses to appear before a magistrate the following morning.

The next day the judge looks at the names and titles of the men before him. "Gentlemen," he notes, "I am distressed to see men of the cloth before me on such a charge, but the law is the law. Unless you can offer some defense, I shall be obliged to find you guilty and fine you severely. Do you have anything to say?"

Father Murphy speaks first. "Your Honor, it is true that we were engaged in a game of cards. But can this really be regarded as gambling? In essence, we were passing time. I am sure none of us was interested in whether he won or lost. And that, after all, is the true test of gambling. So, in that sense, we were not really gambling at all."

"I suppose that is one way of looking at the matter," the judge agrees.

Reverend Sloan eagerly adds: "You see, Your Honor, the money on the table was only being used to mark and measure who was doing better; there was no intention for anyone to keep any more or leave with any less than the amount with which he started."

The judge notes: "A reasonable viewpoint. And you, Rabbi Solomon, would you hold that you were gambling?"

To which the rabbi replies: "Gambling? With whom?"

How far these ecumenical japes can go is illustrated by the following, which takes us right up to the present.

An ecumenical conference is going on with members of the three major faiths in attendance. After many speeches, on the second day a minister, a priest, and a rabbi, who have become friendly, decide that they have had enough for a while and get out of the conference hall. The go to a nearby bar for a refresher. Little do they know that it is a gay bar! Having ordered their drinks, they become engrossed in their own conversation.

Now the minister is a very handsome young man, and within a few minutes one of the local attendees sidles up to him. "Bud, you and I could have a good time," he tells him.

The minister grasps what is going on and says, "Please, don't bother me."

But the gay blade won't take no for an answer. In a few minutes he's back again, propositioning the minister.

At this point, the rabbi turns to the other two and says, "I think I can handle this." He says a few words to the gay man, and his two clerical friends see the latter nod his head, wave his hand, and march off.

"Morton, what did you tell that fellow to get him off our backs?" the minister wants to know.

"Oh," the rabbi answers. "I just told him that he has to respect the fact that you two fellows are married to each other."

Once again, we're being told, the rabbi is a wise man.

You've already seen other rabbi jokes in earlier sections of the book, and there will be more. Read on.

How about a Second Helping?

Jewish tradition and law frown on excessive drinking but have no restrictions for the heavy eater. Countless jokes reflect the Jewish inclination toward eating.

The pleasure of eating so-called Jewish cuisine is one feature of this subject. The German poet Heine, who converted from Judaism, has a story about a medieval knight who is, similarly, a convert. But "His nose has kept the faith," and he comes to the Jewish quarter not because he wants to meet Jews but to eat.

Similarly, there is an old story about a convert from Judaism who comes to a Jewish delicatessen to eat goose, chopped liver, and equally delectable delicacies. He sighs, "Should one really separate oneself from such a religion?"

As though Judaism centered on diet! You may sometimes hear contemporary statements that sound like this.

Yet Jews have not always cracked jokes about eating. Eastern European jokebooks contain very little about this subject. Hospitality was very important, though. In the *shtetl* it was common for Jews to bring home an *oirach* or guest for a meal during the Sabbath, and there are jokes centering on that custom.

> A student in the local Talmudic academy is invited to the home of a local family for a Sabbath meal. The entree is a platter of fish, and it turns out that the fish is already smelly. What is the young man to do? How should he bring the matter to his host's attention without insulting him? His solution is typical of the subtlety of many Jewish stories.
>
> The *oirach* thinks for a moment and then puts his ear down right on the fish.
>
> His host looks at him, astonished. "What are you doing?" he wants to know.
>
> "Just a minute," says the young man. Then he lifts his head and explains. "You see, in the town from which I come, we had a drowning not long ago. So I was just asking this fish whether he had seen that man."
>
> The host looks at him and laughs. "So what did the fish tell you?" he asks.
>
> "The fish told me that he doesn't know because it's been a long time since he was in the water."

Indirect, ironic, and subtle, but it gets the point across. Note that bringing these guests home was actually a sign of poverty. These were not friends invited to a party, as in America. What was involved was an obligation to those in need of food.

Such jokes do not occur, to my knowledge, in Jewish-American humor. And yet we know that Jewish immigrants placed a great value on food and eating. (They are not alone in this; Italian immigrants also emphasize *mangia, mangia,* and Italian-American humorists also get into this subject.) In earlier Jewish-American humor, then, one of the stereotypes deals with eating. Here's a classic story, which takes place, say, about seventy years ago.

A man comes into one of the famous Lower East Side restaurants and has his meal. In such a place, the owner was always around, and he walks up to the customer and asks how the meal was.

"Not bad," says the customer, but it's not nice to put down just two slices bread on the table. What's the matter, you can't afford to give some bread with the meal?"

"Oh, don't say that," the owner holds up his hand. "Come back. Next time you'll get, you'll get."

Several days later when the same man returns, the owner tells the waiter to put a half dozen pieces of bread on the plate.

"Well, today was plenty bread, right?" the boss comments at the end of the meal.

"Better than last time, but still a little skimpy," is the patron's reply. "When I sit down to a meal, I like to see bread, not just a few pieces."

"I understand, I understand," the owner assures him. "You'll come next time, you'll be happy with the bread."

Sure enough, two nights later our friend is back. This time the owner's instructions to the waiter are to take an entire loaf, cut it in half lengthwise, and put it on the plate. At the end of the meal the owner, beaming, asks the customer, "Nu, today was plenty bread, true?"

The customer looks at him and shakes his head. "What, plenty, Rabinowitz? You went back to two slices."

But diners do not live by bread alone.

The story is told about a man who comes to a banquet and proceeds to eat—first the chopped liver appetizer, then the fish appetizer, then the soup, then the entree of chicken with vegetables and roasted potatoes, plenty. Then he asks for and eats another piece of chicken. Now comes the dessert, a big slab of cake. And now the waiters start pouring the tea. As he is drinking his second glass, he develops the most intense gastric pains.

He is moaning, "Oy, oy, oy my stomach!" The ambulance to take him to the hospital arrives, and as they are shifting him to the gurney to put him in the ambulance, he turns to his friend and exclaims, "Oy, that last glass of tea killed me!"

Of course, it's a dig. No one ever said humor was supposed to be kind. And note this irony:

Two friends go to eat in a restaurant they have never tried before. At the end of the meal, one turns to the other and says, "The food here is terrible . . . and such small portions."

Women naturally play an important part in food jokes— and not because they eat so much.

A lady is deeply depressed and decides to commit suicide. She is about to put her head in the oven and turn on the gas. But she decides that she should also put the pot roast in so that her husband will have something to eat when he comes home from work.

The stereotype should by now be clear to you. And you will understand the invention, by some Jewish-American comic, of the following riddle:

How do we know that Eve was really Jewish?
Answer: Because she said to Adam, "Eat, eat, here, have an apple."

Elia Kazan, the famous Turkish-American movie producer, claims to recall Jewish mothers telling their children: "Eat, eat!

May you be destroyed if you don't eat! What sin have I committed that God should punish me with you? Eat! What will become of you if you don't eat?! Imp of darkness, may you sink ten fathoms into the earth if you don't eat! Eat!"

All of this in Yiddish, of course. The translation doesn't convey the real earthiness of such remarks.

At least in humor, Jews like to eat. Here's an overworked story to remind us again of that.

> Mrs. Cohn is visiting Mrs. Moskowitz. They're sitting and having tea, naturally with cookies. Mrs. Moskowitz picks up the plate of cookies: "Mrs. Cohn, have another cookie with another glass tea."
>
> "Moskowitz, I already ate half a dozen cookies!"
>
> "Well, actually, you ate seven, but who's counting?"

So you will understand why a gag writer tells us that the first ship in the Israeli shipping line was named, *S.S. Mine Kind* (translation: "Eat, eat, my child").

So-called Jewish cooking has tended to be like Central and East European, heavy on the potted and roasted side. Buddy Hackett used to tell about his problem after being inducted into the Army. He complained to the doctor that he thought he was dying, because the internal flame had gone out—that is, no more heartburn. The undeniable fact is, however, that this stereotype has a basis in fact. It has been said that Jews tend to suffer in larger numbers from diseases sometimes associated with overeating, such as diabetes.

But you should certainly not get the impression that all Jews are gourmands, well, heavy eaters. Wait a minute! If that's a French word, it tells you something. And maybe you have heard or read about the way the Romans ate. Enough said!

The Yiddishe Mama

You got a mother; I got a mother; all God's children got a mother. So why does Jewish humor pick on them? I guess the answer lies somewhere almost halfway between nurturing and smothering. What comes to anyone's mind upon hearing the words "Jewish mother"? Chicken soup, of course! Naturally, not all Jewish mothers are represented by this caricature, and, in fact, they are not much different from non-Jewish mothers in their reactions. But folklore and Jewish comedians have cut this stereotype so prominently that most people are now aware of it.

Basically, the Jewish mother has a multiple image: suffering, overprotecting, displaying motherly pride, nurturing.

Let's consider the classic sufferer first. There is an Old World Yiddish saying—"One mother can support ten children but ten children can't support one mother"—usually accompanied by a *ziftz*, which translates as a sigh but is somehow more evocative in Yiddish, done with folded hands.

One classic story of this kind, made famous years ago by Mike Nichols and Elaine May presents the sterotypical Jewish mother.

> The telephone rings and Mom picks it up. "Hello."
> From the other side: "Hello, Mom."
> Dead silence.
> "Mom, it's Sidney, calling from Los Angeles."
> Silence. "Mom, are you there? Is everything all right?"
> Cold response. "Is this Sidney Abramowitz, my son?"
> "Of course, Mom. What's the matter?"
> "Already it's six weeks since you called. I thought you forgot already about your mother."
> "Well, Mom, you know how it is when you start a new business. I've been over my ears in work."
> "So you couldn't find even a couple minutes to call your own mother here in New York?"
> "Oh, Mom, honest, I meant to. And besides I didn't want to tell you something, but you're making me."
> "What do you mean?"
> "Well, I had a bad case of the flu; high temperature, you know the whole business that's going around here. I was in bed for the last three weeks."

Pause. Then: "Sidney, you know, if I could just believe that, I'd be the happiest woman in the world."

Note the fancy equation here: a good excuse is at least equal to a telephone call. This story also demonstrates the demand for displaying affection, for consideration of what Mama has done for you. A neat example of this point is the following:

A young man is clearly beset by neurosis and ends up going to a psychiatrist. His mother is consumed by curiosity as to what is going on and what treatment is needed. "So what did the doctor tell you?" she asks.

The young man looks at her, wondering how to explain the psychoanalytic language he has heard and decides to come straight to the point. "Well, the doctor told me that my problem begins with my relation with my mother. I have never resolved this initial problem and he says I have an Oedipus complex."

Impatiently, the mother cuts off the conversation. "Listen, Oedipus-Shmedipus, so long you love your mother, you'll be all right."

How Mama suffers is also illustrated by the following.

Four ladies have assembled for their morning coffee klatsch. As they sit down, one of them sighs (or *ziftzes*, if you prefer) and says, "Oy!"

At this point the second sounds her note: "Oy vay!"

Not to be outdone, the third one looks at the first two and gives out with, "Oy vay iz *mir* !" (a subdued version of "Woe is me").

The fourth one looks around at the other three and announces, "I thought we agreed that we weren't going to talk about the children today!"

The Jewish mother as nurturer is likewise a staple of Jewish jokes. Thus:

A young man is eating in a restaurant. Suddenly, armed men break in and start shooting at one of the diners. In the general melee, our young man takes a bullet in the shoulder.

He lives in the neighborhood, so he drags himself to his apartment building, struggles up three flights of stairs, knocks at the door as strongly as he is able. His Mom opens the door.

"Mom, I'm hurt," he gasps. "Get me help!"

Mom looks at him. "Come bubbele, eat something. We'll talk later."

The chicken soup as Jewish penicillin is always prepared and offered by Mom. Perhaps all the emphasis on food that we hear in Jewish-American jokes is, in fact, the result of the difficulties carried over from the Old Country, where food was frequently scarce.

Now let's look at Mom from a different angle. In Jewish jokes, she also shows up in the overprotection mode. As my mother used to say, *Mir zoll zine fahr dir*, which loosely translates as, "Whatever bad thing might happen to you should, instead, happen to me!" That's no joke, but this is:

A Jewish mother has brought her little boy to the beach. The kid begins to run around and this is what we hear:

"Benjie, don't go near the water. You could fall in and drown."

"Benjie, don't kick in the sand. You'll get sand in your eyes. I'll have to take you to the doctor."

"Benjie, put on the clothes here. Otherwise, you'll get a sunburn, you won't be able to sleep all night."

Another woman seated about four feet from Mama has been looking at Mama and listening to these warnings. Mama notices and turns to her and says, "My son—such a nervous child!"

This should give you some idea of why Jewish kids might become nervous. Author Barbara Gordon, describing her childhood:

Everything was a threat to our survival. Don't touch the toast in the toaster or we'd be electrocuted. Don't swim right after eating or we'd drown. Don't use a public toilet or we'd die of some dread disease.

Levenson picked up this idea beautifully in one of his stories. He and his brothers had been talking about taking a hike. Then came Mama's final instructions:

> "And remember one thing, don't tear your pants; and remember one thing, don't eat wild berries and bring me home cramps; and remember one thing, don't tell me tomorrow morning that you're too tired to go to school; and remember one thing, wear rubbers, a sweater, warm underwear, and take an umbrella and a hat; and remember one thing, if you should get lost in the jungle, call up so I'll know you're all right. . . ."

All this protection doesn't necessarily mean that Mama is always benevolent. Far from it. The mother of the little boy at the beach, with her continual injunction not to do this or that, may have spoken softly, but Levenson's mom was evidently louder and more caustic. He has told us (I don't vouch for the truthfulness) that when his mother died, his older sister said to his brother and him: "Now you'll have to be good on your own. Nobody's ever going to yell at you again!"

Sometimes coddling and overprotection take strange forms:

> A Jewish mother comes to school to find out how her little boy is doing. The teacher tells her that he is very bright, a report that leaves Mama beaming. But, the teacher adds, he has a tendency to be unduly talkative and unrestrained in class.
>
> "Oh, my Julius is a nice boy," Mama informs her. "If he gets a little too energetic, just slap the kid next to him. Julius will shape up."

I promised to remind you of Jewish-American *chutzpeh* jokes. This one comes as close to a Hershele Ostropolier as any you might find.

> Two ladies meet. They haven't seen each other for some time, so naturally, they exchange various bits of health and family information.
>
> "How's the family?"

"Thank God. Everyone is in good health."

"By me, too. So, Mrs. Becker, how are the children?"

"Oh, they should live and be well, they're all grown up. Married, too."

"That's nice. If I remember right, you had two, a boy and a girl. Both married and happy, I hope."

"Well, my son could have a better life. Married *eppes* a *passkudstveh* (abominable woman). Never gets up to make his breakfast. All day long she's in the stores, or she's in the beauty parlor, or she's taking tennis or golf lessons. My Marvin comes home from work tired, and right away she *shleps* him out to the restaurant."

"Is that so? And your daughter?"

"Oh, my Joanie. That's altogether different. Her husband is a jewel. Whatever she wants, she gets—the *telerel fun himmel* (usually translated as the moon from the sky). Brings her breakfast every day in bed. Tells her to get out of the house and use her credit cards. Every night he takes her out to dinner. What a contrast!"

Finally, here's a lulu showing another image. What you should note here is the pride in "mine." This attitude is spelled out in the sardonic definition of a Jewish genius: An average kid with a Jewish mother.

Three Jewish women meet. They once lived in the same neighborhood but haven't seen each other for a while. Obviously, they exchange all kinds of information about what has been going on in their lives since they last saw each other. Before long, the subject gets around to the children.

"Oh, my son Leonard," says Mrs. Berkowitz. "How did he turn out? I don't want to brag, but what can I tell you? He's a doctor! But not just a doctor! He has opened three clinics in different neighborhoods in the city. Written up in the papers and everything."

"Very nice," says Mrs. Cohen. "My son David is not doing so badly either. He's a lawyer. Not just a lawyer. He's the managing partner in his firm."

Mrs. Davidson remains silent.

"Bertha," Mrs. Cohen finally asks her. "What happened to your son Murray? He was such a nice boy."

Mrs. Davidson shakes her head sadly. "Not so good. He turned out to be a homosexual."

"Oh, my God. Too bad!" from the two friends.

"Well, it's not altogether bad. You see, he told me the other day that right now he has just left one, you should excuse the expression, one lover and has taken up with another. The one he just left was a doctor, I think he said he runs clinics here in the city. The new one is a managing partner in some law firm."

They say that pride goeth before a fall, and that's what this sardonic story is about. Pride shows even more clearly in the following.

Two Jewish women meet. After a few inquiries about health, Mrs. Lefkowitz says: "Mrs. Solomon, I heard your son went to medical school. He's already a doctor?"

"Of course! Two years already he's in practice. Knows all about modern medicine and treatment. A top internist. I know it sounds like I'm bragging, but it's true. But listen, don't take my word for it. You could find out for yourself. Go to him. You'll see a real doctor."

"But Solomon, there's nothing wrong with me. So why should I go?"

"Go, go, you'll see. He's sure to find *something!*"

A fitting finale. Life with Mama *must* be clear to all by now, at least in the image developed by comic writers and speakers. To some extent, it was based on fact; humor normally is. Maybe it's a little exaggerated—okay, maybe more than a little.

The Female of the Species

Neither men nor women are spared in the Jewish joke, but, as you have just seen, women do get a sort of special place, certainly in matters that deal with provision for the home. The Jewish jest picks up women's behavior in many ways, some already discussed, and offers us a set of stereotypes about Jewish women. Let's look at these.

In the old country, women's jokes have a different character than they do in the Jewish-American humor. Let me illustrate.

> A woman is standing in the market square of her *shtetl* (village) with a basket of eggs slung over her arm. Another woman from the village walks up to her and announces: "Soreh Layeh, did you hear? Chaye passed away last night!"
>
> Soreh Layeh stares at her. "What are you saying? You mean Chaye, the baker's wife?"
>
> "That's right," the other woman says.
>
> "Please, Dvoshe, hold my basket."
>
> The second woman takes her basket and now Soreh Layeh clasps her hands, turning them inside out (a typical gesture of Jewish women) and says, *"Oy, ah broch tzu mir."* (a very strong version of "woe is me," more like "disaster is mine").

Now what is funny here? The joke maker is lampooning the necessity to fold hands in that characteristic way in order to express grief. You would never get that in a Jewish-American story, but the East European Jews understood and laughed at this habit.

The next one shows another genre of joke about women.

> A wife asks her husband for a ruble. His response: "I just gave you a ruble yesterday (note the culture of poverty)."
>
> So she says, "So, I spent it. What did you expect; it should last forever?"
>
> The husband's eyebrows go up. "You spent the whole ruble?!"
>
> And now she ignites. "So what did you want me to do, save it for my old age? Of course I spent it—for things that we needed."
>
> He shouts: "So what do you think, I go out and pick rubles off trees? What kind of business is this? Every day a ruble!"
>
> Angrily, she screams back at him, "So what do you want, an accounting?"
>
> He answers: "Of course! After all, we're talking about a whole ruble!"
>
> Her turn. "Okay, here goes. Meat cost 50 kopecks. Flour,

another 10 kopecks. Makes 60 together. Raisins cost 10, makes
70. Ten kopecks for sugar, so you have 80 already. And now 10
kopecks for . . . an abscess in your head, is 90. And 10 kopecks
for a bellyache for you. So there, you've got a whole ruble. And
you can rot in your grave with your ruble!"

This sort of cursing was common among women from the
lower rungs of society. The famous Jewish humorist Sholem
Aleichem claimed to have written down a collection of the
curses and swear words that his stepmother used to insult him.
Unfortunately, these lose something in translation. Their hearty
flavor comes through far better in Yiddish.

In some earlier stories we already met the *shadchen*, the
Old World marriage broker. To illustrate the attitude toward
women shown in stories about the *shadchen*, we turn to a jape:

A marriage broker comes to a young man and tells him,
"I have a girl for you, pure gold!"

"Please," the young man pleads, "I've told you; I don't
want to get married. So don't bother me."

"What do you mean you don't want to get married. How
can you live without a wife?" And the sales pitch goes on: "Don't
be a child! You have no idea how good it is to have a wife. Let
me explain it to you. Without a wife you will be lonesome, alone
like a stone. But if you have a wife, as I have (she should live
in good health) it's a totally different life.

"You get up in the morning; your wife gives you a glass
of warm tea, or coffee, or whatever you prefer. She prepares a
good lunch for you upon your return from town (like my wife
does, she should live to be 120 years old).

"Then you can always be together. And especially when
the Sabbath arrives on Friday evening, she makes everything
clean and spotless in the home, puts the large silver candlesticks
on the table, says the blessing.

"She will sit and look at you with large, liquid eyes; she
will smile like my wife does (long may she live). You sit together
and converse; your wife tells you one story, one bit of gossip,
after another, and you listen. She speaks so sweetly, so gra-
ciously, does my wife. You sit and listen and she talks . . . and

she talks . . . and she talks . . . may a fire grip her tongue how
she talks and talks!"

And what was the rabbi's response to the student who
asked why God made Adam first? "He didn't want advice on
how to make Adam!"

Sexist? Sure! So have been hundreds of jokes in every
language at least since the Middle Ages. Notice too how this
joke gives you an idea of the woman's role in the home. Note
also that here the *man* uses a sort of curse at the end.

Yiddish joke collections in the United States continue this
male chauvinist tradition. Thus:

A doctor is called in to examine a sick woman (in those
days, doctors made house calls). He asks several questions and
places a thermometer under her tongue to determine whether
she has a fever.

Immediately, the husband asks, "Doctor, how much will
you take for that instrument?"

Audiences in the United States might not laugh at this
kind of joke today, but East European audiences and immigrant
groups thought they were funny. Of course, the talkative
woman is not uncommon among some other ethnic groups as
well, but she has been a staple in Jewish comedy.

Recall an earlier story in this book about the wife who tells
her husband that if he would burn like the Sabbath candles he
would bless him too. All of these give you some notion of how
women appeared in Old World humor. In these stories, there
are insults, kidding about mannerisms, and other characteristics and stereotypes. Look at the following early immigrant joke:

A lady enters a photographer's studio. "How much will
you charge to photograph my children?" she inquires.

"Three dollars a dozen."

"Oh, if that's your price, I'll be back in two months. Right
now I have only eleven."

This joke rests on assumed misunderstanding, a basic mechanism. But, can you imagine such a story even being considered in these days?

Here is some more recent stuff.

An older Jewish woman likes to spend her day going to various stores and just looking around. On this day, she is trying out a new mall. She sees a line and promptly gets on it. As it happens, her eyesight is not very good, so after a minute or two she taps the shoulder of the young man in front of her. He turns and she asks, "Young man, what's the line?"

"Well, ma'am," he replies, "I'm waiting to go into the theater. Isn't that why you're on line?"

"Not exactly," the old lady responds. "Tell me, what kind theayter is it?"

"It's a rerun house. They show movies that haven't been seen for some time, maybe even years."

"Oh," says the lady. "You mean it's a movie theaytre. I see. So what picture they're showing today?"

"Today, it's *Dr. Zhivago*."

"And how much they charge to go in," she wants to know.

"The admission price is ten dollars," the young man tells her.

"Ten dollars! Such a high price!" the old lady is aghast. "He must be a specialist!"

Again we meet the price consciousness, a stereotype that we saw earlier.

Another aspect of the basic commonsensical character of women is revealed in the following.

A Jewish lady is reading the paper while her friend is knitting.

"Sadie, would you believe it?" the reader asks her friend, "they sent a man into orbit in a space vehicle, around the world 28 times—at a cost of 14 billion dollars!"

"Sure," the knitter observes. "The same old story. If you got money, you could travel!"

A little edge to the humor, a little malice, an attempt to make women look inferior. But it's not only Jewish humor that does this, it has been characteristic of joking for centuries.

Some of the nastiest creations of Jewish-American comedy writers concern the Jewish woman and sex. It's very doubtful that there is any basis for this, but the stereotype that has been offered is that of a woman verging on frigidity, especially after marriage. So we get a malicious jokebit like this:

> How do you stop a Jewish girl from having sex?
> Marry her.

Or a story about sexual intercourse:

> The husband, in the normal missionary position, is busily and ardently engaged and is approaching climax, when his wife speaks up: "You know, Max, the ceiling needs painting."

Funny? Maybe, but definitely nasty. Equally derisive is the following.

> Sam, having a free afternoon, has decided to visit a cinema showing "adult movies," which means, of course, pornography. Well, he returns home in a state of excitement and tells Jenny all about it.
> "You should see what they do in the pictures. All kinds of actions that I never imagined. And all kinds of positions we never knew about."
> "So what do you want from my life with all this telling?" Jenny wants to know.
> "Well, we could try something. For instance, in the movie all the girls moaned when they were in the middle of sex. It was sort of nice. You could see they were all excited. Let's try sex with a little moaning."
> Jenny agrees. And as the process develops, she is moaning: "Oh, oh, oh, oh . . . was there a long line at the supermarket checkout today!"

No doubt there are plenty of non-Jewish women who would fit these stereotypes just as well.

To conclude, I remind you of the derisive jokes about JAPs, the so-called Jewish American Princesses. The attitude of these pampered women supposedly has its origin in overprotection and indulgence. For the three readers who don't know about these jokes, let me include just one. Frankly, I'm tired of them and there are indications that they have become staples of anti-Semitism. Anyhow:

> Question: What does a JAP make for dinner?
> Answer: "Reservations."

Now it may be true that these stories have some basis in fact. I quote from the autobiographical account given by Barbara Gordon, referred to earlier in the Jewish mother section. She tells about her youth in Miami Beach "where most girls grew up to be veritable Jewish princesses, safe and spoiled by their parents until they made the 'right' marriage. Mindless, non-thinking, shopping, cooking, they then disappeared in the shadowy nonworld of their husbands."

Pretty rough, but of course that's only one view. But enough picking on the ladies for now.

So When Are You Getting Married?

The question above introduces a well-known stereotype. Any number of young Jewish men and women will tell you that the question has been asked of them, often. This is undoubtedly not only a Jewish tradition but a common one among many ethnic groups. Among people everywhere and at all times, marriage has been an important event in life and has received a great deal of attention. Since medieval times, it has been held to be so important in Jewish life that it was customary for Jewish communities to provide dowries for poor girls so that marriage would not be foreclosed for them.

To a great extent, this emphasis on being married arises out of religious prescriptions, but in Jewish jokelore it has become an accepted symbol. And so Jewish jokes deal with the getting married, being married, children, and family life.

In the culture of Eastern Europe, selecting a marriage partner was not based on free choice. Early on, there appeared a professional, the marriage broker, or *shadchen* in Yiddish. Anyone who has seen *Fiddler on the Roof* knows about these brokers.

As time went on, Jews discovered that the *shadchen* could be stupid, offensive, dishonest, and all those nice things. So the *shadchen* entered into Jewish humor in a big way, becoming the butt of many jokes. By the nineteenth century he was a well-established comic figure, and the whole marriage-brokering process had become a subject for laughing. In most of these stories, the salesmanship of the *shadchen* comes under the axe. It turns out that he is something of a con artist. Freud tells the following story.

> A *shadchen* has assured the prospective groom that the girl he has for him comes from a fine family but that the father, *alav hasholem* (rest in peace) is no longer alive.
>
> During the period of engagement, the groom learns that the father is alive but is serving a prison sentence. He runs to the *shadchen:* "How could you lie about such a matter? Why did you tell me that the man was dead?"
>
> To which the *shadchen* responds, "You call that living?"

There is also this one:

> A *shadchen* proposes a bride to a young groom, and an initial meeting is arranged. Afterward, the groom is outraged.
>
> "You told me the woman was charming, and good looking, a splendid specimen of womanhood. You are making fun of me!"
>
> "Not at all," the *shadchen* answered him. "What did you see here that was so objectionable?"
>
> "The woman is blind! She could hardly see what I looked like. She had to walk up to peer at my face."
>
> "So you'll be able to do whatever you want without her noticing. Is that bad?"
>
> "And she's deaf! I had to scream to get her to understand anything I said."

"Is that a fault? She'll never hear anything you don't want her to know. Many husbands would be happy about that."

"And she's also a mute!"

"That's a fault? It's a blessing. She will never tax your patience with all the drivel women talk about. You'll never hear a bad word from her."

"And to cap it all, she's a hunchback! What sort of a beauty did you bring me?"

"My young friend, what is it with you? You want perfection? Not even a single fault?"

Finally, an example that is very suspicious. It is probably not authentic, but rather the creation of an American gag writer.

Again, the prospective groom is in a tizzy. "You told me that this girl was a picture, something unusual, a regular beauty. So when I saw her last night, what did I see? One ear is larger than the other, and higher too. The eyes are crossed, the nose is crooked, and one side of her face droops. A real monstrosity."

"All right, all right," says the *shadchen*. "I see already. You don't like Picasso!"

A more authentic Old World story runs like this.

A *shadchen* is trying to persuade a young man that a certain girl is ideal. The young man is hesitant. Finally he makes an outrageous demand.

"You know," he says, "before I marry any girl, I want to see how she looks undressed. Maybe there is some imperfection on her body that I ought to know about."

The *shadchen*, stunned, argues with him that this is improper under Judaic law. But the young man is insistent. And the *shadchen*, after all, is in the business of arranging marriages, not teaching law.

The prospective bride and her father are thunderstruck by the request. But the girl is not so young and does not have too many chances left to get a husband. So they finally agree.

The time is arranged; the place is to be the bride's home. She gets totally undressed and walks around. With some respect for decorum, the young fellow stands not too close, but near enough to get a good look. The *shadchen* thanks the father and leaves with the prospective groom.

"Nu," he says to the young man, "now you're satisfied?"

"No!"

"What's the matter? It's a nice young woman. What did you see that was wrong with her?"

"I don't like her nose!"

Although most of the stories about *shadchonim* seem to show them as slightly on the unethical side, there are reversals on this too. For instance:

A young man comes to the *shadchen* to request his services. "As you see, Reb David," he says, "I am not a very good-looking fellow. And to tell the truth, money I don't have either. And I'm not all that learned in the Torah. Nevertheless, I'm looking for a good match. What do I mean by a good match? I want a girl with a good personality. And good looking, too. And if she's intelligent, I won't object. And best of all, she should bring a good dowry."

Reb David, the *shadchen*, thinks for a minute. "Mendel, I have the girl for you. She meets every one of the conditions you just laid out. But I must tell you she has a serious defect."

"With all those good things, what kind of defect can she have?"

"Every year she goes crazy, becomes a maniac for a whole month!"

"Well," Mendel reassures him, "I'm not so perfect myself. And with all those good qualities, I can bear with her for the one month. So when can I see her? I want to arrange our marriage as soon as possible."

"You won't have to wait long," the *shadchen* replies. "We will put the matter before her next month when she is crazy."

In the West, these matters work out differently. How many marriage brokers have you met? It must have been different years ago, however. Remember *Hello Dolly?* During this century, though, the issue is love, and worry for the parents. One of the chief concerns is marrying out of the religion.

One lady tells another: "I'm so happy. Until recently my Irving was running around only with *shiksehs* (non-Jewish girls). Now I see he's finally taking out a Jewish girl."

"How do you know?" asks her friend.

"Well, I had to take his suit to the cleaners, so when I emptied the pockets, I found a lipstick with the girl's name on it—Helena Rubenstein."

This falls into the category of credible ignorance. Here's another:

A woman says to her friend: "You remember the Zabladofskys? A fine family, rabbis and cantors. Well, the son, Milton, converted, became Episcopalian. And furthermore, my Margaret is going out with him. She brought him home already for us to meet him. It looks like a *shiddach* (a match)!"

"Well, how do you feel about it?" her friend inquires.

"How do I feel about it? To tell you the truth, that's what we always wanted—a nice Christian boy from a good Jewish family."

A wonderful example of paradox and irony together.

Most of these jokes fit into the Jewish mother category. Mama is certainly concerned about her marriageable children. But Papa is not far behind. Nevertheless, the jokes do concern Mama mainly. Witness again:

Martians have just landed on the beach. They are 8 feet tall, move mechanically, have faces that are not human at all— one eye, no ears, no hair, and so on. They are advancing up the beach toward the buildings. There is pandemonium. People are running from the beach, screaming in hysteria.

But one Jewish woman is running toward the monsters. As she approaches the first one, she yells out to him, "Ooh, have I got a goil for you!"

Of course this is exaggerated. And yet, Kenneth Libo, who has written several books about Jewish life in America, once described a visit to a Southern city. He told how the Jewish mothers paid him all the attention in the world when they learned he was unmarried. Why? Their daughters, what else?

Do you remember the man who didn't want a son-in-law who did not own a watch? Don't parents always want to evaluate the candidates who want to marry their children? Of course. Look at the following:

> Esther has taken up with an actor and wants to marry him. She tells her father she intends to get married and he naturally wants to know who the young man is.
> "He's on Broadway."
> "What do you mean on Broadway? What is he, a street walker?"
> "No, Pop, he's an actor."
> In earlier times, actors and actresses were considered out of the question as spouses. So Dad explodes. "An actor?! That means he's a bum. Don't you know what actors are? Immoral, no shame. Never will you marry an actor while I'm alive."
> Well, Esther starts crying and the argument goes on. Finally, after several weeks, she says to her father: "At least you ought to see what he looks like. Please come with me to see the Broadway play he's in."
> Father agrees and, during the performance, sits there watching the man more than the play. As the curtain falls, he turns to his daughter: "Esther, you could marry him. I can see he's no actor!"

Marriage, of course, leads to children. Interestingly, in East European humor you will find few jokes dealing with the problems created by children in the family. But as the last two jokes reveal, the story is quite different in the United States. Part of it, of course, is wrapped in the picture Jewish-American writers and comics have painted of the Jewish mother. Part is due to the concern about marrying out of the religion, also touched on in a couple of the stories above. Part is also related to upward mobility. For example, there is the wisecrack about the Jewish couple who have just become parents of a baby son, and who send out the following announcement: Mr. and Mrs. Larry

Goldberg are pleased to announce the birth of Dr. Michael Goldberg, who weighed 7½ pounds.

Of course, all parents take pleasure from their children and their achievements. But it does seem to show up conspicuously in Jewish humor. Why? It may have something to do with (1) the strength of family feeling in Judaism and (2) the heavy emphasis on performance which is common in Jewish life, as expressed in a significant term: *tochlis*. The word translates as "practical result," and the sentence *"Vuss vet zein der tochlis?"* (What will the practical outcome be?) has been a staple in Yiddish conversation. Jewish parents, like all others, are very concerned about how well their children do. Thus, in jest:

> Two women who have not seen each other for a long time meet outside a supermarket.
> "How are you, Mrs. Axelrod?"
> "Fine, Bernstein, and you?"
> Well, they converse for several moments and then Mrs. Axelrod gets to the inevitable. "Your daughter Marion, such a lovely child. How are things going for her?"
> "Very well!" says Mrs. Bernstein. "You know, she went to a fine college, Wellesley, and graduated with honors."
> "And marriage?" (the natural next question).
> "Five years ago she married a dentist," Mrs. Bernstein notes.
> "That's very nice," from Axelrod.
> "Yes. But after a year, they divorced. But she married a CPA later that year."
> "That's probably even better," Mrs. Axelrod reassures her.
> "Well, that didn't last either. A year ago they got divorced," Mrs. Bernstein explains.
> "Is that so?" Mrs. Axelrod asks rhetorically.
> "Anyhow, now she seems happy. Three months ago she married again, this time a doctor."
> "Really!" Mrs. Axelrod exclaims. "Isn't that wonderful! From one child to have so much *noches!*"

Having *noches*—pleasure, satisfaction, proud enjoyment—from children has been one of the great aims of family Jewish life. As noted, although families are important in all cultures,

Jews seem to place extraordinary emphasis on family life and togetherness.

European Jewry generally regarded the father as the stern figure, the disciplinarian. Of course, you and I know that this was not always true; in many families, the wife ruled the roost. Yet this is a common stereotype, both in Jewish and many non-Jewish families. Even in America, it was common to hear, in early immigrant days, "Wait until your father comes home." Sam Levenson has given us the wonderful crack: "When Father comes home, he should immediately hit the kid. Father won't know why, but the kid will!" Note how the father's role figures in the following story.

Esther Cohen returns home from college. When her father comes home from his job that evening, he is, of course, overjoyed to see her.

"Esther, my doll, it's so nice to see you. We are so proud of you. After all, you're the first one in our family to go to college."

"Gee, Dad, it's great to be home."

"So how is everything going for you? You're doing well in school?" (always the first question).

"Pretty well, Dad. I think I'm going to end up with a B minus average for the semester."

"B minus? What's the matter with an A?" (another typical comment).

"Well, Pop. I have to admit the work is hard. And you know, I have to have some social life."

"Oh, social life! It means you have a boyfriend?"

"Well. . . ."

"It's all right. I suppose a young girl, you need a boyfriend."

"Papa, there's something I have to tell you."

"Oh, it sounds serious. Must have to do with your boyfriend."

"Well, you see, Papa, I found out that I'm pregnant!"

There is silence. Then: "Pregnant! What are you talking about? Who's the boy?"

"Well, Papa, to tell the truth, I'm not sure."

Her father looks at her with his mouth open. A moment

passes and then: "What's the matter? I send you to such a fine college. Didn't they teach you yet to ask—with whom am I having the pleasure?"

Now actually, first, the dialog could involve the mother rather than the father, but that wouldn't ring right. And second, this could be a non-Jewish joke, but the kind of dialog, with its sharp edge at the end rather than merely cold fury, seems to sound more natural when it's told about a Jewish family. Try it out yourself.

Despite the Talmudic emphasis which reminds the man over and over to be kind to his wife, to cherish her, it is also true that Jewish humor celebrates differences between man and wife. Here is one of the most marvelous classic Old World stories:

A rabbi has a servant who is not well versed in Jewish prayer and who therefore prefers to pray at home so he should not become an object of ridicule. One day the *rebbitzin* (rabbi's wife) comes into the kitchen and hears him intoning a prayer which says, "God, thank you that I was not born a woman" (yes, there is one such).

Outraged, she screams at the servant and berates him and then wallops him. He, in turn, sets up a yammer. The rabbi, who is in his study, comes running in. "What's going on here?" he demands to know.

The wife explains how she was insulted and then the servant explains that he is reciting an actual prayer. The rabbi listens, turns to his wife, and says, "Ettel, the man is right; there is such a prayer. In fact, one commentary says that the worst man is better than the best woman."

The wife is enraged but how do you argue with the rabbi and the commentaries?

That Friday night the rabbi comes home to the Sabbath meal and finds that the fowl he is eating is very tough. It happens again the next Friday night. On the third Friday, his gums ache again. So he inquires: "Lately, the chicken you serve has been so tough; it's hard to chew. Why are we getting such tough ones?"

"Who said it's a chicken?" is the reply. "I've been buying roosters in the market."

"Roosters," the rabbi exclaims, in astonishment. "You always bought hens. Why all of a sudden roosters?"

"It's like you told me, from the commentaries—the worst male is better than the best female. So I thought we should have the benefit of the tradition."

The rabbi shakes his head. "Ettel," he remarks, "you're right. But that tradition only applies as long as the male and female are alive!"

How do you like that fencing match? Smart woman, the *rebbitzin*, and the rabbi is no fool either.

Here's an old and unusual story, sometimes found in jest-books about Chelm, the town of fools mentioned earlier.

A woman, a *klippeh* (shrew), is wailing: "Oh, woe is me that I should be such a fool, such a cow. How could I let myself be married to such an idiot, such a *shlemiel*. To do that I must have been an absolute imbecile!"

At this point, the husband leans over and slaps her, exclaiming, "There, that's for talking so much. And now, shut up!"

The wife looks at him, astonished. "What's with the slapping? For years I've been laying all kinds of curses on you and delivering insults by the dozen and I never even heard a word of protest. What happened? You finally woke up?"

And he answers: "You may insult me as much as you like. But under no circumstances do I allow anyone to say a bad word about my wife!"

And so the Jewish shrew becomes the object of the traditional respect with which the husband is expected to treat his wife—a real twist.

Jewish-American comics and joke writers have found man/wife relations a fertile field. Thus:

Mrs. Cohen and Mrs. Klotskin meet for the first time at a social gathering. Each examines the other according to the normal tradition, clothing, makeup, jewelry, and the like. After a few introductory words, Mrs. Cohen remarks: "That's a beautiful diamond you're wearing. And so large. How many carats is it?"

The other woman looks at her ring and replies: "Yes, it is big—eight-and-a-half carats. Costs plenty, too; my husband bought it for my last birthday."

"You know, it's big enough to be in a museum," Mrs. Cohen observes. "Like the Hope and the other big diamonds."

"Yeh, and like those it comes with a curse!" the wearer answers.

Mrs. Cohen's eyes widen. "Really? How interesting! What kind of a curse."

"Mr. Klotskin!"

You might ask yourself, why is the Klotskin joke Jewish? Well, we could argue that.

You Wanna Fight?

Do you think Jews are a peaceful, nonviolent people? Have you looked in your Bible lately? Some Israelites certainly were gentle folk. But if you read your Scripture thoroughly, you'll see that the old Hebrews were fighting men. David was as renowned for his abilities as a warrior as for his other accomplishments. In fact, beginning with Joshua, we see military campaign after military campaign. And Samson?

Historians will tell you that when the Crusades began and the first object of attack was the local Jewish communities in the Rhineland, the Jews resisted fiercely but were overwhelmed. Let me remind you of the battle of the Warsaw ghetto. In fact, here is an old joke that reflects the Hebrew fighting spirit.

A Judean appears at the gates of Heaven. On this day, it is Abraham's turn to greet incoming Jews.

"Descendant of Abraham, Isaac, and Jacob, welcome to *Gan Aden* (Paradise) and to eternal life with our people. It is our custom here to test your true worthiness. First of all, can you give me an example of your courage as a mortal man?"

Shimon, the Judean, nods his head. "Truly, I can, Father Abraham. I remember the time when I went to talk to the Roman proconsul. He had just put into effect an anti-Judean edict. So I walked up to him and told him how we felt about him, that he was a vulture, a beast of prey, and not worthy to live, much less to govern. And then I spat in his face. Does that not prove my worthiness in this respect?"

Father Abraham glowed. "My son, indeed it does! And were there soldiers with the proconsul at the time?"

"Of course," Shimon replied. "It was at the regular time when the proconsul saw supplicants and appellants."

"And, my son, can you tell me when all this happened?"

"Yes, Father Abraham. About five minutes ago."

So the portrait of the quiet, nonviolent, pale Jewish man devoted only to study of the Torah is not inaccurate. It just doesn't apply to all Jews in all times.

In Europe, the Jews learned over time the truth of the old saying, "Discretion is the better part of valor." Many Jewish mothers urged their children not to get into fights—to put the matter simply, the odds were wrong. So, there developed the image that Jews don't believe in physical violence and that they prefer to avoid physical combat. Listen to this Old World joke as a stereotype.

> We are in the *shul* (synagogue) during the High Holy Days. A fairly young man is expressing his penitence for all the things he has done wrong during the past year, by beating his breast fiercely, very hard. An older man approaches him and says, "With such violence you will get nowhere with God!"

This objection to violence also shows up in Old World humor frequently as objection to serving in the army, which was itself a very bad experience for Jews in that part of the world.

> A Jewish recruit is being drilled and drilled in the use of weapons. Now the sergeant is giving an oral test. He comes to

Chaim and asks, "Now tell me, what is your most important weapon?"

Chaim replies, "The rifle."

"And what must you learn to do with it?" is the next question.

"You must learn to shoot straight," is Chaim's reply.

"And why is that so important?" the sergeant demands to know.

"So that when the enemy charges, you will shoot to kill— God forbid!"

Or take this example of the so-called Jewish attitude:

A Jewish recruit deserts his regiment. After several months, he is picked up by the military police and brought before a tribunal.

"After we had spent so much time training you and inculcating the hatred of the enemy, why in the world did you desert?" he is asked.

"Your training was so excellent that I learned to hate the enemy so much that I never even wanted to look at him," is the answer.

The stereotype that developed from these attitudes is the Jew who lacks physical courage or will to fight. Thus, another Old World story takes verse 3 of the Song of Songs, in which it is said that King Solomon needed 60 men to guard his bed. If they had used Gentiles, says the jester, only one would have been needed.

Stories of this kind transferred to the New World too. American comics like Jackie Mason and Mel Brooks have carried this Old World tradition along. Thus:

Two Jewish lads are walking along an unfamiliar street in the city. Two tough-looking boys fall in behind them. The Jewish boys can hear the footfalls, so one says to the other, "Someone is behind us."

The second boy takes a quick look and says: "We'd better get out of here. There are two of them."

And one of the most famous jokes:

> Three Jews have been sentenced to be executed by a firing
> squad. Now the corporal addresses one of them: "Do you want
> a blindfold? Or a cigarette?"
> "A cigarette, please," the man answers.
> The corporal asks the same question of the second.
> "I'll take the blindfold," he responds.
> Now the same question to the third man.
> "From this miserable regime, I have expected nothing and
> will take nothing," the man shouts back.
> The second Jew leans over and whispers, "Simcha, don't
> make trouble."

This story reflects again on a let's-not-get-into-any-argu-
ment-with-them," a supposed cowardice. An Israeli psychologist has used the above joke in research. He tells us that when
he tells the joke about three Frenchmen, it just doesn't get the
same laugh.

Now contrast the above jokes with those that developed
about Jews after the Arab wars.

> Two Israeli lads are reading the paper. It says that the
> Russians are getting ready to get troops into action (the Yom
> Kippur War). One turns to the other and says, "It took us six
> days to beat 100 million Arabs, so we'll need twelve days to deal
> with 200 million Russians!"

Pretty brash, for sure! And it does show the difference in
attitude under changed conditions.

Finally, a rather gruesome joke told by a member of the
Palmach, the Israeli shock troops of the War for Independence.

> A young soldier and his girlfriend take a hike into a moun-
> tainous area. Suddenly they are attacked by three Arab men. In
> short order, the Israeli disposes of two of them and compels the
> third to hoist the two dead men on his back and drag them back
> to a settlement.
> He is asked why he did not finish off all three.

"What?" he answers. "Did you expect *me* to drag three carcasses to the police station?"

On this matter of fighting, then, the jokes of an earlier time and of more recent times don't match up at all. Some of the jokes in this section should prove that aversion to physical combat is no inborn Jewish trait.

Self-Disparagement

Some of the stereotypes of Jews in this chapter are not very flattering. Many of the people who look at jokes seriously believe that self-disparagement is the most important aspect of Jewish jokes and that Jews are unusual in this respect. For example, Freud made the point that Jewish jokes about themselves were often self-criticisms. Furthermore, he thought these jokes were excellent, in contrast to "the brutal buffooneries" offered by non-Jews, in which the Jew appears merely as a comic figure. He noted: "I do not know whether one often finds a people that makes merry so unreservedly over its own shortcomings." Here is Freud's own illustration:

> A Jew has entered a train compartment and immediately made himself comfortable: shoes unlaced, placed on the seat next to him, coat and even shirt unbuttoned, feet on the seat across from him.
> A well-dressed man enters. The Jew immediately puts his feet down, gets his shoes on, buttons up, and straightens out.
> The stranger is examining a book, reading, leaning back, and apparently thinking. Finally he asks the Jew, "Are you Jewish?" The answer is, of course, yes.
> "Good. Can you tell me when Yom Kippur comes this year?"
> "Sure," the first Jew replies and immediately begins to unbutton his coat.

Freud sees this as follows: ". . . The Jew in the train [that is, the first one] immediately abandons all sense of decency of deportment as soon as he recognizes the new arrival in his coupe as his co-religionist!!!" If you are astonished that buttoned coat and feet on the seat are tests of decency, you are thinking like a contemporary American. Remember this is an Old World joke of the nineteenth century. But why would someone like Freud, a native of Vienna, find such attention to dress so significant?

There is a reason. The Western Jews always looked down their noses at those from Eastern Europe who were filtering into Western Europe with the "backward" ways of the *shtetl*. What this joke says, then, is that such Western Jews as Freud see the relaxed behavior of Polish and Russian Jews as indecent or indecorous. In effect they are seeing themselves as an upper class and are making fun of the conduct of "inferiors." (Remember the superiority factor in jokes.) Probably, too, they were embarrassed at being seen by their Gentile neighbors or colleagues as fellow Jews of these "barbarians."

You should realize, however, that most of the *non*-Jews in Eastern Europe would probably behave in the same way as the Jews, and probably receive the same reaction. If not, then why did the National Origins Immigration Law of 1922 discourage immigration from Southern and Eastern Europe?

There are other stories in which Freud makes the same point.

> Two Jews meet and get into conversation. Their talk gets to the point of taking baths. One says to the other, "You know, I take a bath once a year whether I need it or not."

Do Viennese Jews really take baths only once a year, or is Freud telling about how one might kid a Jew from Galicia or Poland? Again, in the following:

> Two Jews have met and are talking. After a moment, one says to the other, "You know, I can tell what you ate yesterday."
> "How is that?" the other man wants to know.
> "Easy. I can see the traces of beans in your beard."
> "You're wrong," responds the alleged bean eater. "The truth is I had beans the day before yesterday."

What is common to all these jokes? They all have to do with cleanliness or clothing—exactly the obvious things that Western Jews *would be ashamed of in looking at their Eastern European fellow-Jews. After all, they might be identified as being characteristic of all Jews, Heaven forbid!*

In my judgment, the whole self-disparagement idea has been overdone. First of all, this is not something that only Jews do. Second, it constitutes only a small proportion of Jewish jokes. Collections of Old World Yiddish jestbooks contain only a scattering of such stories that reflect badly on Jews as a group. It's true that they make fun of *shadchonim,* or of Chelm fools, or of crooks or rabbis or *shlemiels.* But these are specific groups; not all Jews fall in this class. Furthermore, some stories of this kind that do characterize Jews as a whole do not necessarily deal with such objectionable traits as uncleanliness. For example:

> Two Jews have met on a Russian street on a freezing cold winter day. One is gesticulating wildly, explaining to his friend all his troubles with his wife, his in-laws, his children, Russian officials. The other is listening patiently, with his hands deep in his pockets.
>
> Suddenly, the complainer stops. "I have been talking to you for ten minutes and you haven't said a word. Don't you have any words of advice or comfort to give me when I'm having such difficulties?"
>
> The second man responds, "On such a terrible winter day, you want me to talk?"

This joke refers to the image of Jews as using their hands generously while speaking. This probably *has* been characteristic of the Ashkenazim from Eastern Europe. But also of many other people from Eastern and Southern Europe.

A similar point was made by the following jokebit.

> It is said that in a non-Jewish restaurant, one sees people eating and hears them talking. In a Jewish restaurant, one sees people talking and hears them eating.

Again, a reference to Old World Jewish manners. As in the next story.

A new immigrant goes out into the street and for the first time sees a policeman directing traffic with hand motions. After a while, he walks up to the policeman and says, "I dun't understend. To who are you tukking?"

The bottom line on this subject is that there *is* some self-needling on certain traits, and it often is tied into what seems to be class and origin differences among the widely dispersed Jewish people After what is called the Enlightenment, during which Western European Jews moved into the mainstream of European culture, it became common to make fun of the *shtetl* Jews from Eastern Europe.

And now here is something that looks like self-disparagement in Jewish-American humor.

A Jew is shipwrecked and cast up on an island, the lone survivor. Fortunately, he has matches and is able to start a fire and keep it going, hoping the smoke will attract some passing vessel. Unfortunately, this is a season when few vessels pass.

After several days, our survivor, Bernstein, realizes that he may be spending an indefinite amount of time on the island and begins to arrange for food and shelter. Soon he has acclimated himself well to the environment. He is a survivor.

Two months pass, and then one morning Bernstein sees a ship at some distance. Luckily, the smoke from his fire is visible, and the ship's crew sight it. A boat sets out and soon arrives at the shore with three men in it. The first to jump ashore introduces himself as the ship's second officer, Patrick Hurley.

Bernstein introduces himself. Hurley asks about the wreck and marvels at Bernstein's survival and his adjustment to island life.

"Let me show you how I've managed," Bernstein tells him. He takes the officer to a compact hut. "See," he informs Hurley, "this is where I eat and sleep—plenty of room. There is also plenty of vegetation on this island, so I was able to build and find food and shelter. Not like Beverly Hills, but passable."

"Remarkable!" the officer observes. "And what is that little hut?" he asks.

"Well," Bernstein responds, "I'm Jewish. That is a little synagogue where I pray every morning and every evening."

"Very good!" the officer notes. "Oh, I see you have another little place down there. What is that?"

"Oh, that," Bernstein replies. "Well, you see I tried to set up everything the way it is back home in California. That's also a synagogue. But that one isn't from my branch of Judaism, and I wouldn't set my foot across the threshold of that one!"

To appreciate the joke, you have to know that there are now three main branches or denominations in Judaism, and the differences among them are sharp. Moreover, it is not uncommon for serious disagreements to develop within a particular congregation, leading to a split and the emergence of a new congregation even within the same branch, and perhaps considerable bitterness between the two. The story reflects this tendency.

In fact, internal dissension among Jews is more prevalent than any general self-disparagement. There are so many serious examples of this that it would probably take up a book in itself. For example Chasidim were mentioned earlier. Some of the northern communities in Eastern Europe had another group called the *misnogdim*. The enmity between the two was so great that it occasionally resulted in violence—and at least one court case. All this is based on difference of opinion.

There was also an antipathy between Lithuanian and Galician Jews, accompanied by kidding that was both serious and humorous. Further, in France in the middle of the eighteenth century, when a group of German and Polish Jews tried to settle in Bordeaux, the local Sephardim asked the French king to expel them!

Along this line, there is a story attributed to William Faulkner, a *non*-Jew. He tells of a situation many centuries into the future, when a catastrophe has visited the earth and only a handful of survivors remain. Their great technological progress has left many space vehicles, and the survivors are embarking on one of these. Even at this last critical moment, what happens? A violent argument erupts among the passengers as to which planet or star they should be heading toward. So maybe the dissension among Jews is just another example of how the entire human race behaves.

In any event, here is another jape.

> In a synagogue on a Saturday morning the rabbi is delivering his sermon. He is most impassioned in declaring the relative insignificance of man when compared with the glory of the Creator. "Who is omniscient and omnipotent?" he exclaims. "Certainly not man. God alone, the merciful, all-knowing dispenser of justice is our shield and our source. And in that perspective, we are as *nothing!*" he stresses. "We are nothing! As the great Rabbi Johanan said, 'The words of the Torah abide only with him who regards himself as nothing.' "
>
> Carried away by the rabbi's eloquence, the cantor intones, "Yes, indeed, we are nothing, we are nothing."
>
> And the congregation president, who is also seated on the *bimah* (platform) next to the cantor, equally excited, also adds, "We are all nothing!"
>
> At this point, a congregant in the back of the temple jumps up shouting, "I too, I too, am nothing."
>
> The congregation president nudges the cantor. "Listen to him, that *shmendrick*" (a derogatory term), he whispers. "Look who wants to be nothing!"

A subtle joke which tells us something about the pecking order.

Jews certainly do know how to apply the needle to themselves. Consider the following jape, which trades on the light bulb stories common some years ago.

> How many Zionists does it take to screw in a light bulb? The answer is four.
>
> One to announce the necessity for such an "event."
>
> A second to travel around getting contributions for this important undertaking.
>
> A third to organize the flow of money as it arrives.
>
> And the fourth actually to set the light bulb in the socket.

This is pretty critical of the way Jews handle communal affairs, sort of half-joking and half-nasty.

The following was making the rounds in Israel several years ago. To understand it, you need to know what a *minyan* is: the ten people required in order for certain prayer obligations to be carried out in public worship.

In Israel, only five people are required for a *minyan*. Why? Because the Jews are schizophrenic.

As in many groups, there is also a reverse tendency—to stick together against an outsider. Look at the following joke, for example, which has the feel of an Old World story.

A beggar knocks at the door of a Jewish household and asks for food. The housewife generously offers the man a meal. And he repays it by walking out with a silver spoon!

But the woman notices it immediately and runs out of the door, yelling, "You, you with the silver spoon!"

As chance would have it, the running beggar/thief notices a policeman rounding the corner and stops. The cop takes in the situation at a glance. He walks up to the man, grasps his arm, and asks the woman, "Is there something wrong here, Ma'am?"

"No, no, no," the woman reassures him. "I just wanted to tell this young man that the spoon I gave him was *milchik*."

Which, for the benefit of the uninitiated, means a utensil to be used only with dairy products according to Jewish dietary law.

It is well-known that Ashkenazi Jews were committed to community. The above example is only a small token. In some cases, a ruler might order the Jews to yield a person to the authorities, under the threat of severe punishment for not obeying. Jews were always enjoined by their sages and rabbis *not* to do so and often took the consequences of hanging together.

So whether we are talking about self-disparagement or solidarity, let's laugh and enjoy it, realizing all the time that we might find similar sentiments in other places and other groups.

3

This Is Your Life

I have already mentioned that there are several classifications of Jewish jokes. First, there are those that might just as easily apply to other people but that become Jewish simply because the narrator identifies the actors as Jewish.

Second are those that depend on a Jewish language, mainly Yiddish, to make their point. More recently, of course, jokes from Israel have increased in number.

Next we looked at jokes of so-called Jewish characteristics or stereotypes.

Now we turn to perhaps the most important and broadest type: jokes that deal with elements of Jewish life, the conditions under which Jews have lived and still do live—in short, jokes concerning the Jewish experience. Of course, some of the jests in earlier chapters belong here too. Remember, *any given joke may fall into more than one category.*

The Torah, The Whole Torah, and Nothing But The Torah

If you were asked what distinguishes Jews from all others, your immediate answer would probably be their religion. Nearly everybody would agree that Judaism has been the major ingredient in the cement which has bound the Jews together over many, many centuries. Over time it has acquired new meanings and interpretations wherever Jews have lived, but for all Jews— Ashkenazis, Sephardim, or Orientals—it has constituted the foundation of Jewish life and the root of Jewish experience.

The "home base" of Judaism is the Bible, what the Jews call the Torah (more accurately, it should be called the *Tanach*, the Hebrew acronym for the three main divisions of the Hebrew Bible—the Torah, the Prophets, and the Writings). Some people have called the Torah "a portable homeland"—something Jews carried with them wherever they went as the basis of their life. All the other works, the Talmud, Kabbalah, Midrashim, and others, are commentaries, interpretations, manipulations of the text of the Torah. For millennia, the Torah was the fundamental study of Jewish boys.

Now you might ask a logical question: Did Jews have jokes before the advent of Yiddish? Don't jokes occur in the Bible? As far as I can see, the Torah is not a book with jokes such as we have talked about here.

There is a story which may be a true example of Jewish wit at an early time. It refers to Hillel, one of the greatest of the Pharisee teachers in the first century B.C.E.

> Hillel was known to be an extremely gentle man, not given to violence or anger. A stranger comes into the city where he is teaching and hears of this characteristic of Hillel in a conversation with one of Hillel's disciples.
>
> "I will bet 10 silver shekels that I can make him mad," the stranger tells the student.
>
> "Accepted," says the latter.
>
> So they arrange for the stranger to visit Hillel. No sooner has he been introduced to the teacher when he begins to make insulting remarks, to taunt him with being an ineffective rabbi, and on and on, in front of all the students there.

Hillel listens and remains entirely calm.

Finally the stranger comes up for air. He pauses, realizing that he has been licked, and he says to Hillel, "Rabbi, do you realize that by your failing to get angry at what I've said to you I have lost 10 silver shekels?"

Hillel looks at the man and observes, "Better that you should lose 10 silver shekels than that I should lose my temper."

This humor is rather typical of these older stories.

The Talmud and the Midrash are said to contain humorous stories. Midrash is an anecdotal compendium of legends which were intended to flesh out what the Bible contains. Following is one of these legends converted into what we might consider a jest.

Some of King David's servants are eating. They have been served boiled eggs. One of them must be starved because he finishes his portion very quickly and turns to the young fellow next to him. "I'm still hungry," he says. "Maybe you will 'lend' me one of your eggs?"

"Okay," says the second man, "but you must promise me, in front of all these witnesses, that you will make good on this loan by giving me everything I would have gotten from the egg by the time you pay back the loan."

"Done!" says the "borrower."

Some time passes and then one day the "lender" informs the "borrower," "The time has come for you to make good on your loan."

So the borrower returns an egg.

"Oh, no," the lender protests. "Remember, the egg would have produced chickens which would have produced eggs which would have yielded more chickens and on and on. I estimate that you owe me either a hundred chickens or a thousand eggs."

Of course, a big dispute develops. They finally decide to take the argument to the Prince, the young Solomon, and he is asked to decide. After some thought, Solomon answers: "Let us suppose you were to take some boiled beans and go out to plant them. And let us say that someone asked you, 'What are you doing?' You might answer, 'I am sowing boiled beans to get a crop.'

"Your questioner would certainly look at you as though you were crazy. Right?

"So boiled beans will not produce new beans, and a boiled egg will not produce chickens. So one egg is enough!"

Or take the following, again probably an old Midrashic story:

The Roman emperor Hadrian calls his court together and announces: "From now on, I am considered as God. Announce this to all of our subjects."

Soon thereafter, a Jew is brought before Hadrian because he has stated that he will not accept the divinity of the emperor. Hadrian wishes to know the reason for the Jew's defiance of his order.

"Great emperor," he replies, "if you are the omnipotent God, will you not aid me in my hour of need?"

"What is it that you need?" the emperor inquires.

"I have my entire fortune in a ship which is now becalmed."

The emperor assures him: "That is no problem. We will send ships with rowers to rescue your ship. So, do you now see my power and acknowledge my divinity?"

"But," the Jew continues, "why should you go to all that trouble? Why not merely send a little wind?"

"What are you talking about?" the emperor asks. "How can I send the wind?"

"If you do not know how to do that, then how can you be the God who created that wind?"

The putdown in the name of religion! And while the story is clever and wry and vaguely humorous, it does not qualify as a true joke as we think of modern jokes. Such stories are really intended to teach a lesson in wisdom rather than to amuse. It is said that the Midrash does contain sections that might be considered jesting, but probably they are somewhat like this one and would not be considered funny by today's standards.

There is a thirteenth-century collection of jokes by a man called Bar-Hebraeus. I can't say that the following story is typical of this collection. Note that it has a more secular tone than those above.

> A poor man dreams that he is frying dung. What can that mean? So he goes to the dream interpreter to ask him. The interpreter listens to his dream and says, "If you give me a zuza, I will explain the meaning."
>
> "Are you joking?" is the reply. "If I had a zuza, would I fry dung? I would buy a fish to fry!"

A zuza is said to be a weight in ancient Palestine, so this seems to be an old joke. But how do you date it?

The commentaries on the Bible and Talmud are said to contain wit and jokes. There is a supposed quip about a third-century rabbi who was asked why the sea was salty and answered that this was so because of all the herring in it. Did this really happen? And if it did, was it a joke or a serious hypothesis? Who can tell?

There are remarks in the rabbinic literature regarding the need for livening Torah and Talmud study by introducing light and humorous touches. Again, I can offer you no instances. Nevertheless, I have no doubt that jokes were told in those days.

It is also said that many rabbis were known to be witty men, given to joking. It's difficult to judge how authentic stories about them are, or whether a particular story involving Rabbi X is true. Jokes tend to travel around. Here is one example, though.

> A Chasid, on a visit to another town, goes to services on the Sabbath. Now the rabbi of this place is known for his quips and jests and he has his congregation repeatedly convulsed with laughter. But not the visitor.
>
> Finally, the man seated next to him turns to him and asks: "You don't feel well today? How is it that you're not laughing at our rabbi's jests?"

"Don't feel well? God forbid! The reason I'm not laughing?
I'm not a member of your congregation!"

This neo-Chelm story has many modern variations. There
is no guarantee that this is the authentic original, nor do we
have any idea of what the rabbi's stories were. People simply
told this story about a rabbi.

On the other hand, humor of a merely jesting kind was
looked down upon by many of the great rabbis as being un-
worthy and deflecting Jews from the path of true study of the
Bible and its commentaries. (The great Greeks like Plato and
Aristotle did not have a very high opinion of humor either.)

And yet here is a rather strange story which gives some
idea of how other commentators felt about jokes and joking.

A rabbi is in a market when the prophet Elijah appears to
him. The rabbi is naturally excited and respectful. He begins a
conversation with the prophet, and at one point, he asks, "Is
there any Jew in the market here who is destined to play an
important part in the World to Come?"

Elijah looks around and answers, "No! I don't see anyone
who would qualify."

Just then two men appear and Elijah holds up his hand.
"Wait, here are two who will do so!"

Then he disappears. The rabbi turns to the two men and
inquires: "What are you? What do you do for a living?"

One answers: "We are merrymakers. We seek to make
people happy when they are gloomy, to make peace where there
are quarrels. This we do by making people laugh."

Well, everyone is entitled to his or her own opinion. Some
commentators placed a low value on merriment and some felt
the opposite.

Most rabbinical anecdotes carry some moral significance,
or they were used to glorify the religion and its major figures—
the rabbis. One example was the Talmudic joke told earlier in
this book about the man who wanted to learn the method of
Talmudic reasoning and was given the puzzle of the two robbers coming down the chimney. Probably all would agree that

it was mildly amusing at best, but it does tell us something about the emphasis on both reasoning and common sense. Similarly:

> A sage is a passenger on a horse and wagon. As they pass a farm, the driver sees some hay. He stops his horse, looks around carefully to make sure no one is watching, runs out, and grabs a bundle of hay.
>
> The sage has been watching and realizes the driver is about to feed the hay to the horse. Quickly, he shouts to the man, "They are watching; they are watching."
>
> The driver immediately drops the hay, jumps on the wagon seat, and, as he starts his horse, he looks around and sees no one.
>
> "Why did you tell me that lie, old man?" he shouts at the sage.
>
> "Lie, what lie?" the sage replies and points to the sky. "*They* are watching!"

These types of anecdotes, common in Yiddish folklore, and also found in Jewish jestbooks, are not the staple of a modern standup comic. But they were widely used in sermons and they do have a witty or humorous way of making an ethical point or a call to better or more devout behavior.

As we have already seen, quite a few jokes celebrate the *wisdom of rabbis*. These men were considered the moral, spiritual, and intellectual leaders of the community, the ones to whom all questions were referred. And so they performed as judges, often yielding jests to illustrate their sharpness. Look at the following story, for example.·

> A poor man finds a wallet containing quite a few rubles. After a quick look, he says to himself: "In this town only Reb Meyer Horowitz could have such a sum." So he brings the wallet to the door of the Reb Meyer.
>
> Well, Reb Meyer thanks him with spirit and says: "I lost it yesterday and we were all worried. After all, it contained 100 rubles. See?" And he proceeds to count.
>
> As he finishes, he turns to the "returner" and says: "What's

this? There are only 90 rubles. Where are the other 10 rubles?"

The other man swears and protests, "I only looked inside. I removed nothing! My children should live so as I am telling you the truth."

But Reb Meyer continues to demand the 10 rubles. So the finder finally says, "Let's take this matter to the *Rov*" (the true title for those rabbis who were really learned and had such jurisdiction).

The rabbi listens carefully to the two stories, thinks for a moment, and then turns to Reb Meyer. "Now you say that your wallet contained 100 rubles?"

"That's right."

Then the rabbi inquires of the "returner," "You say that you took nothing from the wallet?"

"I will swear to that on the Torah!" is the response.

"Well," the rabbi concludes. "I assume that you are both telling the truth; in that case, Reb Meyer, this cannot be your wallet which contained 100 rubles. So, Dovid (the finder), you may keep this wallet until the true owner is found."

King Solomon would not have done better.

The Chasidim were a group more likely to be jokesters. And even with them, the stories are often offered to prove a point.

A Chasidic rabbi known for his ability to get donations from wealthy Jews is asked whether it is really dignified for him to "stoop" to solicit the unwilling rich for the charity fund.

"Well," he replies, "let's look at it this way. In God's scheme of things, nothing is higher than man. And, tell me, what can be lower than a cow? And yet man has to stoop before a cow in order to milk her!"

A story with a moral, but here it has become sharper and perhaps funnier.

The Talmud contains commentaries on the Torah, which in turn is like a combination constitution and code for daily living. Therefore in both you will find stories, ethical rules of conduct, and advice on how to do nearly anything you can imagine. The Talmud is not a simple encyclopedia but a set of commentaries, and commentaries on commentaries, running to many volumes. To give you a taste, from a humorous point of view, here is a story, one that has the flavor of an Old World Yiddish story.

A young man who has recently gotten married decides to build a house. He goes to the rabbi for advice, and the rabbi tells him: "You came just at the right time. I was just looking at the section in the Talmud that deals with that."

So the rabbi turns to the part in question and tells the young man what the Talmudic instructions are for building a house, ending with the instruction that after it is all put together the last thing that must be done is to nail up the *mezuzah* on the doorpost. (The *mezuzah* is a little box containing the name of God and some appropriate prayers; devout Jews kiss it on the way in and out of the home.)

The young man goes back and does as he has been told. When he has completed building the house, he starts to nail on the *mezuzah*, and lo and behold, the house falls apart.

Upset, he rushes back to the rabbi and tells him what has happened. The rabbi shakes his head: "Is it possible? I'll tell you what. Write down all the instructions. Find a friend. Have him read them to you, one at a time, and carry them out exactly. I'm sure you must have omitted something in what you did. Or else you misunderstood."

Said and done. With the help of a friend, our young man goes through the same exercise, finishes the house, starts to nail on the *mezuzah*, and boom, down comes the house.

Very much upset, he once again rushes back to the rabbi and tells him. The rabbi shakes his head, puts on his glasses, takes a volume of the Talmud down from the shelf, and starts to read, turning pages and nodding as he reads. "Aha," he exclaims. "Here it is. Rabbi Akiva says the same thing happened to him."

If this story fails to make sense, you must understand that it's illustrating that the Talmud is very complex, that it contains additions and modifications of what rabbis have said in explaining Biblical instructions, and it further has observations on these additions. In that sense, it reflects the conditions of Jewish religious thought.

East Europe: Chasidim versus Misnogdim

In the late eighteenth century a charismatic figure, nicknamed the Baal Shem Tov, or Master of the Good Name, emerged as a teacher in Southern Poland. He emphasized the importance of joy, song, and happy prayer, rather than rigorous Talmudic training, as being in consonance with the will of God and the true meaning of Judaism. This period was a low point in the life of Eastern Jews, following a period of dreadful pogroms. Chasidism, the name given by historians to the Baal Shem Tov's notions (never systematized in any way or even in writing) swept across Ashkenazi Eastern Europe. Rabbis devoted to these ideas appeared in a large number of towns and cities, each a sort of local authority. At least one of these is said to have devoted part of his Saturday worship to jokes as well as singing, although we have no record of the stories.

A countermovement developed, mainly in the north and most notably in the important city of Vilna, a center of Jewish learning and erudition. There was extreme antagonism between the *Misnogdim*, as they were called, and the Chasidim, and you can feel the sarcasm in the following story.

> A Misnogid once came to a city where there was a Chasidic rabbi. Since it was Friday night, the beginning of the Sabbath, the Misnogid went to the shul to pray and listen to the rabbi speak. On his return to his native city, he was asked about his trip and he described it all, including the following.
> "At one point I sat with all the old Chasidim as though I were one of them. For a whole hour, we just sat there and listened to the rabbi keeping silent!"

Sarcasm? You bet! It points to the claim by the Misnogdim that the Chasidic rabbis were not learned enough to have anything significant to say because they were not really scholars.
Now the other side of the coin:

One Chasid asks another, "What is the difference between a Misnogid and a dog?"

"I don't know. What is the difference?" is the response.

"I don't know either!"

Pretty crude putdown!

A Misnogid is *davening* (praying) in a Chasidic shul. In a Chasidic shul there is usually a very relaxed atmosphere—much noise, loud singing, the bodies moving vehemently. In short, one throws oneself into the activity.

Accordingly, the misnogid asks one of the Chasidim: "Why do you create such a tumult in shul? In our Misnogdic shul, the service is quiet, respectful, as it should be in a house of prayer, where one is addressing God."

"I understand," the Chasid replies. "You see, we see ourselves as God's children. And as children do when they feel at home, we fool around, joke, and carry on. And the parent is not at all concerned. If we were stepchildren, we would tiptoe around and be afraid to upset our parent with any kind of raised voice."

This is less sarcastic, but still there is a subtle hostility in the putdown. And now, to give equal time:

A Chasid is describing to a Misnogid the miracles performed by his rabbi.

"Yesterday," he tells him, "we were driving through a village. Suddenly several Gentile boys came running out and started throwing stones at us. The rabbi happened along and immediately uttered a curse on the boys. Immediately, one boy's hand became paralyzed!"

"Wait a minute. Didn't I notice that the rabbi's eye is all swollen today?" the Misnogid observes. "How did that happen?"

"Well, you see, the second boy's stone hit the rabbi," is the answer.

The Misnogid's eyebrows go up. "How come the rabbi's curse didn't stop the second boy?" is his obviously skeptical question.

"Well, you see the second boy was deaf and didn't hear
the rabbi's curse."

Here is another lively jest in the same vein.

> A Chasid is bragging about his rabbi to a Misnogid: "I can't
> begin to tell you what a wonderful man this is! Would you
> believe that every Friday night he flies up to Heaven to converse
> directly with the Lord?"
> "Flies to Heaven? And how do you know this?"
> "How do I know it? The rabbi himself has told us."
> "Well, let me ask you; isn't it possible that the rabbi is lying
> to you?"
> "Lying!? Would a man who flies to Heaven to talk to God
> tell a lie?"

There is an interesting side effect to this antagonism. Remember that the Misnogdic centers were in northern Europe,
especially in Vilna, which is in Lithuania. The Lithuanian Jews
speak a Yiddish that is somewhat different from that spoken
by Polish Jews. A strong antagonism developed between the
Litvaks and the *Polyaks* or *Galitzianer* (Galicians). This animosity
is partly the outcome of the Chasidic/Misnogdic controversy.

The Litvak/Galitzianer clash also shows up in Jewish jokes.
As a sample, first, a very crude jest from the Polish side.

> A little boy asks his father, "Dad, why are Litvaks called
> *tzalemkep* (cross-heads)?"
> "You see," the father tells him, "in every Litvak's head
> there is a cross. How can I prove it? If you were to take an axe
> and split his head, you would find it. And even if you didn't
> find one, it's not so terrible either; there would simply be one
> fewer Litvak in the world!"

This is translated almost literally from a Yiddish jestbook.
Not very funny, true, but it tells us something about attitudes.

Litvaks, on the other hand, believed they were superior
to and smarter than the people on the other side. Witness the
following:

Two *yeshiva bochrim* (students at an academy of Jewish learning), one a Litvak and the other a Galitzianer, confide in each other that they are full of forbidden thoughts—about a young girl, the pretty daughter of the innkeeper where they are staying.

Such a matter requires intervention, so of course they go to consult the rabbi.

"This is serious and it requires penance," the rabbi tells them. "Before you go to sleep tonight, get some peas, place them in your shoes, and spend several hours walking around on them. Doing this should help you get rid of such thoughts and atone for your past imagery."

The next morning the young Galitzianer is hobbling around. The Litvak seems perfectly fit and in good spirits.

"How come you're in such good shape?" the hobbler asks. "Didn't you follow the rabbi's advice."

"What do you take me for?" is the answer. "Of course, I followed his counsel. I put the peas in my shoes and walked around on them for over an hour. But first, I cooked them!"

I myself can still remember the razzing between the two "factions" in my own childhood, often jokingly, sometimes very seriously.

The Enlightenment As a Source of Humor

Another important development began around this time, this one in Germany. Here the Jews were strongly discriminated against, but nevertheless, some were quite successful. Moreover, they were much closer than the East Europeans to the great changes then occurring in the culture of Western Europe, known in history as the Enlightenment. Voltaire, Diderot, John Locke, and others were calling for massive changes in European culture and politics, changes which also included greater tolerance with respect to religious differences.

Naturally, Jews would show great interest in such a movement. The outstanding figure in this respect was Moses Mendelssohn, a brilliant man who studied not only the Bible (translating it into German) but also the same things Western students were learning—mathematics, philosophy, history, and the like. Mendelssohn and his colleagues and disciples felt that the Jews generally were behind the times, too deeply steeped in their religious ritual and not knowledgeable about the winds of progress blowing in the outside world. Some of his students came from Eastern Europe, and they returned to the *shtetlach* there with the message of the Enlightenment, known in the Jewish community as the *Haskuleh*. They taught that Jewish life as it had existed, with its emphasis on religion—the Torah as the alpha and the omega of all things—that notion was wrong. The superstition of the common folk was out of joint in "modern times." What superstition? Here is an example from humor:

> A young woman has given birth to a nice-looking baby boy. In the traditional mode, she is afraid that someone who comes to view the newborn will cast the "evil eye" on the baby, a common superstition of the time. What to do? She decides to place a dog wrapped up in baby clothes in the cradle for visitors to see.
>
> Sure enough, one of the visitors is an old crone from the village (a perfect candidate for the evil eye). She hobbles over to the craddle, squints at the dog inside, and says: "May your little boy have a long, healthy life. You know, he looks exactly like his father."

This refers to only one of the many superstitions in which Jews, as well as many other people of the time, believed. So the followers of the Enlightenment, called *Maskilim*, set out to "reform" and "improve" Jewish life. Thus, for the first time in Ashkenazi history, serious internal divisions have developed, centered on religion! Criticism and antagonism are sure to breed satire, sarcasm, and humor. That is why psychoanalyst Theodore Reik states that the Enlightenment was the source of much Jewish joking. Basically, he is right insofar as jokes concern religion.

Observant Jews, both Chasidim and Misnogdim, found a common enemy in the free thinker. Some of these were agnostic or even atheistic, who naturally aroused the anger of the pious. One thing they could do was, of course, make fun of these "new wave" people—which means jokes. Thus:

> A local free thinker, a professed atheist, reaches the age of 70. That year, on Yom Kippur, he shows up in the shul and is observed in fervent prayer throughout the service.
>
> The *shammes* (sexton) sidles up to him during a break in the prayer. "Yonkel," he observes, "what are you doing here? For so many years you have told everyone you don't believe in God!"
>
> "True," the atheist rejoins, "but let me ask you. Suppose I was wrong?"

A gentle ironic poke at the nonbelievers. Also note a kind of practical, common-sense approach, one of the characteristics mentioned in the discussion of Jewish stereotypes.

How about one that's not so gentle?

> A *Maskil*, one of the new breed of reformers, comes to a rabbi. "Rabbi," he says, "I have a problem based on Talmudic lore. We are told that when we are outside and see a rabbi, we should stand up; and also that when we see a dog, we should sit down. Now, what should I do if I were to see a dog and a rabbi on the street at the same time?"
>
> "We do not have a specific rule for such a case," is the rabbi's answer, "but let's both go out together and see what people do."

Not quite as insulting, but also caustic and sarcastic, is the following story:

> The son of a pious *shtetl* Jew leaves to go to the big city to improve his fortune. While there he becomes a *"Deitch"* (literally, a German, the term used for the followers of the Enlightenment).
>
> Now his sister is to be married in his home town and, naturally, he returns for the wedding. The beard is gone, and so are the long sidecurls. The dress is modern, no longer the long gabardine. His parents are astonished and disturbed.

While he is out, his mother examines his suitcase. She discovers no *tallis* (prayershawl), no *tefillin* (phylacteries), not even a *yarmulke* (skullcap). And so, on the morning following the wedding, she says to her son with a sigh: "Oy, what has become of you, woe is me! No *tefillin*, no *tallis*, no *yarmulke*, no *tzitzis* (the tasseled undergarment worn by the pious). Tell me. Are you still circumcised?"

Needless to say, the free thinkers didn't spare the religious folks either. Satire answered satire, and jest replied to jest.

A free thinker is asked why he becomes so frightened whenever he hears thunder and sees lightning.

"This is a fearful prospect," he answers, "because we all remember Mount Sinai."

"What Mount Sinai? What are you talking about?" he is asked.

"Every time I hear the thunder, I'm afraid that the Master of the Universe will hand down another Torah," is his answer.

Here is another story about one of these heretics.

A modern free thinker would go out to tend his orchard and eat some fruit, on Yom Kippur, in full sight of the Jews who were fasting. One day, someone asked him, "Don't you believe in anything? Have you forsaken the faith of your fathers altogether?"

"Well, there is one thing I still hold to," he answered.

"And what is that?" the natural question.

"I still believe in resurrection."

"Resurrection! What makes you pick that out?"

"Think about it. Here is a Jew who comes home from praying on Saturday night. He sits down to the Saturday night meal, the *tcholent* (combination of meat and vegetables) which has been cooking since Friday afternoon. With that he will down his radish with chicken fat, a dish of jellied calf's foot, a pudding, some stuffed derma, one or two meat dishes, a couple of potatoes which have also been roasting since the day before. Then he will get to eat some strudel and stewed plum pudding for dessert. After that, he puts away a quart of cold water and lies down to take a nap.

"If a person can get up after such a meal, I have to believe in resurrection!"

Have no fear. The pious answered joke with joke:

A wealthy man who is also a free-thinking atheist has died and is about to be buried. The burial society demands 500 gulden for the burial plot, for which the normal charge is 50. The heirs bring suit to set aside the fee.

The judge wishes to know the reason for the high price.

The chairman of the burial society informs him: "Your Excellency, pious Jews believe in resurrection. So some time in the future, when the Messiah comes, we will get the burial plots back as community land. But an atheist who does not believe in this plans to rest in the plot forever and should pay for permanent occupancy."

By the beginning of our century, religion had become fair game for jokes. If the numskull stories about Chelm are any indication, it's likely that at least the common folk were jesting about rabbis even earlier. Now the division of the Jewish community was much more obvious—and reflected by jokes. Still, we can't tell for sure just when any given joke was created. Here is a jokebit to illustrate the point.

Two free thinkers are discussing Judaic holiday observance. One says to the other: "Of course, I don't fast on Yom Kippur. But I do make it a point to go to hear a concert of classical music on that day."

Obviously, we have rebellion in the ranks here. In the joke, the man still needs to observe the holiday in some significant way, even one against the ritual. Or listen to this one.

Several Jews who are on their way to shul for the Sabbath services happen to look into a window and see a young man smoking a cigarette, something totally forbidden on the Sabbath. Immediately, they run into the house, calling for the young man's father-in-law: "Shloimeh, what kind of son-in-law do you have? This *opikoiris* (heretic) doesn't observe the Sabbath. He needs severe punishment!"

"Just a minute," the young man protests. "Let's not get so excited. It's just that I forgot," he explains.

"You mean you forgot that it's Saturday? How is that possible?"

"No, not that," is the answer. "I forgot to pull down the shade!"

Some would consider this *chutzpeh* with a capital C.

This sort of insolence is carried even further in the following:

> A young man is talking to several pious Jews. "I have to confess. Recently, I sat down and ate without saying the proper blessing."
>
> "Oh, that's not right," one of the older men tells him.
>
> "I know, but the reason that I didn't say the blessing is that I didn't wash my hands as one is supposed to do before eating."
>
> "That makes it even worse. How do you come to do a thing like that?" he is asked.
>
> "Well, you see, I was eating nonkosher food!"
>
> "That's outrageous! A Jew eating *trayfeh* food!"
>
> "But you see," the young man continues, "I had no choice. All of our kosher restaurants were closed."
>
> "What are you talking about? Jewish restaurants closed?"
>
> "Well, you have to keep in mind that it was Yom Kippur."

Obviously the person who created this joke was trying to needle his observant fellow Jews. The attitude seen in these jests shows us that some Jews were no longer attached to the faith of their fathers, even though they considered themselves to be Jews—an important development in the Jewish community of the nineteenth and twentieth centuries.

But in the midst of all these controversies, Jews continued in many of their old ways. For the great majority, religion and the emphasis on study and Torah remained central, even in the rapidly changing world. And Jewish irony, aware of where Jews stood in Eastern Europe, could sound like this:

A poor but learned scholar in a small town is hard at work on a manuscript of Biblical interpretation. A "reformed" visitor from a large city comes to the town and, in the course of his visit, he finds the scholar hard at work.

"What are you writing?" the visitor asks.

"I am working on an interpretation of some of the laws in Deuteronomy," is the answer.

"Of what use is that? Stop your writing. It will get you nowhere."

To which the scholar responds, "Nu, and if I stop my writing, will it get me somewhere?"

Notice the typical answering a question with a question. And what does his question mean? He is saying that he thinks he has, what we call today, no other "marketable skills."

Most of the above are almost certainly Old World stories. You might be wondering what was happening in the United States.

New World Jokes about Religion

What happens to religion as a source of humor when the Ashkenazis come to the New World?

First of all, the Enlightenment movement produced a change in Germany in the way Jews worshipped. This has been termed the Reform movement, because the rabbis who developed it sought to change the nature of services. In general, one can say that they wanted to make the service more like those of the Western churches. Needless to say, this movement caused consternation and opposition from the more traditional.

What does this have to do with jokes? Well, to start, let's look at Ireland. Most of the Jews there lived in Dublin and were, apparently, Orthodox. When the Reform synagogue, an impressive building, was established, it became something that was shown to tourists.

As you know, Ireland is well over 90 percent Catholic. When Catholic taxi drivers or guides would show the Reform synagogue, they frequently referred to it as "the Protestant synagogue."

In the United States, the first large-scale immigration of Jews came from Germany in the 1840s. Thus, the Reform movement became established here early and very strongly. Orthodox Jews had also found their way to these shores, but the great mass immigration from Eastern Europe came between 1880 and 1920. A middle-road denomination called Conservative also developed. The antagonism among the three groups showed up in Jewish-American jokes. In general, there is a strong tendency to lampoon Reform. For example:

> A Jewish family wants to set up a Christmas tree for the children, but they want to know what would be an appropriate blessing. Since they are obviously not familiar with religious observance, they go to a nearby shul and ask for the rabbi, who happens to be Orthodox.
>
> "Rabbi," they inquire, "we are Jewish but don't know much about the religion. We are putting up a tree for the Christmas season, but we would like to use a Judaic blessing for it. Can you help us?"
>
> "What!" the rabbi shouts. "You're putting up a Christmas tree, a symbol of Christianity, and are looking for a blessing? That's outrageous. Get out of my sight!"
>
> Chastened, the couple decide to try another rabbi. This one is Conservative. After listening to their question, he chides them gently. "It is not appropriate to set up such a tree in Jewish observance. I would urge you not to do this. And there is no appropriate blessing."
>
> The couple would now just as soon forget about the whole thing, but what doesn't one do for children? Asking around, they learn that there is a more "liberal" rabbi in the community and they approach him.
>
> After hearing their plea, this Reform rabbi tells them, "I know what a Christmas tree is, but what is a blessing?"

This rather ridiculous jape should nevertheless help you understand how Jewish jokelore reveals the division between the religious groupings. A similarly malicious story runs the other way:

An old Jewish man is sitting in a shul on a Friday night. Suddenly he spits on the floor. The man behind him interrupts his prayer to chide him, reminding him that it isn't nice to spit on the floor, especially in a shul.

"What's the matter?" the old fellow asks in reply. "Where do you think you are, in a Reform temple?"

Remember also the story earlier about the man who was shipwrecked and built two huts for worship, one of which he will not go to. There is a saying that when three Greeks meet you get a restaurant and when three Jews meet you get two synagogues.

Another aspect of this newer type of joke is the change in the attitude toward the rabbi. No longer the joshing about the marvels of competing Chasidic wonder workers. Now the calling itself comes into questioning.

Two Jews meet who have not seen each other for some time. There are exchanges about health, employment, and business, and then they come to the children.

"I remember you had a smart young boy. How is he doing these days?"

"Oh, my Morris," the other answers. "He's doing very well. He's going to a *yeshiva* (an academy for religious training). He thinks he will go to study further and wants to become a rabbi!"

"A rabbi?" the other exclaims. "A rabbi? Is that a job for a Jewish boy?"

Why would someone question such an occupation for a Jew? Well, this joke dates back to the time when rabbis, like schoolteachers, lived in genteel poverty. It is still being told, however, and is obviously ironic in its intention.

Other stories also demonstrate how the rabbi may be viewed by members of the congregation. Here is one reminiscent of the Old World comparisons among Chasidim.

Two men are discussing their respective rabbis. "Rabbi Stone, our rabbi," says one, "a marvelous speaker, unbelievable.

He keeps you interested all the time. And, you know, he can speak for an hour on any subject, on anything!"

"That's nice," says the other man. "But take our rabbi. He's *really* remarkable. This man can speak for an hour on nothing!"

These jokes reveal a kind of ambivalence toward rabbis. On the one hand is real respect for the learning of these men, as a class; on the other is a sort of good-natured, freely expressed kidding, somewhat similar to that directed toward professors. But it is hard to imagine stories like these about Eastern European rabbis, except in the satiric ones of the factions— Chasidim versus Misnogdim, or free thinkers versus rabbis, or, of course, Chelm.

But not all jokes involving religion are about rabbis. Since most Jews attend services in synagogue or temple on the High Holy Days, this phase of Jewish life does not escape the eyes of jokelore.

In Eastern Europe the shul was supported by the local community to the best of its ability. I do not recall ever having seen any references in buying tickets in order to attend holiday services. But the more businesslike atmosphere of the United States finds business practices applied to admission. So we have the following example, a classic:

It is Yom Kippur. A man comes to the synagogue in a state of obvious excitement. The *shammes* (sexton) is at the door looking at admission tickets. As the man tries to walk in, the *shammes* stops him: "Let's see your ticket."

"I don't have a ticket. I just want to see my brother, Abe Teitelbaum. I have an important message for him."

"A likely story. There's always someone like you, trying to sneak in for the High Holy Day services. Forget it, friend. Try somewhere else."

"Honest. I swear to you, I have to tell my brother something. You'll see, I'll only be a minute."

The *shammes* gives him a long look. "All right," he says, "I'll give you the benefit of the doubt. You can go in. But *don't let me catch you praying!*"

Even more bizarre stories have developed around religion in the United States. To wit:

The people are assembled in the shul for the service. Suddenly, the president of the congregation announces that the cantor has become ill and will not be able to lead the singing. Moe Klein walks up to the president and says: "You know, I practice all the prayers at home. I can't sing, but my dog has learned all of them. And can he sing? You wouldn't believe! If you want, I'll get him and let him do the cantor's part."

"C'mon, Moe," the president tells him. "This is no time for jokes."

"I should live so; it's absolutely true!"

Well, the president turns to the other bigwigs on the *bimah* (platform)—the rabbi, the head of the Men's Club, and the president of the Sisterhood. There is a hurried conference. The rabbi is outraged but the lay members, who no doubt consider themselves more in touch with real life, carry the day. The president turns back to Moe. "Okay, Moe, we'll try it. But please, no jokes, no kidding."

Moe is back with the dog in fifteen minutes. He escorts him to the podium with all eyes focused on him and a lot of whispering and talking going on.

The service starts. And what can I tell you? The dog is marvelous. Nuances never before heard, cantorial inflections, the whole ball of wax. At the end of the service, there is an ovation. Everybody wants to know more about Bruno.

The president approaches Moe. "You should get the dog into cantorial training. He will be a first-rate cantor, a phenomenon."

"Melvin, that's easy for you to say! I would do it but he refuses. He wants to be an accountant!"

A *real* shaggy dog story!

In addition to worship and prayer, there is another aspect of religious jokes. Jewish-American jokesmiths have also taken a look at the rituals of Judaism.

The religion places great emphasis on the proper observance of the Sabbath. However, the economic conditions faced by the immigrant in the United States made strict observance difficult. So we get the following New York East Side story:

> *Kalman:* "You, Zalman, a pious Jew, a man with a long beard, how is it that you keep your clothing store open for business on Saturday?"
>
> *Zalman:* "Kalman, I sold a suit today for 17 dollars that cost me 25. You call that business?"

True or not, it's an ironic twist and illustrates what the New World often imposed on the new immigrant. Another aspect:

> A bus driver stops for a light. Suddenly a woman who has been standing on the sidewalk darts out in front of the bus. Standing directly before the driver, she places her hands on her breasts. The driver shakes his head from side to side.
>
> Now she places her hands on her buttocks. The driver shakes his head up and down. And off she goes as the light turns to green and the bus moves on.
>
> A man, seated directly behind the driver, has watched this scene with amazement. He leans over to the driver and asks him, "Say, Buddy, what was all that about?"
>
> The driver replies: "Well, you see, I'm Jewish, and that lady is my wife. Every day she waits out there for me in the early afternoon to ask me whether I want *milchik* (dairy) or *flay-shig* (meat) for supper."

Jews, of course, may not eat dairy and meat at the same meal. Incidentally, that's why another joke writer said that Jewish women wear two-piece bathing suits so that one covers the milk portion and one the meat.

Devout Jews put on *tefillin* (phylacteries) while praying in the morning (except Saturdays), to remind them of the necessity to remember and love God. They are in the form of two small leather boxes inside of which are written passages from the Bible. Each box is attached to a strap, one wrapped around the left upper arm and the other around the top of the head, to hold the boxes in place.

A young Orthodox Jew has been admitted to a hospital. The nurse comes in to get his temperature, measure his pulse, and record his blood pressure.

The next morning, the man gets up, finds his phylacteries, and puts them on. Just as he is doing so, the nurse peeks in to check on things and sees him placing the strap around his left arm. She walks back to the nurses' station and tells the nurse-in-charge: "You know that Jewish fellow, Robert Cohen, that we admitted yesterday? Already he's showing off. Would you believe he's taking his own blood pressure?"

We already had a section on food and eating, but there are also jokes about food that have a religious connection as well.

A priest and a rabbi again have become very good friends. The priest invites the rabbi to his home for dinner. Unfortunately, the priest has forgotten about Jewish dietary restrictions, and a pork dish is served after the salad.

"Timothy," the rabbi reminds his friend, "you have forgotten that I observe *kashruth*" (under which one prohibition is the eating of pork).

"Good Lord," the priest exclaims. "You are right, Ezra, and I do ask for your forgiveness. But," he adds playfully, "when will you enjoy a pork dinner?"

Quickly, the rabbi replies, "At your wedding, Timothy."

Here we have shifted to the quick-thinking stereotype. Score one for the rabbi.

During the Jewish High Holy Days—Rosh Hashanah, which marks the beginning of the Jewish year, and Yom Kippur, the Day of Atonement for sins committed in the old— Jews are supposed to reflect on their relations with others and actually ask for forgiveness for any nastiness or evils they have committed. So we have the following:

Two Jews have had terrific arguments about their roles in the temple during the past year, and now, right after the Yom Kippur service, Max Birnbaum has decided to make up with Lou Moskowitz and let bygones be bygones.

So on the way out, he approaches Lou and says to him: "Happy New Year! For the coming year, I want to wish you everything you would wish for me at this time."

Moskowitz replies, "You're starting in again?"

And now a different scene.

An older gentleman has worked all his life and has now reached an advanced age. His son is a well-to-do businessman and he is after his father to give up the little store in which the old gentleman has labored so long.

"Dad, you don't have to do this any more," he tells his father. "Retire. Living here in New York is too hard on you physically."

"So what do you want me to do?" the older man asks him.

"I'll tell you what. We'll fly down to Miami Beach. I know you eat only kosher food, but there are a number of hotels down there that strictly observe the dietary laws. We'll find a nice room. You'll see—the climate is better for you. I'm sure you'll find many people with whom you can become friendly. And I'll keep in touch with you all the time."

After resisting for a while, the old man accedes. "All right, you want I should go, I'll go. What I'll do there, I haven't any idea."

Well, they fly down to Miami Beach, find the best hotel with an American plan, kosher food, and a decent room. The son arranges for all bills to be sent to him, and the hotel owner, Mr. Bergman, assures him that he will keep an eye on the old fellow and see to it that everything goes well.

The son flies home. Two days later he decides to check up. He calls the hotel and asks for Mr. Moskowitz. Imagine his surprise to learn that there is no Moskowitz registered. Upset, the son asks for Mr. Bergman. The hotel owner gets on the phone and tells the younger Moskowitz: "Oh, yes, I was about to call you. Your father checked out this morning. He told the clerk here that he could be found at the Hotel Joyland further up the beach. It's on 65th Street."

Well, I don't have to tell you that the son is shocked. He flies down that very afternoon, and a cab takes him to the Joyland.

"Do you have a Mr. Moskowitz registered here?" he asks the desk clerk.

"Yes sir, checked in earlier today," is the reply. "He's in Room 507."

The son gets into the elevator, goes up to the fifth floor, finds Room 507, tries the door, finds it open. He steps into the room and there is his father in bed with a gorgeous young woman.

Sputtering, the son looks at his father and gets out the words: "Dad, what's going on? I went to all the trouble of finding a good kosher place for you. Why did you move? And what are you doing in bed with that *shiksa* (Gentile girl)?"

The father replies: "Marvin, it's all right, it's all right. Don't get excited. I don't eat here."

As you see, some Jews are very cautious about adhering to strict dietary law.

Similarly, when writers of japes look at Jewish history, they see a lot of raw material. Every week a portion of the Torah is read in synagogues during the Sabbath service, according to a certain cycle so that the whole thing is covered over a year's time. So we get the following jest:

A little boy, going to services for the first time one Saturday, hears the story of how Jacob sends Joseph out to his brothers and how these envious fellows sell him into captivity. The boy is both impressed and depressed by the story.

Exactly one year later, this boy is again at services and hears the same portion of the Torah being read. So the youngster shouts: "Idiot! They sold you last year. Why did you go back again?"

Or, take what Jews know as the *Motten Toireh*, the giving of the tablets and the Torah to Moses.

Moses speaks to God. "Lord, all this business with getting the Jews out of Egypt and across the desert is very stressful. And now you've had me come up to the top of this mountain. Frankly, I'm exhausted and I have such a headache, you wouldn't believe!"

God responds in his kindliest way. "All right, if you feel that way, take two tablets and contact me tomorrow morning."

Not only does this joke writer put the famous tablets in play, but he also sideswipes the medical profession. The following sees the same event from a different perspective.

God offered the commandments to the Egyptians.

"What are they?" the Egyptian head man wanted to know.

"They are rules that I want you to observe. For example, 'You shall have no other gods beside me, and. . . .' "

"No, no, no—we don't want to give up our great gods."

So God turned to the Assyrians with the same offer. And the Assyrian ruler also wanted to know what it meant. God, already forewarned by his previous experience, explained: "It's a set of rules. For example, 'You shall not murder.' "

"Forget it! We have a military campaign to complete. And we don't spare our enemies."

So the Lord turned to the Canaanites, repeated his offer, and got the same question.

"Commandments," said the Almighty, "you know, like laws, rules of conduct. For example, 'You shall not commit adultery.' "

"Wait a minute!" the Canaanite leader said, "I'll never be able to get my bunch to agree to that!"

So in desperation, God turned to the Israelites. And Moses asked: "You're offering us commandments. What does such a commandment cost?"

The Master of the Universe answered: "Cost? They will cost you nothing!"

Whereupon Moses replied: "Nothing! Okay. Put me down for ten!"

Another sideswiper. We're back to stereotypes.

The Exodus itself is raw material for the Jewish-American joke:

Moses has asked for help in escaping from the Egyptian chariots which are chasing the Israelites, and the Lord is about to part the waters of the sea. But just at this moment, Satan observes, "Before that's done, it will be necessary to get an environmental impact report!"

And one that I especially like.

A youngster has just come from his Sunday school session at the temple where his father is a congregant. His father thinks it important to keep in touch with his youngster's education, so he asks him, "Well, what went on today at Sunday school?"

"Oh," the boy answers, "Like it was an interesting story. All about, you know, Moses and like the way the Jews got out of Egypt."

"The Exodus," the father observes. "And what did the teacher tell you about it?"

The boy is thoughtful for a moment, obviously trying to recall the story. "Well, Dad, it was like this. Moses and all these Jews are you know, like, running away. And they reach this sea, I think it's called the Red Sea. And, you know, their scouts tell them that the Egyptians are, like, coming after them to wipe them out. So this man, Moses, he's their commander-in-chief, he gets them all to build bridges over the sea and they all get across to the other side. And then, you know, the Egyptian riders show up all of a sudden and, like, they want to cross the bridges to get hold of the Jews. But this fellow, you know, Moses, he gets his artillery going and they blow the bridges to pieces, you know. And all the Egyptians get, like, drowned."

The father's eyebrows are up to his hairline. This is Exodus like it's never been told before!

"You're telling me that that's the story your Sunday school teacher told you today?"

"Well, no Dad. But I figured you'd never believe the story he told us!"

Now let's look at another section of Biblical history.

A minister of a modern church (no organ, no formal services, but rather guitars and rock music) is talking to a friend of his, a rabbi. "What you fellows in Judaism need is more pizzazz in your synagogues, less heavy stuff. You have to think of it in terms of entertainment of your public. Even advertising

wouldn't hurt. Better still, you get some publicity in the newspapers. That'll pull them in."

"Oh," the rabbi responds, "we know about that. You talk
about publicity. Don't you remember when Samson got two
columns and brought down the house?"

Modern humor leaves no stone unturned, no area un-
spotted.

Anti-Semitism—Can It Be Funny?

Does anyone still need a reminder about this fundamental fact
of Jewish history? The Jewish people have obstinately clung to
their religion for millennia—and survived. But their stubborn
independence has also caused them much grief.

In the biblical story of Esther, the basis for the Purim holiday, the Jews refused to worship the Persian king, and Haman,
the first authentic anti-Semite, sought to destroy them. The
record of hate and death and expropriation and discrimination
have been virtually without end. Whether the Jews of ancient
times generated jokes to deal with this problem, I don't know,
but the Yiddish-speaking Ashkenazis of Eastern Europe certainly did. Remember the bitter irony of the medieval Jews who,
unable to get more cemetery space, asked for a law to prohibit
dying. Let's consider some less unpleasant examples drawn
from Eastern European experience.

> Yakov, a wagoner, having delivered a load to a distant city,
> is returning. Singing, he is driving along at a leisurely pace,
> when suddenly, out of the woods comes a Cossack riding his
> horse directly toward Yakov. The wagoner stops and waits; the
> Cossack dismounts.
>
> "You, Jew, get down here," he orders, flourishing a hand-
> gun. Yakov naturally obeys.
>
> "Give over all your money you collected today," the Cos-
> sack orders. Having no choice, the wagoner complies. "And
> now, go, and be thankful that I am in a generous mood."
>
> Yakov turns to him. "Please, *gospodin*, have mercy on a

poor man," he entreats. "If I come home without a penny, I will never hear the end of it from my wife. All I will know is drunkard, bum, go make a decent living for the family. She will never believe it if I tell her that someone took my money. So please do a favor."

The Cossack, obviously amused, asks, "What do you want, a few kopeks?"

"No, that's not necessary," Yakov responds. "You have there a gun. So put a hole in the coat here." The Cossack laughs and complies. Yakov adds, "Put here also in the other side a couple, and here in the hat too."

As the Cossack enjoys himself firing his gun, Yakov is counting the number of bullets. When the Cossack has fired six times, he knows the gun is empty. Himself a big, burly man, he suddenly turns and jumps on the Cossack, beating him mercilessly and retrieves his own money as well as lifting whatever the Cossack has in his pockets.

Now the Cossack looks up at him and says, sadly: "I should have listened to my mother. She always told me—never trust a Jew!"

Needless to say, this is a delicious joke for Jews. It lets them enjoy what, in real life, was almost never possible, a victory both mental *and* physical.

There is an interesting variation on this joke.

A Jew is walking to the synagogue in a Russian town when he sees a mounted Cossack bearing down on him. He knows that it is customary in such situations for the rider to lash him with the whip at least once. So he stops and bends over to catch the whip on his back.

But the Cossack, evidently in a hurry, rides right by him. The Jew straightens up and says out loud, "He was supposed to hit me with the whip but Cossacks never behave correctly toward us!"

How's that for resignation? More often, though, the Jew in anti-Semitic stories triumphs because of cleverness, a kind of outwitting. For example:

Jews were restricted by the czar's decrees from entering major cities without special passes. A Jew wishes to go to the city to get something he needs that can be bought only in the city, but he has no pass. One of his acquaintances, who deals with officials, does have such a pass. "Come with me," the pass holder advises his friend. "Probably no one will bother you, anyhow."

But no sooner have they come to the downtown area when they see a policeman, and when he sees them he starts marching toward them with an obviously official air.

The Jew with the pass tells his buddy, "You just keep on walking as if no one is interested in you."

He, on the other hand, suddenly starts to run. The policeman immediately gives chase. After a few hundred feet, the policeman catches him and at once demands to see his papers. He produces them.

"Everything is in order," says the officer. "Why did you run?"

"Oh, that," the Jew responds, "you see, my doctor told me that I need to run every morning for 10 or 20 minutes."

"But," the cop reminds him sternly, "when you saw I was chasing you, how come you didn't stop?"

"Well, I thought maybe you go to the same doctor."

Of course, irony is the method for outwitting in this case. But anti-Semitism does not always come through so happily. Another ironic Old World story illustrates the Jewish attitude toward anti-Semitism.

A man is sitting in a cafe, sipping coffee and reading a newspaper. Another man enters, recognizes the reader, walks over to him, leans over, looks at the paper, and exclaims: "Jacob, how come you are reading that scurrilous trash. That newspaper is anti-Semitic garbage. Are you trying to punish yourself?"

"Not at all," is the response. "I really enjoy reading this paper."

"Have you gone crazy? After all the attacks that rag has launched against us, how can you even pick it up in your hands?"

The reader remains calm. "Let me explain it to you," the

reader responds. "When I pick up one of our Jewish dailies, what do I read about? Here, vandalism against a synagogue. There, a bomb has been placed in or near a Jewish home. Or someone is calling for Jews to be thrown out of the country. Right? But what do I see here? It's a pleasure to read that the Jews own all the banks, they control all the newspapers, and a secret 'Zionist' cabal is getting ready to take over as a world government."

Now a much grimmer story, real gallows humor:

In a town in Russia, a rumor begins—a young girl has been murdered. The Jews in the town begin buzzing about this and soon one of them comes with the news that the girl was Christian.

Now the Jews gather in the house of study to express their worries. "What are we going to do? Right away the Christians will blame some Jew and we will have a pogrom! What should we do? What should we do?"

Right in the middle of the hand wringing, one of the town's Jews comes running in. "Jews, Jews, stop worrying. I have just learned that the murdered girl was Jewish!"

When things get too tough, we turn to jest.
A more recent story describes anti-Semitism in present-day Russia.

Word has gotten out that a shipment of meat is arriving in the city, and people line up at the butcher shops. They wait and wait. An hour passes, then two hours, and still no meat.

Now the militiamen show up. "We have just learned that the shipment will be smaller than expected, so all Jews are hereby ordered to leave."

So all the Jews, obviously dejected, get out of the line and leave.

Another hour passes, and the militiamen appear again. "The news is bad. Something has happened to the shipment. There will be no meat today. You had better go home."

As the lines break up and the people move off, some sorrowful, some angry, we hear the following conversation.

"Isn't that terrible, Natasha. We waited for three hours for nothing."

"That's right, Anya. And you see, they sent the Jews home an hour ago. Like I always tell you, the government always favors the Jews!"

Sometimes one gets the feeling that the tragic history of Jews has given them a jaundiced world view. This is an old story that illustrates the point.

A man brings some cloth to a Jewish tailor to have a pair of pants made. (This was one craft traditionally carried on by Jews.) The tailor promises to have it "by next week."

But the next week comes and goes and still no pants. To make a long story short, it takes a month for the tailor to get the pants finished. The customer finally picks them up and says to the tailor: "It took so long to make just a pair of pants? You remember that God made the whole world in seven days. It took you a month to make one pair of pants."

The tailor looks at him with a smile and replies: "So—look at the world and look at those pants. There are so many things wrong with this world that I think the Lord could have taken a little more time, too!"

One could argue that many other groups in this world might have originated such a jest, but Jewish history should testify to the fact that this is an authentic Jewish story. Their history has left the Jews somewhat defensive and perennially worried, as we can see in the following story.

A circus comes to town and sets up. Suddenly the news gets out that the lion has escaped from the circus and is roaming the streets. Pandemonium.

At this point, an older Jew comes out of his hovel and walks to the tavern nearby. He notices all the rushing about. "What is going on in town?" he asks the *kretshmer* (tavern owner).

"Haven't you heard? The circus lion is roaming the streets!"

"A lion roaming the streets! Is that so? Tell me, do you think that's good for the Jews?"

A psychologist might say—in-group sensitivity.

During some periods in Russian history, young Jewish lads—age 10 or even younger—were required to serve many years in the Russian army. Many of them were never heard from again! Naturally, there were many attempts to evade such unfortunate service.

Now, the czar permitted some exemptions, such as married men. To Jews, this exception provided a loophole through which they were able to save their children. This situation naturally became fair game for jesting, bitter as it was.

> A 7-year-old boy is playing in the street, wearing no shoes and no trousers. An older Jew passes by and asks, "How come you're not in *cheder* (the elementary school for Jewish studies)?"
>
> "Because I don't have to go to *cheder* any more. I got married the day before yesterday!"
>
> The older man needles him: "If you're married, then you're an adult. So where are your shoes and your pants?"
>
> "Oh, that," the kid responds. "Well, I wore them when I got married. But today my younger brother is getting married, so he has the pants and shoes."

A sad jest, true. It reminds one of an old Yiddish saying: "When your heart hurts, just laugh it off."

In any group, you can always find those who work with the powers that be, even if doing so is against the interests of their group. There were even paid informers (*masrim*, meaning tattlers or snitches) in the Jewish communities whose job it was to keep Moscow informed about any activities that might merit scrutiny from "upstairs." Do you think these fellows were admired?

> One of the *masrim* is charged with not having supplied good and sufficient news, and the local authorities sentence him to a solid flogging. (Remember this is Czarist Russia in the nineteenth century.) Further, the Jewish community leaders are ordered to watch.
>
> After the flogging, one of these leaders asks Shimon, the

informer, "Cursed one, what were you giggling about during the flogging?"

"It always makes me feel good to see a Jew punished," is the answer.

"Is that the way a Jew should talk? But, wait. If you were so happy, why were you also screaming in between the chuckles?" the community leader probes further.

"Because," Shimon answers, "it's a shame that a Jew should have so much satisfaction."

A wonderful ironic twist. First it gets revenge on the informer—he gets his. Then it exposes his supposed sadomasochism. The end result is black or gallows humor, Jewish wry.

So there you have Jewish anti-Semitism at work. Let's look at a type of Jewish anti-Semitism from another angle. This is from the New World.

Levinson is on his way home. Things have not been going well and he is short of money. He walks by a church and reads a sign: JESUS SAVES. IF YOU ARE NOT YET A CHRISTIAN, JOIN THIS CHURCH TODAY AND RECEIVE 100 DOLLARS AS A GIFT.

Just what the doctor ordered, Levinson says to himself and takes advantage of the offer.

When he arrives home, he explains to his family what happened. There is a long silence. Then his wife says: "You know, Sidney. I need a new coat. I saw one for just 50 dollars yesterday. I really should get it. The old one is a shame to wear."

Levinson gives her a long look, takes out 50 dollars, and gives it to her.

Immediately, his daughter brightens up. "Daddy, how about the new tennis racket you promised me?"

"How much?" Levinson inquires.

"Oh, 25 should do it."

Levinson hands over 25 dollars.

His son looks at him. "Dad, won't you help me out, too? You know I've saved up nearly enough to get the English bike I want. Twenty-five bucks will do it."

Without a word, Levinson gives up his last 25 dollars, looks around at his family, and says: "That's the way it always goes. As soon as a Gentile gets a little money, Jews take it away from him."

Silly as it is, it has ironic truth. It turns the anti-Semitic canard into a joke.

Even in the United States, where the government, at least, has not been officially anti-Semitic, the presence of anti-Semitism has been felt and molded into humor, again ironic and somewhat bitter. Such jokes tend to reveal the absurdities that often underlie anti-Semitic practice.

Harry Davidson, a successful Jewish realtor, has long sought to join a certain golf club, but without success. Now, suddenly, a non-Jewish acquaintance approaches him and tells him: "Harry, I've been in favor of getting you into our club for a long time but I couldn't get the others to agree because, quite frankly, we had an unwritten restriction against Jews. Now we're making a drive for new members and I've been told that the restriction has been lifted. If you would like to join, I'll sponsor you and I'm sure you'll get in."

Davidson guesses that they need new money but he is so eager to join that he agrees. Sure enough, he is accepted and inducted. But he discovers that he is the only Jew who has been permitted entrance.

After several months, he begins to feel somewhat of an outsider and decides to try to get some Jewish friends to join. He proposes a name. The president informs him that the membership will act on the recommendation at their next meeting. Furthermore, he is told that the voting is secret and that a majority of affirmatives is all that is required.

The meeting convenes. Finkelstein's name is proposed and the ballot slips are passed out, then turned in. The president announces the vote: one in favor and 43 against. Finkelstein has been turned down.

On the way out, Davidson, dejected, is walking behind two other members. He hears one of them say to the other: "Well, we saved the club. But, man, are those Jews clannish!"

Sometimes, instead of irony, the Jew responds with sarcasm when being treated like an outsider. The following is a story told about Groucho Marx.

Groucho, his wife, and his daughter are driving on a very hot day. They pass a road sign which advertises a hotel and has a picture of its swimming pool, and they decide that this would be a pleasant place to pass some time.

At the hotel, the desk clerk recognizes Groucho and informs him, with regret, that Jews are not permitted in this hotel.

"We only want to use your pool for a short time," Groucho points out.

"Sorry, it's the regulation of the management," is the answer.

"Well," Groucho points out, "my wife is Gentile, so she can use the pool. And my daughter is only half Jewish; can she go into the pool up to her waist?"

Again, needling, but with unhappiness just below the surface.

Jews even make fun of their own views about anti-Semitism. The classic American story:

A man is coming out of the building that houses a major broadcasting company. Just outside, he meets a friend.

"Hey, what are you doing here?" the friend asks.

"D-d-did y-you kn-n-now th-that these b-b-bastards are a-anti-Semites?" is the response.

"Really?" the friend asks. "What makes you say that?"

The stutterer responds. "I-I-I w-was l-l-looking f-for a j-j-job a-and th-they t-t-turned m-me down f-flat. W-W-Wouldn't e-e-even t-take m-my a-application."

"That's too bad," the friend agrees. "What sort of a job were you looking for?"

"I-I-I w-was a-p-p-plying f-for a j-job as a r-r-radio a-announcer."

Anti-Semitism turned on its head. Supersensitivity exploded. In a milder form, another classic:

Four scholars go to Africa to study the elephant. One is English, one French, one German, and one Jewish. Two years later, their reports are read to a scholarly conference. The titles:

> The Englishman's: "The Elephant and the British Empire"
> The Frenchman's: "The Sexual Behavior of the Elephant"
> The German's: "The Biological Adaptations of the Elephant
> to African Civilization"
> The Jew's: "The Elephant—Is it good for the Jews?"

Even as dreadful an event as the Hitler regime evoked jokes. In fact, Hitler himself became an actor in some of them.

> Hitler has come to inspect a boatyard and a crowd has gathered, among them a young Jew who has managed to get to the front to watch what is going on. Suddenly Hitler slips and plunges into the water. Acting on reflex, the young man quickly dives in after him and pulls him out.
>
> Puffing and gasping, Hitler turns to the young man and says: "I am indeed grateful for what you have done. Anything I can do for you as a reward, I shall be happy to do. You need only name it."
>
> The young man looks at Hitler for a moment, pauses, and then says: "There's only one thing I would like you to do. *"Don't tell my father what I did!"*

And another great classic:

> Two young Jews in Berlin have secured automatic weapons and are determined to do away with Hitler. They have been studying his movements and have learned that he comes past a certain point on his way to the Chancellery every day at precisely 11:00 A.M.
>
> Finally, the big day comes. They are stationed on the first floor of an apartment directly across from where the Chancellor will pass, and all is in readiness for the assassination. The gun has been tested, the ammo carefully checked, the window raised only enough to poke the barrel out a tiny bit.
>
> At 10:55 the two men get on their knees and move the gun into position. Now it is 11:00—no Hitler; 11:05—no Hitler; 11:10—still no Hitler. The men are getting restless. At 11:15, when Hitler still has not shown up, one turns to the other and says: "By God, he's late. I hope nothing has happened to him!"

An attempt to kill has been transformed into the genuine concern one feels for a family member.

Survivors of the concentration camps have reported that even in those dreadful circumstances Jews told each other horrible jokes. Some, at least, believe that doing this helped them survive.

A less jovial side to anti-Semitism is the anti-Jewish joke. Earlier in the book you read about two businessmen in Florida who were vacationing and one asks the other about how to make a flood. There is a whole library of such jokes about Jewish businessmen and fires. For example, the following obviously anti-Semitic one:

> A tailor has a fire in his shop. He and his friend are talking when the insurance man arrives.
> "What happened here?" the man wants to know.
> "I think it was the gas light," the tailor tells him.
> "I thought you said it was the electric light," his friend butts in.
> "Okay, never mind," remarks the insurance man, and notes down on his pad, "Cause of Fire—Israelite."

To Jews this is not much of a joke. Of course, Jewish merchants have sometimes committed arson, and so have other businessmen, but no other nationality seems to have such a stock of fire jokes.

There are still cruder and more obnoxious anti-Semitic jokes. Just for the record, here's one nasty example:

> A Jewish man arrives at the New York airport with a number of bags. He is on his way to Israel and, as we know, the Israelis are very careful about examining luggage.
> The Israeli agent points to the first bag and asks, "What's in that bag?"
> "Oh, in that bag is a lotta money, hundreds and hundreds of dollars. It's for Israel, you understand."
> The Israeli's eyebrows go up. "Money? What is the source of all that money?" he queries, obviously suspicious.
> "If you have time to listen, I'll tell you," is the answer.

And without waiting, the traveler goes on. "You see, I believe very strongly in Israel, so I wanted to raise money for the country. So for the last few years I been going into mens' rooms all over. I go in, I take out a knife, and I tell whoever is there, 'Gimme a contribution for Israel or I'll cut off your balls.' So you can see I collected plenty money."

The agent explodes with laughter, opens the bag, and, lo and behold, there are stacks of dollars.

"And what's in this bag?" the agent asks.

"Oh, in that bag," the traveler answers. "Well, you see, not everybody wanted to give a contribution."

Maybe it's less anti-Semitic than it is tasteless. But here's a jokebit that is a record breaker for disgusting:

Question: What happens to a Jew with an erection when he walks into a wall?
Answer: He breaks his nose.

No wonder Freud referred to the anti-Semitic jokes created by non-Jews (as I assume this one was) as "gross buffooneries."

There are also some Jews who say and do things that can be considered anti-Semitic. For example, early in this century, the Jewish director of the Hamburg American Line (shipping), in order to curry favor with the German Kaiser, bought vulgar Jewish jokes from a Budapest comedian and related them to the Kaiser. Anti-Jewish behavior has been more pronounced in ex-Jews, that is, converts. In the Spanish Inquisition such *Conversos* played an important role in accusing their former co-religionists.

Freud offers us a word play which gets to this issue.

An ex-Jew has just made an anti-Semitic statement. A man who has known him for some time turns to him and remarks, "I am familiar with your ante-Semitism, but your anti-Semitism is new to me."

Isn't it sad that, funny or not, jokes of this kind should exist at all?

Assimilation and Beyond

Jews have maintained their identity over several thousand years—and with no end of trouble for doing so. Now how many must have said during these many years: "Enough already! Being one of God's Chosen People is too much trouble for my taste." Eastern European Jews had a saying, *"Shver tzu zine ah Yid,"* meaning "It's difficult to be a Jew."

We have no census to tell us how many Jews have passed into the general population of their countries. Some were compelled to convert, especially in Christian Europe, and more particularly in Spain. Sometimes they mixed into the general population when permitted to do so under some degree of freedom. This happened, for example, to most of the Sephardic Jews who settled in New Amsterdam and New England, as well as to many of the Jews in Germany in the nineteenth and early twentieth centuries. The efforts of the Hitler regime to discover ancestries sometimes turned up people who had no knowledge of Jewish forebears because their ancestors had long before entered Gentile life through conversion or intermarriage.

In the last hundred years, forced conversion has, of course, disappeared. The nearest thing to it has been the attempts by priests to convert Jewish soldiers on the battlefields of Eastern Europe. Jewish jesting picked up on this practice as follows:

> A Jewish soldier has just been badly wounded. As the battle ebbs, a priest walks around the battlefield offering solace and last rites where needed. He comes to the young Jew, notices how badly wounded he is, leans over and asks him, "Do you believe in the Father, the Son, and the Holy Ghost?"
>
> The soldier looks up and answers, "I'm dying and he's asking me riddles."

The major path to the checking-out process has become what Jews call *assimilation,* that is, permitting oneself to blend into the environment. The degree of a person's assimilation varies. Sometimes it's total, with the person actually converting to another religion. More often, it means dropping all the observed rituals even though one remains, by admission, a Jew. Frequently it means dropping most observances but retaining some pro forma adherence such as synagogue membership and attendance during the High Holy Days.

All of this becomes, of course, part of the Jewish fun. Here is an Old World story.

> Four men are sitting in a railroad compartment (where so many Old World stories occur). A conversation begins among them. One introduces himself as a Hungarian. "My name," he tells them, "is Kemeny."
>
> "Oh," says another, "I'm from Budapest myself. My name is Kamory."
>
> "Well, what a coincidence," the third man observes. "I, too, am Hungarian. My name is Kovach."
>
> And the fourth man chimes in: "I'm also Jewish, and my name is *also* Cohen."

We go to New York for a similar story about names.

> In a courtroom, Monte Stafford is before the judge petitioning for a change of name. The judge looks at his papers and says: "Everything seems in order here. But, Mr. Stafford, weren't you in my court some time ago petitioning for a change of name?"
>
> "That's right, Your Honor," Stafford replies.
>
> "So why are you back now? Is there something about your name that is unsatisfactory?"
>
> "No, sir. Let me explain. Last year, when you permitted my name change, I went from Moe Schwartz to Monte Stafford. Now I want to change it to Monte Stone so that when people ask me, 'What was your name before you changed it,'. . . ."

Finally, one superb example.

> A man goes into an art gallery in Manhattan and is immediately approached by the gallery owner who says, "Good afternoon, I'm Charles Lincoln. This is my gallery. What can I do for you?"

"I'm Maurice Rubinstein. I live in the Bronx and I've come down to buy something good. I've just made a killing in the market and I want to get into buying art. But I've got to tell you, I know nothing about it. What can you suggest?"

"I think I have something for you." Mr. Lincoln leads him to a small oil painting. Two fine nude figures face the viewer, with superb skin tones obvious even to a beginner.

"This little painting has just come into the gallery. As far as anyone can judge, it dates back to the middle of the seventeenth century. We have no provenance on it. If we had that, it would probably be worth at least $100,000. Without it, it goes for much less. We think it must have been done by a student of Peter Paul Rubens, Mr. Rubinstein." The dealer permits himself a smile: "A relative of yours?"

"Was he Jewish? I never heard of him," is the reply.

"No, Mr. Rubinstein, I'm afraid not. In any case, I think a painting with this quality is what you should begin with. I can let you have it for $25,000."

"Fine," Rubinstein assents. "Wrap it up."

Several months pass. Rubinstein again comes into the Lincoln Gallery. Mr. Lincoln either has a good memory or was very much impressed by the previous transaction, because he recognizes Rubinstein and walks right up to him.

"Oh, Mr. Rubinstein, so nice to see you. I trust you are. . . ."

Rubinstein interrupts. "Just a minute, Mr. Lincoln, let's get this straight. I'm no more Rubinstein; now I'm Reeves. Also, I don't live in the Bronx. Now I'm living in Bronxville. And before we go any further, I don't want any more Rubens type paintings. What I want is a Goya."

For those who need an explanation, Mr. Rubinstein obviously has moved up in the world, changed his name (normal for those seeking assimilation), and moved to Bronxville, a fashionable part of Westchester County, not always known for its receptivity toward Jews. And the name Goya, the Spanish painter, involves a pun, since in Yiddish the word *goya* means a female Gentile. The joke is poking a little fun at the process of checking out. So is this one:

Jacob Shmulevitz wants to join an exclusive club. His friend Aronson tells him: "You'll never get in. That club is restricted. No Jews allowed."

"You'll see," Shmulevitz insists. "I'll prepare myself with a new personality. They won't even know I'm Jewish."

So he goes to a speech teacher and takes lessons for three intensive months; he buys a complete Brooks Brothers wardrobe, gets his nose bobbed, takes a severe haircut, and replaces his eyeglasses with contact lenses.

Now he appears at the club. He tells the receptionist that he is eager to join, and the receptionist takes him to meet the membership secretary.

"Very well," the secretary says to him, after having looked him up and down. "We will need some basic information. Your name, please."

"John Simmons."

The secretary gets the other basic data—address, age, years in residence, and so on.

"Of what university are you a graduate?"

"Yale. Majored in economics and finance."

"Business connection?"

"I'm a food broker" (actually he's a produce wholesaler).

"Married?"

"Affirmative!"

"Children?"

"Yes. A son at Amherst; my daughter is at Mount Holyoke."

"And what is your religious preference?"

"Oh, I'm a *goy*, like all you fellows."

Another aspect of assimilation has to do with Jews being absorbed into the general life of the country. American Jews often move away from their background in religious education toward general education and the business of the world outside Judaism.

A congregant has made a large contribution to his synagogue. But he has long since forgotten what meager knowledge of Hebrew he did possess, so he asks his rabbi not to call him up to say the blessings when the Torah is read.

"Please," he says, "every eye will be on me. Some of my friends will be there and I don't want to appear like an ignoramus!"

On the following Saturday, what does the rabbi do? He promptly calls the man up to say the blessings.

Having no alternative, Howard Lieberman walks up. He is, of course, furious. The rabbi is standing next to him. Howard looks down at the blessings printed there and mutters, out of the side of his mouth: "Rabbi, what did you do to me? I specifically asked you not to call me up. I don't mind being an anonymous donor. But you have embarrassed me in front of everyone. I can't read Hebrew. Honestly, I'm really angry with you!"

At this point, the rabbi turns to him and sings out loudly, "Amen!"

Some Jews do not merely escape the Jewish community, they actually convert to another religion. Naturally, Jewish jokes pick this up without fail. For instance:

A man has gone to hear a Christian spellbinder and is so impressed that he's gone right up as a witness for Christ, gone through baptism, and is now a convert. All excited, he goes racing home.

He dashes in the front door and sees his wife at the hall mirror putting on her lipstick, obviously ready to go out.

"Listen, Charlotte," he begins, "I've just been through one of the most tremendous experiences of my life. Let me tell you about it."

But Charlotte's hand goes up. "Not now; I'm already late for my bridge game." And out the door she goes without even saying goodbye.

Down the stairs comes a young man, tennis racket in hand. "Chester," the new convert begins, "this will be of interest to you."

"Sorry, Dad; can't talk now. See you later. My tennis lesson starts in five minutes and I'm late already. Tell it to Melissa; I think she'll be down in a minute."

Sure enough, the daughter appears on the stairs.

"Melissa, darling, I've got something important to tell you!"

"No way, Dad. Corliss is waiting for me in the car outside and we have to get started. Some other time." And out she goes.

Our convert stands there with his mouth open. After a minute, he mutters: "I've been a Christian for only about an hour, and already I hate three Jews."

This is obviously a dig at anti-Semitism at the same time that it gets at conversion. And to make it a triple play, it also throws a bit of a zinger at upward mobility.

Thus, many Jews do disappear into the general population. But it isn't always easy, and Jewish humor "celebrates" this difficulty in several ways. As we've already seen, it pokes fun at the assimilationist and obliquely criticizes anti-Semitism. It also works in another interesting way, as in this one.

A magnate is walking with a friend, who happens to be a hunchback. As they walk and talk, they pass by a splendid church. The magnate observes: "Oh, Lester, we are congregants at this beautiful church. And, by the way, did you know that we used to be Jewish?"

Lester looks at him and observes: "Is that true, Otto? You know, I used to be a hunchback."

This joke is telling us that conversion doesn't work, that you remain a Jew forever. Even if you're a pope or a bishop, you are eternally identified with that culture. The converted Disraeli was regarded as a Jew in Parliament. And it is not uncommon to see Karl Marx, who wrote vitriolic anti-Semitic attacks on Jews, described as a Jew.

You have already read about the Nazis' search for Jewish ancestry which turned up some individuals who had no idea that they were of Jewish descent. The following, therefore, should not surprise you.

An older Jewish man is listening to younger friends talking about a young woman singer with a superb voice who is a convert to Christianity. The older man observes, "In her youth, she already had a fine matzoh-soprano."

The next one is less sarcastic.

A young Jew not only converts but becomes a priest. On
the occasion of his first sermon, the bishop attends as an ob-
server. After the sermon, the young man comes to him, very
excited, and asks for his evaluation.

"Excellent," is the bishop's verdict, "you were really first
rate in showing your knowledge of the Bible and its implications
for Christian behavior. But I must caution you to avoid one
phrase which you used a number of times. You must stop saying, 'We *goyim.*' "

Goyim is the plural of *goy,* or Gentile. Obviously, the joke
is letting us in on the fact that this priest still has a Jewish
residue. And now one step further—an Old World story.

One of the Rothschild women is about to give birth. The
doctor has been called to the home. He examines her, comes
down from her bedroom, and says: "My dear baron, not yet.
Let us relax and play some chess until the the moment comes
when she will need me."

A short time passes and suddenly there are groans from
the room upstairs. The baron looks up sharply and asks, "Is it
time, doctor?"

Without even looking up, the doctor answers, "Not yet."

The chess game continues, and after several minutes the
groans become louder moans and one can hear from upstairs,
"Oh, *mon Dieu,* how I suffer, the pain, the pain!!"

The baron, his face white, jumps up from his chair. "Doctor, you must go to her. Don't you hear her cries of anguish?"

The doctor remains calmly seated at the chess board. "My
dear baron, believe me, the time is not yet here."

Despite his anxiety, the baron tries to continue at the chess
board. About a quarter hour passes and suddenly there comes
a shout from upstairs: *"Gevalt, gevalt!!"*

The doctor rises quickly and turns to the baron: "Now!"

You won't get the point of this story unless you know that
the word *gevalt,* which literally means "force," has become, in
Yiddish, a sort of all-purpose cry which conveys the meaning

that something dreadful is happening or about to happen. A similar point is made in the next story.

> Mr. Cowan receives a telephone call from the United Jewish Appeal. The caller begins: "Mr. Cowan, we are asking all the Jewish people in this area to contribute so that we can help meet the needs of both local Jewish. . . ."
>
> Cowan interrupts: "But I'm not Jewish!"
>
> The caller pauses and observes: "That's strange. The names I have on this list were guaranteed to be those of Jewish residents."
>
> "Well, that is strange," Cowan repeats. "But you've got the wrong family."
>
> "I wonder how your name could have gotten on this list," says the UJA man.
>
> "I certainly don't know. All I can tell you is that my daughter is a nun, my wife teaches in a Christian Sunday school, and my father, *alav hasholem*, is buried in a Catholic cemetery!"

Once you know that *alav hasholem* is Hebrew for "may he rest in peace," the rest should be obvious.

What these jokes turn on is the notion that there is a Jewish nucleus inside of the individual Jew, no matter how eminent and assimilated he or she may be, and it is likely to show up no matter how many layers have grown over it. Of course, such an idea can be neither proved nor disproved. Nevertheless, it is fairly common in Ashkenazi folklore.

Finally, here is a jest that shows a very modern aspect of this same issue.

> Mrs. Greenberg goes to her travel agent. "Mr. Fishman, I want to go to Nepal," she says. "Arrange for me a trip."
>
> "Nepal! Mrs. Greenberg, that's not an ordinary vacation area. I must call to your attention that most of the country is high mountains. And I have to remind you that for people at our stage in life such altitudes are not always healthy."
>
> "Fishman, are you a doctor or a travel agent? If I want medical advice, I know where to go. From you I want a ticket. Yes or no?"

Confronted by such an attitude, the agent works up the trip and Mrs. Greenberg is off. She lands in Katmandu, is taken to her hotel, and while the bellman is moving her luggage to her room, she is already at the desk where trips are arranged.

"How do I get to Mount Kucheraj?" she inquires. (Don't look for it on your maps. It's imaginary.)

The man at the desk stares at her.

"Madame, you can get there only by bus. It's a difficult two-hour journey over very rough terrain. And there are no especially interesting things to see or do there. Are you sure you want to go there?"

"Young man," Mrs. Greenberg responds, "if I want to go to Mount Kucheraj, why are you giving me all this nothing information. Can you get me on that bus or can't you?"

Confronted by such determination, the man writes out her bus ticket, tells her where to get the bus, and off she goes. As they warned her, it is a very tough ride; she's thrown around for two hours on the bus, all the while muttering: "*Vay iz mir* (woe is me); will I get there alive?" But she arrives. She gets off the bus slowly, walks to a little stand, and asks, "Can you tell me where I will find the guru who teaches here?"

The man points to a building several hundred feet away and Mrs. Greenberg marches off. She arrives at the gate, which is open, and walks through. An attendant, a tall young man dressed all in white, asks her, "Madame, you wish to speak with the guru?"

"Why would I be here if I didn't want to talk with him?"

"As you can see, madame, the line of those waiting to see the guru is long. It will take no less than half an hour before you can see him. Can you wait that long?"

"If I came up on that bus for two hours, another half hour won't make any difference. I'll wait on line."

The young man looks at his watch. "One more thing, madame. By the time you reach the guru, it will be almost time for him to commence his meditation. It will be possible for you to say only three words to him. Do you understand?"

"Only three words! Hmm. Well, I came so far, it will have to do."

"Very well, madame. Get on line—and remember, only three words."

So Mrs. Greenberg gets on line and it moves slowly toward

the shrine where the guru is seated. In exactly 33 minutes she enters and walks up to the guru, looks at him, and says: "Sheldon, come home!"

The joke may seem funny to you and me, but the movement of a number of young Jews to Far Eastern cults has made many Jews very unhappy. After you've laughed at the way Jewish-American comic writers pick up every nuance in Jewish-American life for their fun, think again about the serious underside of this joke.

Anti-Gentilism

If you were subjected to oppression, humiliation, discrimination, restriction, and intermittent violence, how would you feel about those who were doing this to you? The most logical answer to the question is, of course, fear, hate, and anger. But what could you do about these feelings? Physical opposition is almost impossible, so you would be left with humor, needling, jokes.

The condition of the Jews in Europe for centuries, and especially in Eastern Europe since the seventeenth century, has had a great deal to do with Jewish humor. In addition, there is another factor.

Suppose most of your contacts with members of the outside world were with poor peasants—unschooled, mainly illiterate, many not very bright. Suppose your contacts with the upper classes were with people who depended on your financial or commercial abilities, who didn't know how to carry on such activity or were not well-informed in this regard. Wouldn't your fear, anger, and hate be mixed with a certain measure of contempt? Your group consists of people who have had some measure of literacy, even if only in Hebrew, who are familiar with and greatly respect learning, who have mastered commerce and finance with success, sometimes great success.

It should not be surprising, then, if some Jewish humor expresses this contempt as well as feelings of superiority. In fact, jokes about outwitting became extremely common. The following, which may be an Old World story, shows it to us.

> A Jew and a Greek are engaged in a dispute about which ancient culture was more progressive, that of Greece or of Israel. At one point the Greek says, "Archaeologists, digging in Athens, have uncovered wires, showing that the ancient Greeks were familiar with the telegraph."
>
> And the Jew, not to be outdone, shouts back: "Yeh, and when they dug in Jerusalem, they didn't find wires. So that tells you that they already knew about wireless!"

Even in a noodle type story we can see the attempt to establish superiority. In Jewish-American humor this is a staple. A sample:

> An Englishman, a Frenchman, an American, and a Jew are discussing a variety of "what ifs." One of them asks: "What if a something from space struck the earth, causing an enormous flood which would engulf the whole earth as we know it. No escape. How would we spend our last few hours before we drowned?"
>
> The Englishman: "I would open a bottle of port, drink as much of it as possible in the allotted time, reflect on my life, its joys and its sorrows, and await the inevitable."
>
> The Frenchman: "I would get hold of a bottle of my favorite wine, look for a beautiful girl, and make love until the end came."
>
> The American: "I would construct a raft and stay on it as long as possible. When it became impossible to stay on it any longer, I would swim as long as I could. Believe me, I would go down fighting!"
>
> The Jew: "Right away, I would start taking lessons to learn how to live under water!"

Again, a somewhat silly story, but it does establish superiority. Many stories of this type appear earlier in the book, and there are dozens more. The next one is less silly:

> In a small village, the priest stops in at the local tavern, owned by a Jew. A conversation begins. The Jew complains

about business being poor. He tells the priest that he can hardly make ends meet. The priest nods and explains that he, too, suffers from inadequate means.

As the conversation develops, they suddenly generate the idea that if they could find something to draw people into the village, it would be helpful. Suddenly the priest remembers that he has an old picture of the Virgin Mary with a halo around her head. Maybe. . . .

And sure enough, with a little word-of-mouth advertising, the picture "acquires" great ability to heal the sick, make the childless able to bear children, provide spouses for the unmarried, and perform similar miracles.

People start flocking to the village. The tavern owner's business improves solidly, and the contributions to the church are proving very helpful to the priest.

On this day, a peasant from another part of the district comes into the village, stops in at the tavern for a drink, gets to talking with the owner, and finally asks, "This picture of the Virgin that everyone is talking about, does it really help the people?"

"Absolutely," the tavern owner assures him. "I myself know two people it helped a lot."

You see in this old Yiddish joke a picture of the attitudes toward the peasantry described above.

But aside from establishing superiority, outwitting, the Jewish jest gives the Jew a chance to get back at anti-Semitism and lets Jews verbalize some of the anger and hatred created by their history. Some of this jesting is in the section on anti-Semitism. And even more overtly hostile jokes were generated. For example:

A Russian (or Polish) nobleman (or landowner) laughs three times at a joke—once when you tell it to him, again when you explain it, and finally when he gets the point.

An official laughs only twice—first when you tell the joke, and next when you explain it. He never gets the point.

A peasant laughs only when he hears the joke. Even if you took the time to explain it, he wouldn't get it!

Or this one:

> A Jew gets on a train and sits down opposite an officer of the Russian army. The officer is holding a small dog in his lap. The Jew, a friendly sort of fellow, tries to strike up a conversation, but the Russian gives him a dirty look and turns his head away.
>
> After a moment or two, the officer begins stroking his dog. "You are a nice animal, Isaac," he repeats over and over, with the obvious intention of insulting the Jew.
>
> After a few minutes, the Jew observes, "Too bad about your dog."
>
> "What are you talking about? What's too bad?" the officer wants to know.
>
> "He has a Jewish name," the Jew responds.
>
> "So what?" the officer asks.
>
> "Well, that marks him as Jewish. If it weren't for that, he too could be an officer like his master," is the reply.

Insult versus insult, a neat case. And now a supposedly true anecdote involving the Anglo-Jewish writer Israel Zangwill.

> Once, Zangwill was riding in the London subway, sitting opposite two well-dressed, apparently affluent women. At one station, a man, obviously a Jewish peddler, got on the train carrying a pack on his back, and he sat down next to one of the women.
>
> Immediately she turned to her neighbor and said, quite audibly, "Good Lord, is there anyplace we can go where there are no Jews?"
>
> Zangwill quickly leaned across and answered, "Madam, why not try going to hell!"

A clean double shot. First, there were no Jews in hell. And also, of course, Zangwill was telling her where to go.

It was common in the Middle Ages to force Jews to dispute matters of faith with Christians. Usually this was a no-win situation. If the Jew did not do well in the dispute, the community was at the least shamed, sometimes punished. If he made the Christian look bad, he was punished, and the community was likely to suffer too. In humor, of course, this dilemma did not hold true.

There is to be such a debate in which the two opponents are to ask each other the meaning of Hebrew words. The first to confess ignorance will pay with his head. The Jewish community is upset. They are sure that no good will come of it, one way or another. If they win, their representative, presumably the rabbi, will probably be penalized in some nasty way. And if they lose, God forbid, they are likely to be hurt also.

So they call for volunteers, and a local drayman offers himself. The people of the community are amazed. But better to lose a drayman than to subject the rabbi to such a hazard.

So the disputants are introduced at the governor's mansion—Father Thomas on one side, and Noiach the drayman on the other. The governor decides to let the Jew ask the first question.

The executioner steps forward and receives his instruction: he is to lop off the head of the first one to show that he cannot answer.

Noiach asks, "What is the meaning of *eyneni yodayah?*"

The priest responds promptly, "I do not know" (which is the translation!).

Immediately, the executioner steps forward and off with the head. The contest is over.

The Jews gather in the shul. There is naturally much joy. The drayman is being carried around amid much merriment. Finally, when things have calmed down a bit, the rabbi asks him, "How did such a wonderful question come into your head?"

"Well," Noiach answers, "I remembered when I was a child studying elementary stuff in the *cheder,* I ran across that phrase. So I asked the *melamed* (teacher) what *eyneni yodayah* means and he told me 'I don't know.' Now I ask you. If my *melamed* didn't know the meaning of it, how could you expect the priest to know it?"

—

Note that in this joke the ignorance, credible ignorance, of the drayman carries the day, a sort of indication that God has not let His people down. If they can't win by cleverness, they triumph by luck. Now consider the following:

There was a wealthy Jew in old Russia who wanted his son to succeed in the outside world, so he sends him to Europe to the *gymnasium* (a secondary school that is somewhat more advanced than our own high schools). But the lad does not do well; he brings home poor grades, to his father's great distress.

"What is going on at the school?" the father wants to know.

"The Christian teachers discriminate against me and the other Jewish boys!" he is told.

After some deliberation, the father decides to have the boy baptized and converted to Christianity so as to avoid the alleged bias.

But at examination time the boy does even more poorly!

The father confronts him. "Well, what can you say now?"

The kid looks at him and says: "It's like you always said, Dad. Gentiles haven't got the brains."

Perhaps in an even nastier vein is the following:

Chaim is on his deathbed, and he knows it. Weakly, hardly able to breathe, he tells his wife: "Faigge, call the priest. Tell him I want to convert."

His wife is thunderstruck. "All your life, you were a *frumer yid* (pious Jew). Have you lost your senses?"

Chaim looks at her and weakly whispers, "Isn't is better a *goy* should die than a Jew?"

This sort of humor has been carried over to the United States, despite the fact that the conditions for Jews here have been far better, by any test. Possibly the memories of the European experience and the residual anti-Semitism which Jews found in the United States have sensitized them. So the jokes show. Let's look at one or two examples.

In the United States, unlike in Eastern Europe, we have developed a good deal of cooperation and friendship between the Christian priests and ministers and the Jewish rabbis. Thus, a rabbi and a priest have become good friends. One day the priest says to the rabbi: "Abraham, I think we know each other well enough so that you will not be offended if I ask you several questions about Jewish matters. First, why do your people place so much emphasis on study for the children? Wouldn't a little more emphasis on baseball be more conducive to their health?

"Second, I've never understood the noisiness of your prayers. The services are so loud. Couldn't you do the same thing in a more restrained way?

"And finally, the same sort of thing characterizes your funerals. So much wailing and screaming. It's most undignified."

The rabbi thinks for a few moments and then responds: "Simon, your questions are fair and they tell me that you still don't know all that much about our people. First, our familiarity with bats and clubs has had to do with pogroms. That's what we saw used against us in the old country, so we feel a little reluctant to pick them up here. They remind us of bad times.

"Second, Simon, you have to remember that our God is a little older than yours and we assume he may be getting a little hard of hearing. So we call more loudly to make sure he hears our prayers.

"As to the third, there I believe you're absolutely right. Frankly, I'd rather go to ten of yours than one of ours."

You might wonder whether this is a recent joke. The fact is that it goes back a long time, before Jewish youngsters began to participate actively in American sports. But it illustrates the point.

A more recent Jewish-American joke gets at superiority differently.

Two friends, one Catholic and one Jewish, are discussing their future prospects. The Jew has indicated that he hopes to become a lawyer. The Catholic says that he will enter a seminary and study for the priesthood.

"Well," the young Jew remarks, "that doesn't seem to lead very far, does it?"

"Oh, I'm sure that if I apply myself, study hard, and get lucky, I could become a bishop," is the response.

"Yes, but even that is not such a big deal. How far can you get in the Church?"

"What are you talking about? Who knows? You know, there's always a chance to become an archbishop, maybe even a cardinal." And then, in an obviously joking way: "With unusual luck, I might even be the first American to become Pope!"

The Jew looks at him: "C'mon John, is even that such a big deal?"

"What do you want, Irving? How far would you like me to go? You expect me to be God?"

And Irving responds, "Why not? One of our boys made it!"

Sometimes the joke intends merely to needle the Christian:

A Jewish painter has been hired to paint the inside of a convent. He comes in on Monday, begins his work, comes back on Tuesday, and finds the Mother Superior waiting for him.

"Mr. Silverman," she says to him, "we must establish some ground rules for you to follow while you are working here. First of all, we want you to remove your hat when you work in our chapel. Second, under no circumstances are you to wash your hands in our holy water. And finally, you will address me as Mother Superior, not Mother Shapiro!"

Or take the following case:

A little Jewish boy has been taken by his parents to see a film about ancient Rome. In the movie, the Roman emperor is shown ordering Christians thrown into an arena with lions. Suddenly the little fellow is crying bitterly.

"What's the matter, Jonah?" his father asks. "Don't cry; this is a story of ancient times. They don't do things like that any more."

"It just isn't fair," the little fellow observes.

"What isn't fair?" his Mom inquires.

"The little lion in the corner isn't getting any Christians to eat!"

Now, obviously this never happened. And sensible Jews are not particularly happy with such jokes. What the jokes reveal is the residue of feeling at having been so badly treated for many centuries.

The following is a relatively recent quip.

> A Gentile woman has married a Jewish man and decided to convert to Judaism. She goes through all the instruction with the rabbi and finally he declares her ready and tells her that he will introduce her to the congregation on the following Friday.
>
> Well, the lady reviews her wardrobe for the big day, makes her selections, and decides to get a new hairdo and a perm. On the Thursday prior to the big evening, she calls the rabbi to confirm and ask about any details she should know. During their discussion, the rabbi asks her, "Have you been to the *mikveh* (ritual cleansing bath)?"
>
> "Oh, heavens," the lady exclaims, "I forgot all about it!"
>
> "You can still go," the rabbi reminds her.
>
> "But rabbi," she answers, "if I go now and immerse myself completely as is required, I will ruin my perm. Would it be acceptable if I just went in up to my chin?"
>
> "I suppose you could do that," is the answer, "but then you will still have a *goyishe kop*."

Goyishe kop translates as a "Gentile head," and what we have here is a language joke which takes us back to Yiddish usage. The term was always used in a derogatory way to denote lack of learning ability or just plain stupidity.

Some such jokes turn really nasty. As you might expect, stories about marriage are among the classics of Jewish humor. But listen to this.

> A young man tells his father that he wants to marry a *shikseh* (non-Jewish girl). The father is arguing the case, trying to persuade the young man, in the classic phrase, "to stay with his own kind."
>
> "I don't want to marry a Jewish girl. I know she'll want an expensive car, a big house with all the latest devices, fancy clothes without end, membership in a country club, a lot of expensive vacations."

"But, Julius, Gentile girls also want those things."
"Yeah, but Dad, if she's a *shikseh*, who cares?"

That's nasty, certainly, though not nastier than some of the anti-Semitic japes heard.

Well, you have seen that the counter to anti-Semitism has been what I call anti-Gentilism. I hope you will understand and remember why this developed among the Ashkenazi Jews.

I've Been Rich and I've Been Poor

Earlier we looked at a stereotype concerning Jews' supposed business acumen (although if I had a dollar for every Jewish entrepreneur who has gone broke, I wouldn't be a poor man). We'll now carry our lesson in applied economics a little further.

A famous comic used to say, "I've been rich and I've been poor and rich is better." Jewish jesting celebrates both conditions. How did that come to be? As many of the japes here have indicated, the Ashkenazim in Eastern Europe were, in the main, people who lived in poverty. In the original Yiddish version of the book *Fiddler on the Roof*, Tevye describes himself as a *koptzin*, a pauper or poor man. Author Sholem Aleichem was reflecting here on the general state of Jews. An earlier writer even names one of his fictional cities *Kaptzansk*, or "Paupery."

For an example of Jewish sick humor dealing with poverty, let me offer the following story.

A Jew is reduced to such a terrible financial condition that he goes to appeal to the community for assistance. They dawdle and deliberate. Finally, he comes to them and tells them: "You must help me! Don't you see how unlucky and poor I am? If you fail to help me, I will become a hatmaker!"

"So you will become a hatmaker!" the head of the community council repeats. "So what?"

"Don't you see?" the poor man exclaims. "With my luck, if I become a hatmaker, children will be born without heads!"

Pretty gruesome, yes. That one isn't intended to make you laugh. It's an example of Jewish wry.

Less gruesome, but still wry.

A Jew comes to the rabbi. "Rabbi, Passover is approaching. We are desperate. I lack money to buy the necessary holiday foods. How can we come to the synagogue on the holiday in the tattered clothing which is all we have. Rabbi, rabbi, what shall I do?"

"Let us think about the matter; with God's help, we can surely find a way out of your predicament," the rabbi answers. "Tell me what and how much you need."

"For matzoh and meat, we need 8 rubles. Throw in another ruble for the other food and 2 rubles for the sacramental wine."

The rabbi nods his head. "That makes 11 altogether. What else?"

"Clothing for the children and for my wife; I figure it would cost me 12 rubles. And something for myself, another 4 rubles."

"Good! So, 11 and 16 make 27 rubles. That's what you need. You see, already you're better off. You don't have to worry about food, wine, and clothing. Now you have just one worry— where do you get 27 rubles?"

You never heard jokes like these from a Jewish-American comedian. Just one more to clinch the point.

A poor shopkeeper comes to see the rabbi. "Rabbi," he begins, "I want to ask you something about your sermon last Shabbos (Saturday). I think you explained to us that those who are poor in this world will be rich in the next life and those who are rich in this life will be poor in the next. Right?"

"That is what the Torah, the prophets, and the Talmud all teach us," the rabbi agrees.

"Rabbi, do you think that will apply to me, too?"

"Why shouldn't it apply to you?" (Note again the old Jewish custom of answering a question with a question.)

"In that case, rabbi, maybe you could lend me a hundred rubles. When I collect my wealth in the next life, I will repay you, with interest, if you choose."

The rabbi begins to count out rubles, then stops. "Tell me, Reb Yitzchak, what do you intend to do with the money?"

"Rabbi, I will buy some fresh new merchandise to offer to the people in the community."

"And you think you will sell your new merchandise?"

"The stuff I have in mind is good, new material. I expect it to sell like hot bagels on a cold day."

At this point, the rabbi puts the money back in the box. The Jew is speechless. Finally, he stammers out: "Rabbi, what is wrong? What did I say that changed your mind?"

"Just think about it. If your goods sell so well here, you'll get rich. And if you get rich here, you'll be poor in the next life. So how will you be able to repay the loan?"

Sometimes the rabbi acts as judge, in such matters as that in the following jape.

A doctor is called to the humble hut of a poor Jewish cobbler.

"Doctor," the cobbler says, "my wife is dangerously sick. I'll pay you anything you want if you can save her!"

The doctor looks at him. "You know, I'm not God or a magician. What if I can't save her? I still want to get paid even if I can't cure her."

"Kill her or cure her—I'll pay; I'll pay! But try, please."

Well, the woman dies. And the amount the doctor wants from the poor cobbler is unbelievable, far beyond his ability to pay.

"Please, have a heart," the cobbler entreats. "I agreed to pay, but so much! Where can a cobbler get so much money?"

The doctor is insistent. Finally, the cobbler appeals to the local rabbi, who invites both men to his home to hear the case. The rabbi listens to the cobbler's story.

"My wife was terribly sick so I called him. And it's true I agreed to pay him regardless of whether he killed her or cured her. But *rachmones* (mercy or pity)! I am only a cobbler. From repairing shoes you don't get the kind of money he is demanding."

The rabbi thinks for a few minutes and turns to the doctor. "Doctor," he says, "obviously, you did not cure this woman."

"That's true. She was too far gone when he called me. I told him I might be unable to do so."

"Now," the rabbi continues, "would you say you killed her?"

"Of course I didn't kill her. She died naturally."

"What Menachem the cobbler told us here is correct?"

"The facts are as he stated them. He agreed to pay, whatever happened."

"Not exactly. What I heard is that he agreed to pay whether you cured her or killed her. But you yourself have just said that you did not cure her, nor did you kill her. So for what reason should you be paid?"

This story is consistent with others about the wisdom of the rabbis. Recall the earlier story of the man who found the wallet with 10 rubles missing and the rabbi deciding it could not be the lost wallet. The rabbis, in the jokes at least, took the side of the poor against the rich. In fact, in Old World japes there is a kind of bias against the wealthy. Here is where the poor can get even, and they do.

Two men meet who haven't seen each other for some time. "So, Pinches, how's it going?" one asks the other.

"Nachman, I think I'm getting rich!"

"What do you mean, you think? Either you are or you aren't."

"Well, Nachman, that's the way it is. True, money I haven't got yet. But I'm beginning to feel like a *shvine* (swine)."

A story attributed to the famous *shnorrer* Hershele Ostropolier, discussed earlier, makes the same point.

It was normal for the Jews in the town to appear at weddings or other celebrations, so Hershele shows up at one of these functions just before mealtime. Since he was a rather poor fellow, his clothes are ragged. The people running the affair take one look at him and tell him to go home.

Well, Hershele, being who he is, goes to the rabbi and "borrows" one of his gabardines, a good-looking one, virtually new. He returns to the meal, which has just begun, and this time he is seated at once.

The soup is just being served and it no sooner arrives than Hershele picks up his bowl and spills it all over the gabardine. The people running the affair rush over. "What are you doing?" they want to know.

"Well, you threw me out before, and when I came back dressed in this nice gabardine you permitted me to stay here. So one must conclude that it is really the coat that you wish to feed, not me."

Thus humor permits the underdog to get back at the upper dog. As we have seen, widespread poverty made it necessary to ask for help, in jests as well as in life—sometimes with surprising results:

A poor *shnorrer* comes to a wealthy man in his city. "Please, I haven't eaten for two days. I need some money to go out and get myself some provisions. Won't you please help me out?"

Well, this wealthy man has a decent heart and he gives the poor fellow some money. Several hours later the rich man is walking on one of the more fashionable boulevards. As he passes by one of the better restaurants, he looks in and, lo and behold, there is the "pauper" sitting and eating an expensive salmon dish.

The rich man walks into the restaurant, goes up to the diner, and says: "What kind of business is this? You come to ask me for money and I find you eating salmon à la Viennoise in this expensive restaurant. With the money I gave you, I would have thought you would be out buying food for a week, not eating in an expensive restaurant like this."

The other fellow looks at him and answers: "Before, when I had no money, I could not afford to eat this wonderful salmon dish. Now, when I have some money, you don't think it's proper for me to eat this excellent salmon dish. Please tell me, so when can I eat this salmon dish?"

Here, irony takes a hand in the life of the impoverished. On one hand, the generous man wants to make sure the pauper is not nearly his equal. On the other, the poor guy is saying, "Sometimes, when I have a windfall, can't I enjoy life in the same way you people do?" It's quite a sociological comment.

So much for the Old World of Eastern Europe. Were things better in America? According to Jacob Riis's description of Jewish life on New York's Lower East Side early in the century, they were worse—overcrowded slum living, dangerous and unhealthy working conditions, low earnings, shocking poverty. These conditions were typical of *all* immigrants, not the least the Jews from Eastern Europe. So you can understand such jokes as the following.

> Two Jews who know each other from the Old Country meet on the street and exchange greetings. Then one asks, "Mendel, how is it going here?"
>
> "You shouldn't know from it. Regular work I can't get. I earn hardly enough to feed the family and, to cap it all, I've been sick for a month. Last week I had to give the doctor 50 dollars!"
>
> "Oy," says the other Jew, "that's terrible. You know, in the old country, you could be sick for a whole year for 50 dollars!"

Or this one:

> A Jew is sitting in a cafeteria drinking coffee. Another Jew comes and sits down at the same table.
>
> "You're in this country long?" the original sitter wants to know.
>
> "About a year," is the answer.
>
> "I'm here only about two years myself. So tell me, where did you come from?"
>
> "From Yehupetz, not far from Kiev," is the response.
>
> "Really? I come from Kiev myself!"
>
> Having discovered that they come from the same part of the Old Country, they enter into a lively conversation. Finally, the man who has been here the shorter time says: "Let me ask you something, Pasternak. I haven't been working for a month. Maybe you could lend me something till I get back on my feet."
>
> His *lantzsman* (compatriot) looks at him and says: "Lend you money?! I hardly know you; we just met!"
>
> At which point the asker observes: "Terrible, terrible! What am I going to do? *Inderhame* (in the old country), no one would

lend me money because they knew me. Here no one will lend me money because they don't know me."

The next one will give you an idea of the general scale of life as seen through the eyes of the joker.

> A woman asks a pushcart peddler, "How much do you want for this fan?"
> "One cent!" is the answer.
> "Too much," the lady says (naturally).
> "Okay," the peddler replies, "so make me an offer."

I can still remember the men who would wheel hurdy-gurdys (hand-cranked music boxes) around the streets of New York City. They usually showed up on weekends and cranked their music out in the street, waiting for coins to be thrown from tenement windows.

> A Jewish *katerinstshik* (organ grinder) is working his neighborhood one day, and another Jew walks up to him and asks, "Tell me, from this you could make a living?"
> "You know," the organ grinder answers, "I would do all right if not for the competition. The Metropolitan Opera House is killing me!"

The tradition of poverty persisted even when immigration from Eastern Europe had virtually stopped in the 1920s.

> Groucho Marx is supposed to have quipped: "When I came to this country, I didn't have a nickel to my name. Now I have a nickel!"
> From Barbra Streisand: "We were awfully poor. But we had the things money can't buy—unpaid bills."
> And from Neil Simon we have the comment that his family was so poor that if there had been log cabins in New York, they would have lived in one.

The above statements may not be totally accurate, but they do confirm that there was much poverty and that the talk about it continued for a long time.

But times change. As the twentieth century progressed, the proletarians became unionized and their wages improved. The peddlers became retailers and their incomes increased. Like most of the other immigrant groups, the Jews moved away from extreme poverty and toward better living standards. And as we move to the present, we find that some moved into middle class status or occasionally even better.

This movement was accompanied by humor. No longer did the jokes deal with poverty. First, there was a waystation. For instance:

> A Jewish man is walking across the street. Suddenly a car veers toward him, tries to check, and hits him, but not too hard. He falls, with a scream. Several passersby rush over. One man picks him up, brings him to the sidewalk, props him up against the wall, wipes the dirt from his face, and asks: "Okay? Are you comfortable?"
>
> The victim looks up and replies, "Well, I make a living."

This joke, of course, rests on the double meaning of the term *comfortable*, which, as the depression receded, came to be interpreted as having a reasonable income.

Even as late as the 1920s many people still made many of their garments at home. There were men who, having been machine operators in one of the needle trades, were in the habit of sewing clothes at home. (I remember my father doing so.) Paper patterns would be set up, material purchased, and the garment constructed.

> One such tailor has gone into business and become successful. The family has finally moved out of the East Side to a more fashionable area in one of New York's suburbs. Now they invite over some old friends, the Berkowitzes, a couple they have known for many years. Food is prepared, the house is cleaned, and suddenly, on this Sunday afternoon, the wife discovers that they are totally out of toilet paper. But all the stores are closed on Sunday. What to do?
>
> Suddenly, an inspiration. The husband tells his wife: "You know, we have a lot of old patterns in the closet, what I used

to use for cutting clothes. We'll never use them again. Let's put them in the toilets. It's better than nothing."

Under the circumstances, the wife agrees.

Well, the friends arrive, there is much talk, plenty of food, wine, the traditional house tour, a period of sitting in the back yard. And during the course of the afternoon both visitors have occasion to use the guest bathroom.

Evening is approaching. Time to take the subway home. The guests depart. Berkowitz observes to his wife, "It's a nice place the Rabinowitzes have, no?"

And she answers: "Oh, it's beautiful. And everything so modern, such nice new furniture. And did you notice, Bernard, the special toilet paper? Really something unusual; it's even marked *back* and *front*."

And here is another one.

A tailor with a little shop in Manhattan was once advised by friends not to keep his money in the bank, but to invest it in a sound security. He chose A.T.&T. Now twenty years have passed. The value of his stock has increased from $10,000 to over $100,000 and he is well off. He decides, finally, to take some time off, and he also wishes to "thank the people at A.T.&T. for what they done for me."

He asks around and is told to go uptown. But he is unfamiliar with travel in the great city, despite having lived there so long, so he gets lost and finally ends up in the Bronx in one of the rather shabby industrial areas. Now he is walking along a street looking from door to door at the name plates, when suddenly, wonderful—A.T.&T.

He walks in. There is a man seated at a shabby desk in a small office, a skullcap on his head. Our tailor extends his hand. "Long life to you, my friend, for the good you have done for me. Now I will be able to live all my years without having to rely on charity or depend on my children. I thank God for you every day!"

The other man takes his hand. "I am happy to do good for other Jews. And many thanks for your kind prayers. But tell me, explain me—what is this wonderful thing that Amalgamated Tallis and Tefillin has done for you?"

To understand this marvelous story, you must, of course, know that a *tallis* is a prayer shawl and *tefillin* are the phylacteries worn by devout Jews during weekday morning prayers.

By now we have moved away from poverty via upward mobility, but we have not yet reached conspicuous consumption. That is the next step on the ladder.

Like many other recent arrivals, the Jews in the United States have finally worked their way up and, again like many others, they tend to show it. Material goods are used to demonstrate that one has arrived, has a certain status. What's odd here is that humor seems to pick on Jews in the area of conspicuous consumption more than on the general population. Doing so may be a leftover from earlier stereotypes. Thus, we get an ugly "little joke" like the following:

> *Question:* What does one mink say to another in the cage?
> *Answer:* See you in the synagogue next week.

Do you see why Jews might resent this? Does anyone really believe that the tiny population of Jews in the country is the total market for mink clothing? Yet I never hear jokes of this type about any other group, maybe because so many of the comedians are Jewish and they draw on the people they know. Anyhow, look at the following.

> A man goes into a store that retails art works. "I made some money in the market," he explains, "and I want you should show me a picture that I could hang in my living room. I don't know anything about art but I want a good artist. Cost is by me no objection."
>
> "Very well," says the dealer looking around. "Oh, here's one that should serve you. It's by the well-known artist Joshua Vulfe." He points to a picture with a blue background and just one black dot on the right side.
>
> "Vulfe is already well-known," continues the dealer. "I want you to admire the way he uses space here and the marvelous contrast between the two colors. The blue is a special color that he prepares himself and it gives a feeling of translucency."

"Well, I don't know much about this. If you say it's so good, I'll take it," the man replies.

Several months pass and the same man returns to the same dealer with his wife. He is warmly welcomed by the dealer.

"Mr. Shoenfeld, I remember you bought that Vulfe several months ago. I have another one that you might like if you're in the market again." The picture is an all-white background with two green dots placed some inches apart on the left side.

The wife says: "Walter, it looks like the other one. Should we take it?"

Mr. Shoenfeld examines it carefully from all sides and then turns to his wife. "No, I don't think so. It's too *ungepatchket*" (translates here as overly busy or overdecorated).

Of course, this joke is Jewish only because of the use of the Yiddish word.

Most ethnic groups make a big thing out of important life ceremonies, such as marriages, births, and deaths, as well as what are called rites of passage, the occasions when the group accepts someone as a member of the adult community. Among Jews, of course, this is the Bar Mitzvah. What this means fundamentally is that the young boy has reached the adult stage and is now obliged to participate in the weekly reading of the Torah and practice and observe all the rituals.

In Eastern Europe this used to be a fairly simple ceremony. In the United States, however, it has become increasingly elaborate. Parents, even those of modest means, feel compelled to offer their relatives and friends, and the friends of the young person a big party or banquet. These usually take place in the temple, in a restaurant, or in some other place that has catering facilities.

The trend in Bar Mitzvahs has been toward more and more conspicuous consumption. Whereas it was once customary to serve a nice dinner to those attending, with wines and liquors, the party has become increasingly fancy. The temple sanctuary, where the religious part of the ceremony takes place, is decorated with flowers, and flowers are also placed on every table at the dinner. These flowers or plants have become quite elaborate.

The jokelore picks on this trend. Here is a description given by someone who recently attended a bar mitzvah.

"I went to a bar mitzvah recently. What an affair! The food was unbelievably good—marvelous hors d'oeuvres, without end. And such a beautiful chopped liver sculpture! And drinks, not just Scotch—only Chivas Regal. Do I have to tell you?

"And the hall had little birds flying around! And instead of flowers, they had trees in the place. And not just trees. They had monkeys jumping around from tree to tree.

"Everything wonderful, except they had a problem. The *yarmulkes* (skullcaps) that the monkeys were wearing kept falling off!"

Remember that we're talking here only about upper-class folks. You're likely to find the same thing among other groups, even if they don't create these exaggerated jests.

And finally, a joke that is both silly and amusing but that illustrates what we are talking about here.

Mrs. Green (formerly Greenberg) tells her butler: "Reeves, I want you to set the table for six for tonight's dinner. The Cowans (Cohens?) and the Goldmounts (Goldbergs?) will be dining with us. Dinner will be at 7:30."

"Very well, mum. Shall I set out the Grand Baroque tableware?"

"Yes, Reeves, that will do. Tonight's dinner is not really formal."

At 7 o'clock, Mrs. Green, now fully attired, peeks into the dining room and is astonished to find the table set for ten.

"Reeves," she calls, "I thought I told you to set the table for six. How is it that you have it set for ten?"

"Oh, Madam," the butler tells her. "I thought it best not to disturb your afternoon slumber. Mrs. Goldmount called and said that she was bringing the Bagels and the Bialys. So I added four places."

I capitalized the Bagels and the Bialys to show you what the butler's (credible) ignorance created. What we have here is a combination of upward mobility (butler, Grand Baroque), assimilation into the larger society (the un-Jewish names), ignorance (the joke rests on that punch line), and the residual use of Yiddish which makes it a language joke as well as one about the Jewish experience in the United States and an illustration of a stereotype. As you can see, any given joke can offer a number of elements.

These are typical of the Jewish-American jokes which celebrate the upward movement of *some* segments of the Jewish population in the United States. I suppose that within this group you might say that it is usual "to try to keep up with the Cohens" just as it is normal to try to keep up with the Joneses in the general American society.

And so we have moved from the jokes of poverty past the jokes of upward mobility to humor illustrating the use of wealth. As you see, jokes are connected with the life led by the people, even when they are stereotypes.

Sweet Charity

As we know, poverty was an everyday fact in Eastern Europe. But this was hardly new in Jewish life even then. In Biblical times the Israelites had been told always to remember the poor. For instance, those harvesting grain are reminded to leave something for the needy so they too can have nourishment. And at one point the Talmud tells Jews that "the command to give charity weighs as much as all the other commandments put together."

Every medieval Ashkenazi community had some forms of help, whether for brides or burial, or holiday necessities. Jews have always been instructed to take care of their own and they have always seen to it. Of course, that's not only true of Jews. We've all heard of faith, hope, and *charity*. Only in Jewish life that trio was worship, study, and charity, according to ancient Pharisees such as Hillel.

Is this a reason for jesting?

We have already met the *shnorrers*, that class of professional solicitors of charity whom Freud, for example, found so amusing. He makes the point that they feel they are entitled to charity according to Jewish law. They are helping those who have the wherewithal to fulfill their Biblical obligation. Humor stresses their *chutzpeh* (gall), rather than this obligation. Here, to remind you, is another *shnorrer* story.

One *shnorrer* has had for years a patron from whom he gets an "allowance" every month. One day he approaches the door of his patron, or "client."

Kugelman, the patron, opens the door. He is unshaven, disheveled, unkempt. The first words out of his mouth: "Didn't you hear that I went bankrupt this week?"

The *shnorrer*: "I know, I know."

"So what do you want from me?"

"I heard you're settling for 10 kopecks to the ruble; so I want my 10 percent!"

Or take the following example:

The magnate Brodsky's secretary asks him: "Are you seeing those who want charity today? There's a real case outside."

"Bring him in," is the answer.

Bergman, in tattered clothing, hollow-cheeked, with a grim cough, is shown in. "Please," he begins, "you are well-known for your charity. I need help. I have a lung disease. My wife is pregnant and ill. I have six children who have no clothes to wear. We eat just once or at most twice a week. . . ."

Brodsky's eyes are tearing. He turns to his secretary. "This man is breaking my heart . . . Throw him out!"

You see how charity can play in Jewish jokes—*chutzpeh* on one hand and hard heart on the other. In fact, there is a whole class of Jewish jokes that deals with misers. (This means, of course, that there *were* some people with money; the number was small, however.)

One such miser is very ill. Just what the disease is we never learn, but the doctors agree that if he cannot rid himself of the congestion by perspiring, he is likely to die.

The news spreads around the town. A small deputation goes to visit him, with the rabbi at its head. They have agreed that they will try to persuade him to leave some money to the town for community purposes.

The rabbi approaches the sickbed. "Reb Feivel, we are unhappy to hear that you are not doing well," the rabbi begins.

"Oy," says the patient, "if I could only perspire. But as you see, all I do is lie in bed and shiver. Rabbi, I'm afraid that my time is near."

"At such a moment," the rabbi continues, "it is time to think of settling your accounts on this earth so that you can appear before the *reboineh shel oilem* (the Master of the Universe) with a good record of many good deeds. For example, if you leave a substantial sum to the community chest, it will surely be remembered in Paradise."

Weakly, the miser responds. "You are right, rabbi. Get the needed paper, write what is required, and I will sign it. But hurry!"

The rabbi quickly secures a piece of paper and starts writing. "Reb Feivel, I am ready. Here is the writ which will accomplish what we want. If I can get you to sit up and sign it. . . ."

Reb Feivel sits up, holds out a trembling hand, and is about to write when suddenly he shouts with all his strength: "Forget it! Forget it! I'm sweating! I'm sweating!"

Rabbis figure quite often in such stories. Here's a rather coarse joke which tells something about their views.

A rabbi is talking to a rabbi from another city about his difficulties in getting contributions from the wealthy to aid the poor. So hard-hearted are they, he explains, that—but let me give you his words:

"If I come to a poor man's house and need to spit, I spit on the floor. But when I come to the home of a rich man, with all the carpeting on the floor, I have no other recourse—but to spit in his face!"

And just to convince you that Jewish humor didn't like the miser, one more:

A *shnorrer* who is in great need decides that he will tackle the town miser for some money. So he goes to see him and makes his request known.

"Reb Hershel," he argues, "I am so poor and you have so much. Do you not think that you are obliged by our Torah at least to give me something to help me out."

"Well," says the rich man. "I see you do not remember that I have a brother who is also very poor. You know, that comes first, in my way of thinking."

Hearing this, the *shnorrer* leaves. Several days later he chances to meet the brother of the miser.

"Hello, Reb Chotzkel," he greets him. "You know, I was talking to your brother only the other day. It is good to know that a family holds together and that brothers help each other."

"What do you mean," Reb Chotzkel asks.

"Well, please forgive me for butting into your business. Your brother told me that he helps you out financially because you are not doing so well."

"What?! That's a lie! He has never given me a penny!"

Obviously embarrassed, the *shnorrer* says, "Please forgive me and let's forget the whole thing."

But it bothers him. The next day he goes knocking at the door of the miser. "Reb Hershel, you told me that you help support your brother and that was why you would give me no assistance. But I met your brother and he told me you never give him a cent. How could you tell such a lie? And in that case, if you do not aid him, you ought to be able to make my life a little more comfortable."

The miser looks at the *shnorrer* with cold eyes. "Tell me," he says, "if I don't help my own brother, why should I assist a total stranger?"

There's a double dose of *chutzpeh* here. Poverty and charity both become the occasion for bitter humor in such jokes. How bitter the humor could be is seen in another Old World story dealing with this subject.

A woman comes to the rabbi in her town. "Rabbi, help me. My husband is so generous, I think he will give away all we own if he continues."

"Have him come and talk to me," the rabbi tells her.

Soon thereafter, a man comes to talk to the rabbi. "Rabbi, my family is in such dire need. We don't even have enough to eat. And worst of all, my brother is wealthy and won't help us at all. Maybe if you talk with him. . . ."

"Have him come and talk to me," the rabbi says once more.

Both men arrive together and the rabbi, for some reason of his own, asks both of them to come into his alcove together.

"Why are you giving away all your hard-earned money?" he asks Mr. Generous.

"Rabbi, we are only human. After all, one can die at any moment. I would be afraid to appear before the Almighty to be judged if I thought that I had not acted properly, in line with what our Lord commands us to do!"

"And you," the rabbi turns to the other man, "how is it that you do not help your brother?"

"Well, Rabbi," is the answer, "we are only human. Who can tell how long he is to live. I am afraid that if I live a long time and don't save my money, I too will end up in poverty."

The rabbi thinks for a moment and comments, "Well, may the Almighty see to it that your fears turn out to be groundless!"

Think about that. It's a subtle putdown, and at the same time a little on the caustic side.

Sometimes the charity jape becomes incredible, as in the following:

A man comes to a wealthy relative to ask for financial aid. After he has explained his needs, the relative says: "All right. I see your problem. Tell you what I will do. I will send you 50 rubles every month."

The other fellow looks at him and says, "That won't do!"

"What? According to what you told me, that should be more than enough for your needs."

"True," the potential beneficiary admits. "But what if you were to die after the first month?"

The great magnates of the Jewish world, the Rothschilds, the Montefiores, the Brodskys, and the Hirsches all enter Jewish humor. We have already seen a number of stories that involve them as participants, normally on one side, as the rich man vis-à-vis the poor man. But there is also an interesting story that involves two of them.

Baron Hirsch comes to visit Rothschild in Vienna. In the course of their talk, the latter describes all the welfare arrangements he provides for his employees in his many factories. Hirsch asks him, "How many workers do you have?"

"Oh, I can't tell you exactly but it numbers in the hundreds of thousands."

"And how many of these are Jews?" Hirsch probes further.

"None, so far as I know. For people of my ancestry I have established very important hospitals all through the Austrian Empire!" is the answer.

Hirsch is thoughtful. "You know, Rothschild," he finally remarks, "I would like it better if you employed thousands of Jews and set up your hospitals for the non-Jews."

Once again, as we have seen so often, the knife cuts deep. This story may or may not be factual, but this form of Jewish anti-Semitism in employment is not unknown, and humor is one way of protesting it.

In the New World the subject of charity was no less useful for jokesmiths, but the jokes were adapted to life here. Philanthropy has become highly organized and professionalized for both Jew and Gentile and it is this fact that Jewish-American jokes deal with. For example:

A trunk is brought up out of the Caribbean Sea. It turns out that it was the possession, of all things, of a Jewish pirate named Henry Morgan Stern. It was claimed by lineal descendants of the man, and with some media attention, it was opened. Guess what!

It contained a fortune, thousands and thousands of Spanish dollars—in the form of pledges!

Charity drives here, of course, run on pledges. Or, look at this one:

> A Jewish salesman is calling on trade in the South. He is in a small town one evening, he has made his calls, and there is nothing to do. So he looks at the bulletin board in the hotel and notes that there will be a meeting of the Sons of the South in the local meeting hall.
>
> With nothing better to do he saunters down to the hall, noting that almost all the seats are filled. He sits down at the end of one of the back benches. Soon a tall, impressive fellow gets on the podium and begins his address. "Sons of the South, we all know that this country is being mongrelized. All kinds of foreign lowlife elements are defiling white, Christian racial purity. Blacks, Jews, and Orientals and their white liberal pals need to be purged from the body politic of this great nation."
>
> Moskowitz realizes that he is in the wrong place. However, he is embarrassed and a little fearful, so he stays seated. Soon the speaker, in ringing tones, is explaining that the crusade of the Sons of the South needs to be "fed" with funds if it is to continue its important work. He adds, "Our worthy brothers will pass among you and accept your cash contributions to the cause."
>
> Young men and women with baskets suddenly materialize. As one of these reaches Moskowitz sitting at the end of his row, he looks up somewhat sheepishly and asks, "Is it okay to put in a pledge for a hundred dollars?"

I don't have to tell you this is wry humor—first the idea of a Jew offering a contribution to an anti-Semitic cause, but second, a little jab at the practice among Jews of pledging.

You have probably heard the following (non-Jewish) joke:

> A man is stuck in a Swiss snowdrift for days. Finally, a rescue party breaks through and their leader can be heard calling, "Mr. Smith, we're here from the Red Cross."
>
> Smith replies, "I gave at the office."

And now here is a Jewish brother joke to that one:

Mr. Cohen gets a call from the Hebrew Home for the Aged in his community, asking for a contribution. So he sends his mother and father. . . .

Both are a sort of satirical commentary on charity, not in the Jewish tradition at all. They would be considered funny only in America. They also would be easy to transfer to some other ethnic group.

Still another way of seeing charity in the New World:

At a country fair, a strongman is performing. He bends iron, tears the telephone book in half, lifts a safe with one hand, and does various similar stunts. Then the barker announces: "And now for his last act, Colossus will squeeze a lemon! But wait, don't leave—there will be something for you in the audience to do afterward!"

The strongman squeezes the lemon until it looks like pulp. Again the barker addresses the audience: "You've all watched Colossus squeeze the life out of that lemon. We will pay 50 dollars to anyone in the audience who can get another drop of juice out of this pulp!"

Several brawny characters come up and try—with no results. Then a short, thin man walks up, takes the lemon, and out comes juice.

Well, the barker counts out the 50 dollars, hands it to the little man, and asks, "Tell me, sir, how is it that you were able to get more juice out of the lemon when all these big strong fellows couldn't do it?"

"You see," the "squeezer" responds, "I worked for many years for the United Jewish Appeal. Compared to that, this is easy!"

Now as a matter of fact, Jews are quite generous and their giving compares favorably with that of any other group, but for jest purposes the joke sounds good.

Finally, another twist to the philanthropic joke.

A man who has not received any education in the religious tradition of Judaism although he is of Jewish birth decides at a rather advanced age to join the synagogue in his area. Not having had a religious education, he knows virtually nothing about Judaism or even about the Bible.

He comes to services one Friday night, watches the prayer session without understanding, and then listens to the rabbi's sermon. He realizes that he has a far piece to go before he will be integrated into this community but his resolution is strong. At this particular service the rabbi announces that the next week's reading and service will deal with the Great Flood.

At the end of the service, our friend approaches the rabbi and says: "Rabbi Berman, I am planning to become a member of this congregation. I found everything very interesting although I have to admit that I don't know much about our religion. Anyway, I won't be able to be here next Friday since I have to be out of town on business. But I want to show that I'm right in there with all the other folks in this congregation. So, put me down for a contribution of 25 dollars for the flood victims."

I leave it to you to decide whether the mechanism here is credible or incredible ignorance.

Home Sweet Home

How many peoples have had to wander as much as the Jew? Maybe the gypsies; I certainly can't think of anyone else since the times of nomadic tribesmen. But what do you do when you are so often unwelcome and persecuted?

By the nineteenth century the main base of Jewry was in Eastern Europe, among the Yiddish-speaking Ashkenazis. As the Yiddish saying has it, honey they didn't lick. Then stories filtered back into the *shtetlach* about better conditions in other places, and so the Jews began a mass migration—to England, France, Italy, Germany, Latin America, Australia, Canada, and, above all, the United States. Millions of people emigrated.

Now suppose you were moving to China. Can you imagine the problems involved, first just in getting there, and second in blending in with the life in that place?

This was no joking matter. Or was it? Of course, Jewish jesters picked up this emigration/immigration business and had some fun. For example:

A Jew has decided to leave the Russian empire and goes to a local official to find out about doing so. After waiting an hour or two, he is ushered into the office. The official is seated behind a large desk and next to him, on a stand, is a very large globe.

The Jew addresses him: "Pardon me, your honor, I want to go to the United States. Can you tell me what I must do?"

The official looks at him and responds coldly: "The United States? You can't get in there for at least three years. All the quotas are filled."

"So where *can* I go?" asks the Jew.

The official points: "There is a globe of the whole world. You decide where you want to go. It's not up to me."

The Jew points to a spot on the globe: "Maybe there I could get in?"

The official responds: "There? Your kind isn't wanted there!"

The Jew points to another spot. "And there, maybe?"

"There?" says the official. "They have all kinds of legal restrictions. Actually, you have to have real money to get in there."

Well, the Jew continues to point and the official continues to discourage. Finally, the Jew stops and asks, "You said this was a globe of all the countries in the world. Is that right?"

"True," the official answers.

The Jew thinks for a minute and then, "Maybe you have another world I could try?"

Bitter, bitter humor, you say—not very funny. Of course not; it's an ironic jest which hurts. Again, *lachen mit yashtsherkes*, laughing through tears. Again you see why the Jews of Europe said, "When it gets too painful, laugh."

And when they got to the United States, millions of Jews (and others) discovered that the streets were not paved with gold. True, here they were tolerated, sometimes ridiculed, but no official policy harmed them. But they still had to find out how to fit in.

For instance, what work could they do? Most of them took marginal jobs, like peddling. Others went to work in the apparel and textile firms where Jews were already settled. Some came with no particular skills. Some may have been Judaic scholars "back home," but here, where did that take you? And so jokes developed around this problem.

A Jew comes to the United States, having no skills and no crafts. He gets a job within the Jewish community in New York. He gets a contribution can (with a slot in the middle, called a *pushkeh* in yiddish) for collecting money. He goes from place to place asking for contributions to help support a Jewish endeavor, the settlement of Jews in the Holy Land. He gets a portion of what he collects so he is managing to get by, but he is certainly not getting rich.

One day he is working a neighborhood, going from store to store and door to door, and he reaches the edge of the neighborhood. The last house on the last block is a two-story building. How should he know that it is a brothel?

He walks up the front stairs to the door, knocks loudly, and as the door opens he holds out both hands, the *pushkeh* in the left, and opens with his usual, *"Shenkt ah nedoveh,"* which translates as, "Make a contribution."

But the madam, a big Irish woman, doesn't understand a word of what he has said. She makes the obvious assumption, grabs his right hand, pulls him in, and yells: "Mary, you got a customer."

A large girl, underdressed, appears, takes the bewildered Jew by the hand, and moves him quickly into a room. He stands there looking around while she invites him to bed. Of course, he doesn't understand a word, but assuming that in this new country this is how things are done, he gets into bed.

I won't burden you with the details you can read about in any modern novel. When it's all done, they both get out of bed and Mary moves him right out of the room. *Pushkeh* in his left hand, he approaches the door where the madam is standing.

"All right, mister," she says, holding out her right hand, "let's have the five dollars" (tells you something about the age of this joke, doesn't it?). Of course, he hasn't the faintest idea of what she's talking about, but he grips her hand and replies in Yiddish, "*Men zol zach nor zen ahf simches!*" which translates as, "We should only meet on such happy occasions!"

This is one of my favorite stories and always gets a big laugh. But behind the very funny punch line we can see the immigrant, unable to handle the language of his new country, unable to find an occupation in the mainstream, a marginal scrounger who, in this case, has managed to get a little accidental pleasure.

There is another side to this situation which was discussed earlier, but let's consider it from the point of view of another joke.

A very improbable situation. A successful Jewish lawyer has recently met and married a very pretty woman who is a recent immigrant. He needs to attend a meeting of attorneys at a fashionable resort. His wife is eager to go along and see the American world in action. He is reluctant to take her but finally she persuades him.

They arrive at the hotel, check in, get to their room, and get settled in. Then he says to her: "Dora (only a few months before she was Dvoireh), I know you can't speak much English. With this group I'm not eager to push forward my Jewishness, so I want you to go to the swimming pool by yourself. Later on, when there aren't too many people around, you and I can do some things together. Just look around, but don't talk to anybody, because I'll tell you the truth, with your Jewish accent, you'll embarrass me."

And she answers: "Don't vurry. I'll be by myself and I vun't talk to nobody. I told you, I just vanna look arond."

Reassured, he goes off. Dora gets into her bathing suit and walks down to the pool. A large number of women and men are seated around the pool and naturally some of them watch when a newcomer approaches.

As luck would have it, the deck around the pool is slippery, Dora is wearing leather sandals, and as she starts to walk toward a chair—plop, she slips and starts to fall. As she is falling, she cries out, *"Oy vay iz mir* (woe is me!)" and then adds quickly, "Votever dot meenz."

So we learn the lesson that children learn at a very early age. If you're different in some way, you stand a good chance of being ridiculed. And when you're ridiculed, you're ashamed. So you can see why Lefkowitz, in the joke earlier in the book, wanted a machine with less of an accent.

Remember that when you move to China.

The Holy Land

As you have seen, the wandering Jew shows up in humor. The Holy Land too is not exempt from jesting. Even the concept of the return to Zion did not escape the wit of Jews. Thus:

> One Jew tells another: "You know, I have steady work now. And not only that, the job is permanent, secure. I can't lose it during my lifetime."
>
> "What sort of a job is that?" is the natural question.
>
> "I've been appointed to sit and wait for the Messiah to come."

You no doubt recognize the appearance of the basic common-sense foundation under the Jewish dream of the Messiah's appearance. Reversing this notion, we have the following:

> A Jew comes home from the Friday night service. He looks glum.
>
> "What happened in shul to make you look so sad?" his wife asks.
>
> "Velvel Bernstein, who is a great scholar in Torah and Talmud, told us that by his estimate the Messiah should be coming within a few months."
>
> "And that makes you unhappy?" The wife doesn't believe what she is hearing.
>
> "He also told us that when the Messiah arrives, all the Jews will necessarily go with him to Eretz Yisrael (the Land of Israel).

And here it is only a few months since we moved into this nice house with a garden where we have just planted flowers and vegetables. To leave it would be a shame. So now you understand why I am gloomy."

The wife thinks for a moment. "Boruch," she tells him, "stop worrying. Remember what the Torah teaches us. God saved us from Haman; He delivered us from Pharaoh. He will protect us from the Messiah, too."

That little diamond has a number of facets. First is the commonsensical approach to the problem created by the notion of redemption. Second, is the wife being ironic or just plain stupid? I leave it to you.

Not all Jews favored Zionism, especially political Zionism, as you will see from the following jape, an Eastern European story which probably goes back at least to the early part of this century.

A Jew is leaving for the Holy Land. He says goodbye to a friend, whom he knows to be anti-Zionist. Nevertheless, he is still trying to convince him.

"Why don't you come with me to Zion?" he asks him. "You know you belong there."

"Eh, I will wait until I am dead," is the response. "I will let the angels bring me there."

"But why bother the angels when you can go there yourself?" is the next question.

"It's no bother for them. The same angels who will bring you back here will take me there," is the response.

A little obscure, but the feeling comes through.

Then there is the establishment of Israel—and the various wars connected with it. So let's look at the unpleasant state of war.

A couple, not too young, have settled in Tel Aviv. It is wartime, and Tel Aviv has begun to have air raid alerts. On this day the warning sounds, and all the people, including our couple, are rushing out of their homes to go to an air raid shelter.

Suddenly the wife is running back. The husband stops and calls to her, "Dvoireh, where are you running?"

She turns around and yells: "I have to go back. I left my teeth in the glass on the table by the bed."

And he shouts back to her: "Forget the teeth, They're gonna throw bombs, not sandwiches!"

Even at such a time, jokes! This one, though, was probably coined by a Jewish comic in the safety of the United States. Authentic war jokes in Israel have a different quality. Here is one attributed to the Palmach, the Israeli special striking force which was very important in the early struggles.

> One of the military instructors is told by the group commander: "I hear all you talk about in your training sessions is rifle, rifle, rifle. Remember, we are Jews, civilized people with a tradition of learning. Talk also about history, culture, sociology, philosophy. At the very least, you should start your instruction with the Bible."
>
> The instructor nodded his head in the affirmative. The next time new recruits arrived, he began his training session as follows: "In the beginning God created the heavens and the earth. After that, he created the rifle. Now this is the rifle. Let's see what we can learn about it."

The Israeli victories over the enemy have encouraged a spirit of bravado. These Jews no longer have to cringe. Recall the joke earlier that since it took only six days to subdue the invasion of 100 million Arabs, it ought to take twelve days to deal with 200 million Russians. Forget the arithmetic or lack of realism.

The performance of the Israeli army encouraged other jests. It was said (this too is probably of American origin) that their troops must have been led by doctors, dentists, and lawyers because they know how to *charge!* Here's another story:

> An Egyptian platoon is reconnoitering. As they come to a hill, a shot is fired at them. The officer says to a scout: "It may be a solitary sniper. Get into that tree and take a look."

Several minutes later, the scout comes running back. "We have to retreat. We're outnumbered," he reports. "There are two of them!"

But the old stereotypes die hard. To wit:

Two tanks, one Egyptian and one Israeli, are approaching each other in the desert. For some strange reason, the drivers do not see each other, and lo and behold—they crash!

The Arab jumps out with his hands up: "I surrender; I surrender!"

The Israeli jumps out: "Whiplash, whiplash!"

I strongly suspect that this too is a Jewish-American jape rather than an Israeli story. When I was in Israel, I inquired about this joke and was met with blank stares. I don't think they even knew what I was referring to.

As everyone knows, Israel has been under the threat of war ever since its establishment. One result has been the creation of one of the best intelligence services in the world, the Mossad. This too gets into the jokes.

A CIA agent finds it necessary to get in touch with a Mossad agent on a super secret mission. He is given an address in Jerusalem which turns out to be an apartment house where the Mossad agent, currently going under the name of Moishe Goldstein, resides.

Smith, the American agent, goes to the apartment building, looks in the directory, and notes Goldstein, apartment 1A. He walks up a flight of stairs, goes to door 1A, and rings the bell. A short, stout man opens the door and says, "Shalom."

Smith offers the code sentence he has been instructed to use: "The grapes are ripe in Carolina."

The Israeli looks at him. "What, what did you say?"

"The grapes are ripe in Carolina."

The Israeli is obviously puzzled. Smith decides to take the bull by the horns. "Aren't you Goldstein?" he asks.

The light dawns. The Israeli starts to giggle. "Yeah," he says, "I'm Goldstein, the *jeweler*. You want Goldstein the *spy*, Apartment 2A."

This is likely an American creation. More typical of Israeli humor is the Knesset story near the beginning of this book, about the Messiah needing a jackass to arrive on and they're all in the Knesset. Israeli jokes appear to have more bite. You'll recall that in Israel only five people are needed for a minyan because Israelis are schizoid? Similarly, a group touring through Jerusalem came to a building which, the guide informed them, housed the Ministry of Finance, or as they call it, "our second Wailing Wall."

The Jew who headed and was most responsible for the creation of the Israeli state was David Ben Gurion. I believe it is Israeli jokesters who have said that he might have become the king of Israel except that he did not wish to be called King David II! (The man, in fact, was a principled Socialist.) He was the prime minister for a long time, and an opponent is said to have remarked, "The Messiah won't come and Ben Gurion won't go!"

I'm not sure whether the following joke is Jewish-American or Israeli.

> In an Israeli high school in the year 2000, a history lesson is in progress. The subject is the modern history of Soviet Russia.
> The teacher asks, "Who can tell me who Khrushchev was?"
> There is a dead silence.
> "Not even one of your knows? Didn't any of you read your assignment carefully?"
> She turns to her star pupil: "Simche, even you don't recall?"
> Simche scratches his nose. "I'm not sure," he answers, "I think he was an obscure Russian political figure during the time of Ben Gurion the Magnificent."

Well, after all, Ben Gurion was a massive figure during the period when Israel was formed. And a country is entitled to its heroes.

One more story of that period.

> Following Khrushchev's speech in which he revealed the atrocities which Stalin had ordered, the Russian government—

in this story only—decided to dig up his grave and have him reinterred in some other country.

Well, the United States wouldn't have him. None of the European countries wanted him. The Soviet leaders wouldn't ask any of the East Asian nations. So they finally turned to Israel.

Ben Gurion was contacted by Khrushchev. His reply: "We here have no particular objection to burying the man forever. But I must warn you of one difficulty. Israel has the highest resurrection rate of any country in the world!"

The fact that Israel accepts Jews from any part of the world without question has created a very mixed population—highly Westernized Ashkenazis from Europe and the New World; old-line Sephardim, many from families that have lived in Israel for generations; and the so-called Oriental Jews from various Asian and African countries, including black Jews from Ethiopia and dark-skinned Jews from some of the Moslem countries. From this, naturally—jokes.

A Yemenite Jew, new in Israel and unsophisticated in its ways, needs something from a public office. He finds his way to the large office building but, once there, he is totally at sea. Someone tells him that the man he wants to see is on the fifth floor and that the elevator will take him there.

But what the elevator is he doesn't understand. However, he stands in front of it and waits for something to happen. An older woman walks up next to him, nods, and as soon as the elevator arrives, she steps in. The Yemenite continues to stand there.

In a minute or two, the elevator door opens and out comes a beautiful young woman who walks by him and out of the building.

The Yemenite quickly walks out the door, goes to his home, and commands his wife to follow him. He takes her back to the building to the elevator. When the door opens, he tells her to get in.

The door closes, opens a minute later, and there, of course, is his wife, looking baffled. As she steps out of the elevator, he says to her, "It's just as our fellow-Yemenites say; these Ashkenazis always discriminate against us!"

And now a contrast to the Yemenite joke.

> On a bus going from Tel Aviv to Jerusalem, suddenly a passenger seated at the back begins to moan and writhe. A fellow passenger approaches him and says: "Can I help you? I'm a physician."
>
> Meanwhile, because of the hubbub, the bus driver has turned around, seen what is going on, and stopped the bus. He walks back to the man and asks. "Can I help you? I'm a trained and licensed medical practitioner."
>
> At this point, the sick passenger looks at the two men and whispers: "Leave me alone. I, too, am a doctor."

Israel has one of the highest ratios of doctors to population. Most of these have come from the Western Ashkenazi group, as a result of the flight from Europe. So Israel sees the humor in this situation, too—precisely the opposite of the lack of sophistication in the previous story.

For some reason, the German Jew (called *Yekkeh* in Israel) has been cast in the role of one who does not understand the life of Israel very well. This story illustrates:

> A *Yekkeh*, walking in Jerusalem, sees a man carrying a grandfather clock on his back. He is, in fact, a porter who moves furniture this way as his occupation.
>
> The *Yekkeh* walks up to him and says, "Pardon me, sir." He points to his wristwatch. "Don't you think it would be more practical to use one like this?"

Obviously, an Israeli version of a noodle story.

Now how do the Jews in the rest of the world feel about Israel? Well, how do American Irish feel about Ireland, or American Armenians feel about Armenia? You may remember how Americans of Greek and Turkish descent reacted when Cyprus was in the throes of a big argument. Similarly, it should not be surprising that American Jews, and Jews worldwide, feel a close kinship with those in Israel. Jokes develop around this relationship as well.

George Burns tells the story about George Jessel, a prominent comic and after-dinner speaker, who was called upon to offer a eulogy for Harpo Marx's cat. After telling all the marvelous things that the cat had done, Jessel added, according to this story, "It would put you to shame if you knew what this cat did for Israel!"

If you think that's extreme, listen to this:

A lady is on her way to Israel. She wants to purchase a seat for her dog, which is in a special cage, but the airline will not agree. After a long argument, she permits the attendants to put the cage with the baggage.

At Lod airport she disembarks, and through some strange circumstance, the dog, cage and all, has disappeared. She keeps needling the airline people, telling them that they should have listened to her and permitted her to keep the dog with her on the plane. Needless to say, the airport personnel are very apologetic, but keep reassuring her that the animal will be found and returned to her.

Sure enough, the cage turns up, but to their consternation they discover that the dog is dead! Swiftly, they contact every kennel in Israel and, luckily, they find a dog that looks almost identical to the dead one. This whole process has taken several hours, during which they have received numerous phone calls and complaints from the lady.

Now the airport manager calls her up and tells her, "Madam, we will have your dog at your hotel within an hour."

And he is as good as his word. Forty-two minutes later he himself arrives at the Hilton with the cage and dog. The lady takes one look at the dog and starts to wail: "That's not my dog! That's not my dog! You liars, thieves. What have you done with my pet?"

Well, the manager sees that he is in the soup; he might as well confess. "Madame," he reports. "unfortunately, when we found your dog, it was dead. So we disposed of it and got you a replacement which is almost an exact replica of the one that died."

But the woman won't be soothed. "You fools, liars, no-goods. That dog was dead when I put it on the plane! Don't

you understand anything? I wanted to bring it to the Holy Land
to bury in sacred soil!"

You see what I mean by devotion to the Holy Land.

The following was reported to me by a friend as an actual
occurrence—one of those unintentional jokes we touched on
at the beginning of the book.

He had come to visit Israel with an older aunt, and, as
visitors do, he took a tour. Part of the tour took the visitors to
the Caesarea area, where there are many Crusader ruins. The
guide was telling about the great building done by the Crusaders, showing the remains of some fine architecture, when my
friend broke in.

"Why are you telling all this about the Crusaders? From
the Jewish point of view, they were deadly. They pillaged Jewish
homes, raped Jewish women, and killed many of the Jews who
lived here at that time."

And at this point, his aunt piped up with, "Yes, and after
all we did for them!"

Honestly, he hadn't the faintest idea wh t she was referring to, nor do I. Did she mean that Christ was Jewish, or was
she just misunderstanding what was going on?

One final point about modern Israel. Yiddish, the great
language of the Jews of Eastern Europe, was frowned on by
the early Zionists as the language of the ghetto and the Diaspora. Hebrew was reestablished and, of course, became *the*
language of Israel. Today Yiddish is not widely spoken in Israel,
except by some of the older folks and a scattering of immigrants.
Knowing this, you should appreciate the following jest.

A grandmotherly lady is on a bus with a little boy, who is
seated next to the window. As they drive along, the boy jabbers
away, as kids do, talking about one thing and another, including
what he sees outside the window. Naturally, he speaks Hebrew.
Every few minutes, the old lady says to him: *"Red Yiddish, red
Yiddish"* (speak Yiddish).

A man seated across the aisle is watching all this with great interest. After a few minutes, the lady turns to this man and explains in somewhat fractured Hebrew, "I'm telling him to speak Yiddish because I want him to remember that he's Jewish!"

That joke should give you some idea of how Jews used to feel about *mameh loshen* (mother tongue). We see again that Jewish wit doesn't shrink from looking into any Jewish experience to find what's odd or funny in that experience.

Jewish Elocution

Let me remind you again that some jokes are Jewish only because the teller makes them so. Some are more authentically Jewish if they come out of the Jewish experience or life; or if they are stereotypes created about Jews; or, finally if they depend for their kick on a Jewish lanaguage, primarily Yiddish.

Jokes in this last category are always difficult to translate and so only a couple of examples have been given so far. In spite of that, Yiddish has been used here occasionally for punch lines or other short "takes." But before we leave the subject, you should get a smattering of some of the *characteristics* of speaking in that language which mark its uniqueness. Remember that this language is part of the life and history of the Jewish people.

As we all know, *how* you say something is as important as what you say. Over the centuries, Yiddish-speaking Jews developed special ways of speaking—not just in the language, but in the way in which they phrase things. To explain, here is an old story.

Two Jews are picked up by the police on suspicion of having burglarized a store. The interrogation proceeds as follows:
"Cohen, will you admit that you broke into the store on 23rd Street?"
"Why should I break into the store?"
"When we arrested you, didn't you have a carton in your possession that had the name of the store on it?"

"What would I be doing with such a carton?"

"Isn't it true that you have a record of stealing?"

"Who steals?"

"So what kind of work are you employed at?"

"Who works today?"

At this point the police interrogator has had enough of this fellow. He turns to the next man.

"You, Levine, what do you do for a living?"

"What do I do? I'm not a crook. After all, is it against the law for me to help out my friend, Mr. Cohen?"

Aside from the absurdity of helping a man who appears to do nothing, notice that this whole exchange has been driven by a series of question responses to questions. In fact, the classic story of this genre goes like this:

A priest and a rabbi have become very good friends. One evening, the priest asks the rabbi: "Morris, I want to ask you a serious question. Why do Jews always answer a question with a question?"

And Morris immediately responds, "Is there a better way?"

This trait may have developed out of the training of Jewish scholars. Jewish students who studied the Talmud and the Torah did so largely by a sort of question-answer technique rather than by listening to lectures or memorizing catechisms. Now see how the question technique has been reversed in the following story.

Two women meet who have not seen each other for some time. One immediately starts to talk and continues for several minutes. Suddenly she stops and says to her silent partner: "Such a long time we haven't seen each other; we meet again and you don't even ask—How are you? How's the family? What's new?"

The other woman takes her cue and inquires, "So, tell me, how is everything going?"

"Oy," says the gabby one, "don't ask!"

This ironic little joke describes one of the characteristic ways in which Jews frequently answered questions. I suppose it's a way of warding off unpleasant recollections. "Better you shouldn't ask" and "Better you shouldn't know from it" are characteristic expressions. As you just saw, such a phrase is easily woven into a joke.

This question technique shows up in other ways, too:

> Aaron Rosenbloom has to spend time in a large city away from his family for a period of some months. He receives a letter from his wife informing him that she has become ill and is going to see the doctor. Alarmed, he sends off a telegram:
>
> SEND INFORMATION PROMPT
>
> Sure enough, two days later he receives a return telegram:
>
> HE SAYS TO OPERATE OPERATE
>
> Immediately, he wires back:
>
> SAYS TO OPERATE OPERATE
>
> Now even in the days of the Czar there was a secret police, and they apparently monitored telegrams to make sure revolutionaries were not communicating in that way. Thus Rosenbloom is visited on the following morning by an agent. He shows Rosenbloom a copy of the telegram and says, in a harsh tone of voice, "Explain the code you are using for these subversive messages!"
>
> "W-W-What code? W-W-When code? Rosenbloom stammers. "I don't know what you're talking about!"
>
> "Do you want me to take you down to headquarters? We can make you tell us what we want to know there!"
>
> "Officer, it is a simple telegram I sent to my wife. There is no code. The words are the words," Rosenbloom explains.
>
> "Do you take me for a fool? What kind of telegram would a man send to a wife that reads like this?" the officer says sternly.
>
> "Let me explain," Rosenbloom responds. "You see the first telegram. I have a letter from my wife that she has become sick. So she went to the doctor. And she let me know what he said. See it means 'Says to operate. Operate?' You see, she's asking me. So I sent her a message. 'Says to operate? Operate!' That's all!"

We are indebted to Sam Levenson for an illustration of a third manner of speaking, again drawn from Old World Yiddish, but translated. He tells the story of an income tax agent who has come to speak to his father. Sam acts as the translator.

Whether the story is true, I haven't the faintest idea. My best guess is that Levenson at least doctored it. What you should watch are his father's alleged responses to the agent's questions.

> The agent inquires: "How much does your father earn in a week?" And Dad responds:
> "His worst enemies should earn what I earn!"
> Obviously this isn't the information the agent wants, but in the story he proceeds:
> "How much does your father pay in rent for this store (father was apparently the proprietor of a tailor shop)?"
> The answer: "My landlord should have so many boils on his neck how much too much I pay!"
> Another try: "Who owned the store before you did?"
> In the classic manner, Dad replies: "Some other poor shnook with a house full of loafers."

While I can't claim that every East European Jew always talked this way, it was not uncommon. It probably developed as a way of avoiding answering embarrassing questions and is really part of the same ironic mode so often seen. It is somewhat similar to children's answers to questions they consider an invasion of their privacy. Another aspect of how Jews speak is shown in the following.

> Three Jews who grew up together in the Old Country meet in New York. They embrace each other and then begin to retrace old memories. One says: "Izzie, you remember Mendel Dvoshe's?" (This refers to the mother's name. In Europe people were often identified either in this way or by the father's name. Thus Mendel Dvoshe's is the son of his mother, Dvoshe.)
> "Of course I remember, Abe."
> "Sol will confirm what I tell you. Mendel came to this country after we did, went into the cloak and suit business, changed his name to Murray, made a fortune, and now he lives on Park Avenue. Tell him, Sol, am I not right?"
> To which Sol responds: "Yeah, it's true but not exactly. First off, he never changed his name. Second, he was always in the grocery business since he came to America. Third, he went

broke twice and I heard he doesn't have a pot to piss in right now. In fact, I just was told that they put him out of a small cold-water flat on the East Side. But except for that, everything Abe told you is absolutely right!"

The penchant for contradicting one's fellow Jews, especially in this satirical, ironic way, is a stereotype—exaggerated, of course, but with some basis in fact. It may have been more characteristic of Jews in immigrant days than it would be today.

Since life has not always been too sweet for Jews, the following conversation should not be too surprising.

> Chaim is speaking to Feivel. "Feivel, my friend, life is too difficult, especially for us Jews. *Siz shver tzu zine ah Yid* (it's hard to be a Jew). But do I have to tell you? Sometimes I think it's better not to be born at all."
>
> So Feivel answers: "You're right. But who could be so lucky? Maybe one in a thousand."

Of course, it's a noodle story, worthy of Chelm. Moreover, why must this be a Jewish joke? In theory, it doesn't have to be. But such a depressed view of life would be characteristic only of groups that have suffered as Jews have. In this sense, the sadness underlying the absurd punch line could also be found among other ethnic groups, but it fits the Jewish manner of speaking very well.

Generally, Jews may be talkative people, but obviously this trait isn't true of all of them, as we see in the following two stories.

> Two Jews who have not seen each other for some time meet. Berl asks Fishel, "Listen, you're making a living these days?"
>
> "Eh!"
>
> "I heard your father died. How's your mother getting along?"
>
> "Ehhhh."
>
> "And your wife. How is she feeling?"
>
> "Eh."
>
> "The children. Grown up already. They're doing well?"

"Uh."

"Is that so? Well, I'm sorry to hear all this. But you know, it's good to get it off your chest."

Another jape to illustrate manner of speech.

The non-Jewish nurse who has been on all night explains to the doctor who has just come in: "The patient's pulse was irregular all night. His temperature went up as high as 102 degrees. I believe he was hallucinating and calling wildly for what I assume are members of his family. He refused all medication."

The next night the nurse is Jewish. The doctor comes in next morning and Nurse Sobel says to him, "Oy, did I have a night!"

Can you imagine how many Jews have asked themselves: If we are God's chosen people according to the Torah, why has life been so difficult for us all these centuries? What have we done that is so wrong? Or is there more here than meets the eye? Did God really mean it? Such questions are going to promote irony. After all, can this be what "chosenness" means, to be continually persecuted and humiliated? This perplexity explains the question Sholem Aleichem's Tevye puts to God, roughly translated as, "Maybe you could let some other people be the chosen people for a while?"

So, it is understandable that with Jews going over these questions and also studying the Torah with questions and disputations, their jests love to play with words and are often so ironic. Of course, so are the jokes of many other people, but Jews carry it to the extreme. This trait can be seen in the following typical joke, normally told in Yiddish.

Two men who are originally from the same *shtetl* meet after one has been away for a period.

"Oy, Reb Mendel, such a long time since I saw you!" says one.

"Nu, Reb Shmuel, if you would come back to your place of birth more often, you would see me!"

"So how is everything going in Shniyadova?"

"Well, not too much has changed. I can't give you a full report. It would take too long. But wait a minute. Just last week Dovid Bashe's (David, son of Bashe) passed on. You must remember him."

"Dovid Bashe's? No, I don't think so."

"Of course you do. He was the one with the crossed eyes."

"Dovid Bashe's, crossed eyes; no I don't recall."

"Yes, with the crossed eyes and the nose turned to one side."

"Dovid Bashe's, crossed eyes, nose turned; you know, I really don't recall him."

"How is it possible? Don't you remember, he had a skin condition all over his head?"

"Dovid Bashe's, crossed eyes, turned nose, skin condition, I should know so from evil if I remember him."

"The *shtetl* hunchback, and you forgot already?"

"Oh, you mean that Dovid. Oh, he died. Too bad. *Azah shaner Yid.*"

Shaner Yid means, literally, handsome man, but it is also used in Yiddish to mean a fine character. So this is word play and irony all at once.

And now let's look at one of the all-purpose words in Yiddish.

A Jew is indebted to another Jew. The creditor has asked many times to be repaid but it's stall, stall, stall. Finally, he decides to send him a telegram (don't ask how a telegraph got into a small *shtetl* in Eastern Europe; it's not important).

The telegram simply reads: "Nu?" (This is an all-purpose word in Yiddish. Here it translates into "Well, how about it?")

Several days later, he receives a telegram in return, which reads: "Nu, nu!"

In this context, the words would best be translated as "Well, it's a long story but. . . ." The term is often used in Yiddish as a sort of conjunction when one has a long story, for example, "Nu, nu, what should I tell you?" It might also be taken as an abbreviation for "Well, you're still going to have to wait." As you see, it has a rich context, but in this case it

certainly says, "Buddy, you ain't gettin' your money just now."
And in two words.

In a more American joke, this turns up as follows:

> A Jewish cattle breeder has finally succeeded in developing
> a new type. He has successfully crossed a Guernsey with a
> Holstein. The result is a Goldstein, which says "Nu" instead of
> "Moo."

Yiddish is extremely rich in such little idioms, and of
course they figure in jokes. Still another favorite Jewish word
expresses much of the pain that Jews have suffered. It's easiest
to explain it in a jest.

> Two Jews are sitting opposite each other in a train. Each
> recognizes a fellow Jew in the other but they sit quietly for several
> minutes.
> Finally, one leans toward the other with a deep sigh. "Oy!"
> comes out in one breath.
> The second leans forward and observes, "That's just what
> I was thinking!"

This business of the sigh and the *oy* is so characteristic of
Yiddish that it is hard to imagine any long dialog in that language without it.

Another all-purpose word occurs in the following joke
roughly translated from the Yiddish:

> Yoineh meets Shmerl. "How's it going, Shmerl? I heard
> you were having all kinds trouble. Is it true?"
> "No, quite the opposite. By me, everything is good!"
> "I'm glad to hear you say that it's going good by you."
> "Of course. Now it's winter; my house is good cold. In the
> summer, it's good hot. My roof leaks so when it rains I get good
> wet. Yesterday my boy got beat up good. My wife is good sick.
> So, as you see, everything is good!"

Old World Jewish people, especially the women, were
always uttering good wishes: May the Lord protect you. May

you live and be well. And of course these resulted in certain idioms which find their way into japes.

> An elderly woman is arriving at Ellis Island. When her turn comes to be questioned by the immigration officer, he realizes that she doesn't speak English. He doesn't want to waste any time waiting for the interpreter, so he decides to question her in the little bit of fractured Yiddish he has learned. The conversation translates as follows:
> "What is your name?"
> "Malke Rubinshtane."
> "And where do you come from?"
> "From the Czar's country, may a plague take him!"
> "And how old are you?"
> "Sixty years old, till 120."
> This makes no sense to the examiner, so he repeats his question.
> "I already told you. I'm 60 years, till 120."
> Just as she is saying this, the interpreter arrives. The examiner explains that he has been unable to get an answer to his question. The interpreter nods, turns to the old lady and asks: "You should live to be 120; how old are you?"
> "Sixty. Sixty. What's so hard to understand?"

So you see, it's the way of speaking rather than the content that often matters in Yiddish.

Sometimes Yiddish word usage seems tortured, hard to believe. An example:

> Two old ladies are sitting in comfortable chairs on a hotel porch in Miami Beach. After some chatting, which tells us that they are old friends, one of them starts to get out of her chair. But this is a real operation. Apparently her arthritis or some similar affliction makes it hard for her to move.
> So we see her getting up painstakingly, bit by bit. And finally, she has risen and taken a faltering step. Her friend, who has been reading a Yiddish newspaper, looks up, notices her, and asks, "Sarah, where you running?"

Now you have to understand that running is used often by Jews in this special way. Thus, if Jewish people invited you for dinner, and after dinner was over and you spent some time in conversation, you finally got up to go, you would be asked the same question. The use of this phrase in this sense does not seem to be common among Gentiles.

Finally, a characteristic which you may find "cute."

During the immigrant days, a lady has just come into a New York Jewish delicatessen and walked to the pickle barrel. She fishes one out, a nice large, fat one, and turns to the store-keeper.

"How much you want for this pickle?"

"It's a nickel a *shtikel* (piece)!" is the answer.

"A nickel! That's too much," the lady protests. She picks out a small one and again turns to the merchant. "And for this *pikele*, how much?"

The owner looks at her and sings out, "For that *pikele*, will only cost you a *nikele*!"

This love for the diminutive was apparently picked up from the Slavic languages. You find it throughout Yiddish. In one well-known play in Yiddish, the 40-year-old central character, a man of great virtue, is called Reb Hershele, not Reb Hersh, and a 20-year-old young man is Motele, not Motel. Similarly, the suffix *nyu* is often used in Yiddish, and in Yiddish jokes, as a diminutive. Thus a little girl might be Faigeleh or Faigenyu.

All these ironic jokes should help you understand Yiddish jests more fully. And, perhaps, who knows, you'll start using some of these speech traits yourself.

4

If You Cut Me,
Will I Not Bleed?

In the sixteenth century, when Shakespeare wrote, there were very few Jews in England. Today there are many charges of anti-Semitism regarding his *Merchant of Venice* because of the way he portrayed the character Shylock, a Jew. Yet Shakespeare, being such a fine dramatist, put what is probably the best monolog of the play in Shylock's mouth when Shylock faces his enemies and asks:

> I am a Jew. Hath not a Jew eyes? Hath not a Jew hands, organs, dimensions, sense, affections, passions? Fed with the same food, hurt with the same weapons, subject to the same diseases, healed by the same means, warmed and cooled by the same winter and summer as a Christian is? If you prick us, do we not bleed? If you tickle us, do we not laugh? If you poison us, do we not die?

How is this speech relevant here? Because it is always said that Jewish humor is different from others. To some extent, as you have seen, this is true, insofar as the Jewish experience and the stereotypes created by Jews and non-Jews are involved. On the other hand, Jews get married, have children, succeed, fail, misbehave, grow old, get sick, die—just like other people! Is it possible that there are *no* jokes dealing with these universals that are not especially Jewish?

In Western countries, where Jews have become increasingly integrated into the general society, there are many such jokes; it is only the narrator's identifying them as Jewish that makes them Jewish jests. But in the Old World, where Jews were not part of the larger society but were marginal—what was the situation there?

Curious about this matter, I paged through collections of Euro-Jewish jokes which, according to the writers, had been gathered directly from conversations with Jews. Most of these are in Yiddish. And what do these collections tell us? Of course—they contain japes dealing with all the matters that other nationalities fool with—misdeeds, marriage, man/wife relations, sex, and so on.

These collectors gathered their material from ordinary people, who related the stories being heard in their communities. Certainly they were edited somewhat as they were being written down, but they must have been based on the originals. Possibly some were invented by the collector, but my guess is that these are relatively few. And the fact that many of the stories occur in more than one collection suggests they were really current. Furthermore, since Jews could not have been completely isolated in Eastern Europe, some of these stories were probably picked up from non-Jewish sources.

In any case, there were stories of a general kind, not merely those dealing with Jewish problems, that did circulate among Jews. These were not merely Jewish stereotype jests, and not only jokes that dealt with the Jewish conditions of life, Judaism, anti-Semitism, the Holy Land, and the like.

So we turn now to a sampling of such stories, drawn from and either translated or adapted from the original Yiddish, or in some cases German.

Crimes and Misdemeanors

Jews are only human, so why shouldn't they have their fair share of crime, drunkenness, and other misbehavior? They do, of course, both in real life and in humor.

Earlier in this book there was a story about a cobbler in Chelm who catches his wife with another man and kills him. I don't have any crime statistics, but the general impression is that crimes of violence are actually not common among Jews. Theft, however, certainly does show up. To wit:

Talmudic students frequently studied by candlelight. One such young man confides to another: "You know, Yitzchak, I had no money and I needed candles so I did a terrible thing, committed a sin—I stole some candles! I feel awful and I know I should do something to atone for it."

"Your right, Maishe," the other one agrees. "A good deed would balance your *ahvaireh* (sin or transgression). Why not bring a couple of bottles of sacramental wine to the shul on Friday evening for the service?"

"Yitzchak, what are you talking about? I have no funds; otherwise I wouldn't have stolen the candles. So how do I get wine?"

"The same way you got the candles, Maisheh."

Of course, this is sacrilegious, but a certain commonsensical characteristic breaks through the preoccupation with religion in an ironic way.

Here is another ironic witness to the way in which Jews might look at misbehavior.

A young woman has just given birth to a nice bouncing boy. In the Jewish tradition, the child is named after a relative who has died, and it happens that both husband and wife no longer have their fathers.

Now an argument erupts. The father wants the child to have his father's name.

She objects: "Your father was a drunkard!" She wants the boy named after her father.

He objects. "Your father was known to be a thief!"

So after a lot of wrangling and screaming, they decide to take the matter to their rabbi. The rabbi listens to the arguments, thinks a while, and then asks the husband, "What was your father's name?"

"Avrom Dovid."

Next the rabbi turns to the wife and puts the same question to her.

"Avrom Isaac."

"The answer is obvious," the rabbi intones. "First, call the child Avrom. Second, you wait and see. If he grows up to be a drunkard, you will name him Avrom Dovid after the father's father; if a thief, Avrom Isaac after the mother's father."

This is clearly a story worthy of the Chelmer rabbi, but it is not attributed to him. While it sheds no glory on the rabbi's decision, it does remind us that the *shtetl* was certainly not without some forms of wrongdoing. And, naturally, the joke-lore picks it up and twists it.

There is a mechanism in jokes which I call the *good and the bad of it*. It's shown in this next jest.

A wagoner comes home and tells his wife that it has been a hard day but, thank the Lord, he has survived.

"What happened?" his wife wants to know, somewhat alarmed.

"Well, I had to make a deal for a new horse. The old one went lame," he tells her.

"Oy vay," is her natural response.

"Don't take on," says the wagoner. "I ended up with a very good animal, worth at least 20 rubles, and all I paid was 10."

The wife claps her hands. "That's good, Shmuel!"

"No—it's bad because this horse is smaller than the one I had before," he tells her.

"So how will he be able to pull the load? You made a mistake. That's bad," she agrees.

"No, it's really good," he reassures her. "He's a very strong horse. The only problem is that he limps."

"Shmuel, what is it with you? Why did you buy a damaged horse? It's a bad bargain," she admonishes.

"Not so fast. It worked out for good. I looked over the feet and didn't tell the seller what I saw, but after I bought the horse, I pulled out a nail from one of the front feet and now he doesn't limp any more," Shmuel explains.

"Thank Heaven you're so smart. So now we have a good horse for only 10 rubles. Good, good, good!"

"But it's still bad," Shmuel notes. "I made a mistake and gave him a 20-ruble note."

"*Vay iz mir* (Woe to me)," the wife wails. "That's terrible, very bad."

"No, it's good." Shmuel smiles. "The note I gave was counterfeit."

So you see why I use the term the good and the bad of it. Such an alternating current story appears from time to time, teasing the listener or reader. Notice also that the Jew in it passed counterfeit currency—misbehavin'.

But Jews were also caught and punished. And that fact leads to the following jest.

A Jew is praying in the synagogue.

"Reboinch Shel Oilem, blessed be Your name. We have so many thieves and pickpockets and swindlers among us, but You see to it that the police are active and catch them. I pray that You will continue to do so. Otherwise, how would a poor thief like me be able to make a living?"

But not all misbehavior is criminal. For example, we have already touched on sharp business practices. Even milder forms exist:

A blind man and his friend go partners on a basket of cherries. They begin to eat, and after a couple of minutes the blind man suddenly lashes at the friend and socks him in the face.

"What's the matter?" the friend asks. "What did I do to you?"

"You *passkudnyak* (scoundrel, lowlife)! Here I am, taking

two cherries at a time, and you aren't complaining! It can only mean that you're taking three or four at a time yourself, you cheat!"

Finally, a story which occurs in a number of variations.

> A man borrows a large pot from his neighbor. The next day he returns with the pot and a small pot.
> "What's this?" the neighbor inquires. "I don't take interest."
> "No, it's not that. What happened is that the big pot gave birth to a little pot."
> Some time later he borrows a sharp knife, and on the next day he returns it with a little pocket knife. The same story: the big knife gave birth to a little knife.
> Some time later he borrows a pair of silver candlesticks. The next day he comes back, this time with a long face.
> "What happened to my candlesticks?" the neighbor questions.
> "Your candlesticks died!"
> "What are you saying? How can candlesticks die?"
> "Look, my friend. If a pot and a knife can give birth, candlesticks can die!"

Jokes about physical violence are rare, but, as you've seen, jests about other actions that we might not regard too highly are found in Jewish humor. Many of these could easily be transferred to some other ethnic group. But we see that Jews do kid around about their misbehavior.

Smart and Outsmart

You will recall the superiority factor, which figures in jokes all the time? Very frequently, one person comes out ahead of the other because he or she is smarter. Remember the story in which Hershele Ostropolier chooses a roll, then a bagel, then doesn't pay for the bagel because he gave a roll for it. It sounds very Jewish, but a columnist in the *Los Angeles Times* put out the same story about booze not too long ago, showing that either the story travels or it can be transferred. In short, although the actor I gave you was Jewish, this is really a universal story. In fact folklorists might trace it back to examples in other places. Basically, *such stories do not involve Jewish stereotypes, Jewish language, or conditions directly related to Jewish life.*

Let me illustrate again with a story that is *not* Jewish at all.

> A man is standing on a street corner with an open suitcase on a camp stool and shouting: "Come and get it! Get the miracle pill just developed by modern science. It helps everybody who takes it. Buy one or buy a bag full."
>
> A passerby stops and asks him, "What are these miracle pills that you're selling?"
>
> "Terrific. I won't bother you with the scientific name— monoglucamate. All you need to know is that you take them and they make you smart! How about a bag?"
>
> "I'll try one anyhow," the passerby tells him.
>
> "Okay. Just gimme a half a buck and it's yours."
>
> The next day the customer comes by the corner and the same fellow is still peddling his smart pills. "Hey, you phoney," the customer says. "I took one of those pills last night. And right away I did some dumb things and my wife bawled the hell out of me. Those pills don't work. Half a dollar apiece. They're not even worth a nickel!"
>
> The vendor looks at him. "Paid half a buck and they're not worth a nickel. See, you're smarter already!"

So again, someone is up and someone is down.

But, here is an example of the stories Jews told *among* themselves. It could, in fact, be told about any two people; it isn't even essential to mention any nationality. Nevertheless, it was told among Jews.

> Two Jews, both hungry, are walking along a street in town. Suddenly one of them notices a bagel on the street. Immediately, they start a dispute as to who should get it. The fellow who saw it claims it. The other man argues that they are friends and were walking together so they should share it.

Finally, they come to an agreement. They will take the bagel to a local park area. They will lie down and take a nap. When they awake, they will compare dreams, and the one who has the most beautiful dream will get to eat the bagel.

They carry out the plan, and now they are both awake. One of them says: "I had the most beautiful dream. I dreamt that a huge white bird picked me up and transported me directly to Paradise! Isn't that a wonderful dream?"

The other fellow stares at him and says: "That's strange. We should both live so that I must tell you that I had exactly the same dream. I saw clearly how the white bird picked you up and carried you to Paradise. Well, I figured if you get to Paradise, why would you want to come back here just to eat a bagel? So I got up and ate the bagel."

Dream stories are very common in jokelore. And they frequently end up with one of the participants getting the best of it, outsmarting the other.

Hey Stupid!

We have already seen that one of the pillars of jokes is hostility, aggressiveness, overcoming, outwitting, outsmarting. There is also malice in making fun of deformity, laughing at the stutterer, the alcoholic, or the person who is stupid. The superiority factor is still at work, but here it's not *inside* the story but rather belongs to the narrator and audience.

We've seen plenty of such stories. In fact, the stories about Chelm were almost all of this type. I'll give you just one convincer. But first, here is a story that I've been telling for decades.

Sam is unhappy. He doesn't seem to be able to get anywhere with the girls. Finally he decides to talk to Marty, an acquaintance who does very well in that field.

"Marty, I can't make it with the goils. I know you and the other guys are gettin' laid reggeler. I don't understand why I can't make out. Couja gimme an idea?"

"Well," Marty asks him. "What are you doin' now? What happens when you meet a girl?"

"Oh, you know, I interdoos myself, I ask her her name and then I usually say sumtin' like, 'Hey good lookin', how about you come up to my place for some fun in bed?' "

"Hey, Sam, you can't be abrupt like that! You gotta buy her a drink and talk about something else first. You could talk about art, the movies, literature, history, maybe even travel."

So Sam, having listened to the advice, goes to a dance and sees a good-looking girl. He approaches her. "My name is Sam. What's yours?"

"I'm Alice; my friends call me Al."

"Great, Al. How about we sit at the table and have a soda?"

So they find a table, sit down, and Sam orders two sodas. Now he remembers Marty's advice. What should he talk about? What did Marty say? Oh, yeah—travel. He turns to the girl.

"Say, Al, ever been to, uh, Siberia?"

"Siberia! No, never."

"Never traveled there? Okay, Al, whaddaya say we go to my place and hop into bed?"

Now let's look at a cousin of this joke, much more elaborate and refined, which circulated among Eastern European Jews.

Again, we have a lamebrain. The *shadchen* is trying to get him married but this jerk can't handle himself when he has to talk to people, and especially young women. So his father decides to coach him.

"Listen, Shmerl, the *shadchen* has picked out a nice girl for us(!). When you go over to her house to be introduced to her, you must talk a little bit."

"But I don't know what to talk about!"

"So let me give you some subjects. You can talk to her about love; you can talk to her about family matters; you can bring in a little philosophy. Just get started. It'll go."

So the boy keeps repeating—love, family matters, philosophy. Now he has arrived at the prospective bride's home. After the meal, the older folks get out, leaving the young pair to get acquainted.

So Shmerl starts: "Malke, do you *love* noodles?"

And she responds in the usual Jewish way. "Who doesn't love noodles?"

Well, he's gotten past that subject, so he turns to number

two, family. "Malke, was that your whole *family* at dinner to-night? Maybe you have a brother, too, who wasn't there?"

"No. That's my whole family. I don't have any brothers."

So he's passed point two, but he still has one arrow left, *philosophy*. Philosophy?! So he turns to a "conditional" question, a question which requires reflection. "Well, now, Malke, sup-pose you had a brother, do you think he would love noodles?"

Need I say more?

All in the Family

What could be more obvious than the man/wife joke? People have no doubt been telling such stories for hundreds of years in every language. Sometimes the man gets the best of it and sometimes it's the woman's turn. And naturally, Yiddish humor has had its share of such jests.

Some of these stories have already shown up in this book. As you know, one story may have several aspects. For example, there was the lady lighting candles who said that if only her husband would burn like the candles, she would bless him too. And also the *shadchen* who is telling about how wonderful it is to be married and illustrating with his own wife, how she feeds and tells him gossip, talks, and talks—"may a fire grip her tongue." These japes merely illustrate the saying that "Love is a sweet dream and marriage is the alarm clock."

Now an anti-wife joke may surprise you because there is a tradition that Jewish husbands are kind and gentle to their wives, in accord with the regulations of Torah and Talmud. It is for this reason that Jewish husbands are supposed to be desirable mates for even non-Jewish girls.

And yet the talkative and bossy wife is a staple in Jewish humor. Thus:

A *melamed* (teacher) in this *shtetl* is moving on in years but is still unmarried. So the local *shadchen* comes to him with a proposition. "I have a spinster for you. It's Yente. . . ."

"Wait a minute," the *melamed* interrupts. "Yente! Everyone knows that she's a shrew, a plague. I don't want to marry her!"

"Listen," the *shadchen* tells him. "You know, you're not such a desirable commodity yourself. You're not young, you're not rich, and you're not handsome, so what do you expect— the Czar's daughter? Moreover, I know that she's got quite a bit of money."

This bit of information apparently impresses our *melamed* and he agrees to the wedding. Needless to say, as soon as they are married, the wife begins to make his life miserable. Comforted by the thought of money, the *melamed* thinks to himself: "Keep this in mind. Whoever dies first, I promise the Lord I will put up a gilded tombstone!" (Note the power of positive thinking.)

And God helps. The wife dies. The *melamed* grieves in the proper manner, and now the funeral procession is on its way to the cemetery. On the way there, it is necessary to pass over a rough cobblestone bridge. The wagon carrying the corpse is bumping up and down. After a particularly bad bump, the corpse suddenly sits up, resurrected!

Of course, she continues to make his life miserable and he continues to hope.

And again, God helps. Within a short time, the wife again dies. Again the tears and the wailing. And again the corpse is properly dressed and on its way to the cemetery. As the wagon comes to the cobblestone bridge, the husband jumps ahead and screams to the wagoner: "Please, please, very slowly, go very slowly over this bridge."

Obviously, such a story could be told in any language or of any ethnic group. The same is true of the following story.

A 70-year-old man comes to the local *rov* (official rabbi) seeking a divorce.

"How long have you been married?" asks the *rov*.

"Fifty-two years."

"And after all these years, you decided that you don't need your wife any more?" the rabbi inquires.

"Well, it's not really like that at all," the old man explains. "You see, mine was an arranged marriage. My father set it up when I was only 18. By the end of the first week, I realized that my wife was a witch! So I went back to my father and told him that I wanted out.

" 'Well,' my father said, 'I can't do that. We will be shamed in the whole community. Wait a bit, in any case. You may find she's not as bad as you think.'

"So I waited a few months and went back to my father again. He asked all kinds of questions and it finally came out that my wife was already pregnant.

" 'How can you consider a divorce when your wife is pregnant?' my father asked me. 'It will shame us in the eyes of the whole *shtetl*!'

"So I waited. And what can I say? The children came, one after another—sons, daughters. So how could I leave her, rabbi?

"But yesterday I married off my youngest daughter, so there is nothing more to be ashamed of. So I want my divorce! Enough is enough!"

Such jokes, found in the Old World collections, are similar to some of the material in Yiddish collections published in the United States in the earlier immigrant period. Some of the latter seem similar to college humor magazines.

That raises the question of where these jokes come from. Were they carryovers from what these people heard in Europe? Or did they originate in other languages, say the English press, magazines, or joke collections, and get translated into Yiddish? That is a mystery that is almost impossible to solve. For example:

Mrs. *Tarnover:* "Our marriage is so happy, Morris! The only cloud is my constant worry that some day I will be a widow."
Mr. *Tarnover:* "Oh, don't worry, my dear. As long as I live, I will not permit that to happen."

For a somewhat different angle, let's look at this.

A bon vivant arives home late one night after a lively session at the local tavern. The door is locked, so he knocks loudly. "Frumeh, Frumeh, let me in. I'm home."

"Go to Hell and bake bagels. Where were you all night?

You didn't tell me you wouldn't come home for dinner, you *shikker* (drunk)!"

"Open the door! Look what I have here. A roast goose and some delicious wine!"

Well, that makes a difference. So Frumeh opens the door. But goose and wine are not in evidence.

"Where are the goose and the wine you were just talking about?" she asks.

The husband pats his tummy. "Right here!"

The next story throws a different light on man/wife relations.

> During the first World War the Russian army was initially successful against Austria. Now a Russian regiment is approaching the large city of Lemberg. There are some wealthy Jews in that city, and when they hear the news, they feel sure that the invading troops will loot their homes. So many of them rush out into their gardens, dig under the vegetables, and hide their gold, diamonds, and other treasures.
>
> A neighbor observed a relatively poor man digging a very large hole. "Why such a big hole?" he asked. "What are you planning to hide?"
>
> The neighbor replied: "Most of you are burying your gold and your diamonds. But for me, my wife is my diamond."

But a family does not consist only of a man and wife. There are also in-laws and other relatives. That they were a real source of humor becomes obvious when we consider what one of Freud's patients said to him: "You know, we all suffer from *mishpochitis* (a word coined from the Yiddish *mispocheh*, meaning family)." So, not surprisingly, Jewish humor also offers us stories about the mother-in-law. Incidentally, I did not find any stories that attack fathers-in-law.

> At Old World weddings every guest was expected to offer a present for the newly married pair. One might present silver candlesticks, another silver forks, others silver spoons, goblets, and other such utensils.

Some people, however, made a symbolic offer of a segment of their life for the bride or groom. At one wedding, a Jew stands up and says: "I present the bridegroom ten minutes of life." Another offers a second ten minutes. Of course, these are cheap gifts.

Finally, a Polish Chasid stands and says: "I'm giving the bride ten years of life!"

There is a murmuring of astonishment in the assembly, and someone yells, "How can you afford to give up so much of your life?"

To which the Chasid replies: "I'm not giving up my life. I'm presenting my mother-in-law's!"

You'll probably agree that such jokes can come from any ethnic background even though they have been told in Yiddish within Jewish communities?

One of the silliest jokes of this class:

A family group is sitting around, drinking tea and talking, when suddenly a neighbor runs and shouts, "*Gevalt*, help, my mother-in-law just hanged herself!"

Well, a furor breaks out—women fainting, children crying. Some men turn pale, and one of them jumps up and starts for the door:

"C'mon let's quickly cut the rope!"

But the young man who came in with the news detains him: "No rush; she's not dead yet!"

And similarly:

The town needs a new bridge to replace the old one which has become dangerous. We're not talking here about engineers; this is going to be a home-made job. So the town council debates the matter of how to test whether the bridge will hold up. One member comes up with, "Listen, let's gather all the mothers-in-law in our town and have them cross over the bridge all at once."

"What? Why the mothers-in-law?" someone else asks.

"As near as I can count, there are close to a hundred of them. If they march across in one procession and the bridge holds, it will mean that it's secure enough. And if, God forbid, it doesn't hold, that's not so terrible either."

Sort of sick, but what does it say about the attitude toward mothers-in-law?

Other relatives also come in for some ribbing. George Burns had his brother-in-law, Jessel had his uncle. Here's one about relatives from a Yiddish jokebook.

A man comes to a relative who is a wealthy businessman. "Since you're a relative, I think you ought to be able to find a position for me," he says.

"Well, what can you do?" the rich relative asks. "Are you versed in bookkeeping?"

"No, I know nothing about that."

"Well, maybe you could handle my correspondence?"

"I really haven't had any experience along that line."

The entrepreneur asks several other questions about competence in business pursuits, each time getting the same answer—no experience.

"Well, what sort of job did *you* have in mind?"

"I know that you are a very busy man," the applicant tells him, "and I'm sure many serious problems confront you all the time. Now, even if I say so myself, I am a man with very good judgment. I would say you need a full-time adviser with you whom you could consult on a day-to-day basis, one who could offer you useful advice."

"Good thinking!" the businessman counters. "I do have a problem about which I can use your advice right now. Tell me, how do I get rid of you?"

Body Language

You ask whether "dirty jokes" circulated among Jews. These are said to be uncommon in Jewish humor. Still, there is a publication titled *The World's Best Yiddish Dirty Jokes*. And the collectors of Old World stories do include some.

Here is one that I had told for many years without relating it to being Jewish; yet in the course of my reading I found it to be told in the Old World too.

A Jew has occasion to visit a town where a former neighbor now lives. Naturally, he looks him up. He finds that this man has prospered greatly, become wealthy, is living like God in France (an Old World Yiddish expression).

The visitor goes to call on his ex-neighbor. After the greetings, he asks, "Well, how are things going here, Reb Hersh?"

"What's this Reb Hersh?" is the answer. "My name is Grigori Alexandrovich! But I'm glad you asked. I am, as you see, with God's help, in good health and business is excellent.

"Moreover," Reb Grigori adds, "I get up in the morning, drink a glass of tea, and lie down on my veranda. When my mail comes, my daughter Regina brings it in, I read it, compose my responses, and lie down again on my veranda. At about 11 A.M. I have my brunch, drink my coffee, and lie down on my veranda. In the afternoon, I spend another hour on my veranda. At about 4 o'clock I take a walk, come back, and lie down on my veranda. And in the evening, I once again lie on my veranda. So you see how well I am living, with God's blessing."

When the traveler returned home, he was asked about his trip and someone wanted to know about Reb Hersh.

"May he be protected from the evil eye, he is doing very well. But I must tell you he has become a regular goy. He has changed his name to Grigori Alexandrovich; his daughter Rebecca is now Regina, and his wife Leah changed her name to Veranda!"

I am a little suspicious about the following, although it is supposed to be an Old World story.

A wife has just died. On the day of the funeral, the procession to take the woman to the cemetery is about to start when the wife's brother discovers that the husband is missing.

After a brief search, he finds him in bed with the maid. Outraged, he screams at him: "What are you doing? Even if you didn't love my sister, do you not have enough respect for the dead to behave yourself on the day of her funeral?"

"You are absolutely right," the husband replies. "In fact, however, I did love your sister. This is a terrible day for me. My grief was so great, I was so distraught, that I did not know what I was doing."

We can always find a good reason to do what we want. It's called rationalization.

Sometimes an extremely pious Jew would leave his home and go to another place for an extended period to pray and do penance for some real or supposed sin or perhaps to study in accordance with what he thought was God's will. His stay might even extend for several years. During this period, the only contact with his wife would be through correspondence.

> One such Jew, after having been away for two years, receives a letter from home that his wife has given birth to a baby.
> He mentions the fact at the house of study and another man looks at him and says, "How can that be, if you are here?"
> "Well," is the answer, "you see, during the time when I am here doing what the Lord wants me to do, my work at home is being done by others!"

Now you might think this is a very unusual story, but consider this American jape.

> A man who has been away on military duty gets the same message: his wife has had a baby.
> He is shocked, but another soldier says to him, "Must have been a grudge baby!"
> "A grudge baby? What are you talking about?"
> "It should be obvious someone had it in for you."

Of course, the two jokes are not the same, but the general topic and the conclusion are close enough to make them relatives.

Here is a little story which may remind some of you of a calypso song with exactly the same punch line.

> A Chasid is sitting at the rabbi's table on this afternoon, watching the rabbi and listening to his humming. Suddenly the rabbi becomes very gloomy. Then a few minutes later, his mood changes and he is once again cheerful.
> "Rabbi, may I ask a question?" the Chasid says.
> "Of course, any time. What is troubling you?"

"No, it's not about me, it's about you. Suddenly, in the middle of your *nigun* (a song without words), you stopped and turned very gloomy, and then your mood changed again. What would make you do that, Rabbi?"

"Let me explain it. While I was singing, I was suddenly carried to Paridise. And suddenly, my father appeared to me, looking ill and very pale. That touched me deeply, that he should still be so weak even in Paradise."

"But then my mother suddenly appeared. And she whispered to me, 'Don't worry, my son. He's not your father.' "

But temptations are not always fulfilled. A story attributed to one of the famous wits of Ashkenazi life runs like this.

In Vilna, several very pious Jews are sitting in shul. With them is the jester, Motke Chabad. They are discussing a variety of subjects of current interest, and a little gossip, too, including tales of wealthy people.

"But," says one of them, "in the end we all die the same death and go to our just reward."

So the *shochet* (ritual slaughterer) remarks, "You know, when I die, I would like to be buried next to the old rabbi; such a holy man I would like to be near."

The cantor speaks up: "And I would like to be buried near Reb Dovid, may he rest in peace. This was a scholar of scholars and I would consider it a privilege to be buried next to him."

Motke has been silent. So the others ask him, "Nu, what's your preference, Motke?"

"Where would I like to lie, you ask?" he responds. "I'll tell you. I would like to lie next to Opatov's daughter."

"What are you talking about?" the others shout. "The woman is in the prime of life!"

"And what am I, dead?" answers Motke.

Sex even enters into *shadchen* stories, as, for instance, the following:

A *shadchen* comes to a young man in Vilna and tells him about a fine family who live in Kutne, not too far away. The parents are ready to marry off their daughter, a wonderful girl.

The young man, with admirable caution, decides to go to the other town and see for himself.

He arives in Kutne in the morning, too early to appear at the home of the Katsenfeld family, so he stops at the inn for a glass of tea. Only one other person is there. This man walks over to the Vilner and asks, "What brings you to Kutne, some business deal, I suppose?"

"No."

"Oh, so I suppose you're here about a *shiddach* (a match). May I ask whom you are considering?"

The young man sees no reason to hold back and answers, "It's Katsenfeld's daughter, Chana."

The other Jew hears the name and jumps up. "Young man, take my advice; forget it, everybody in town knows that she is making it with all the officers in town!" And he says goodbye.

Thoughtfully, the young man asks for a second glass of tea. And as he's sitting there, a second Jew comes into the tavern. Soon the latter wanders over and the opening remarks are repeated—business here, no must be a *shiddach*, who, Katsenfeld's daughter Chana.

The other Jew's eyebrows go way up. "Chana Katsenfeld? Young fellow, I advise you to be very careful. Let me tell you something. There isn't a policeman in Kutne with whom she hasn't been seen. Take my advice and go home." And he waves goodbye, too.

By now, the young Vilner is thoroughly upset. He pays for his tea, walks outside, and observes an old Jew coming toward him. He decides to try for one more opinion. "I hope you'll excuse me, sir. I'm a stranger here and I'm looking for information about the Katsenfelds. You see, a *shadchen* has told me that their Chana is a very good match. Do you know them?"

The old fellow looks around to see if anyone is listening and whispers: "You want to listen to me, young man; don't go near the place. Everyone knows she's carrying on with all the doctors in town."

By now convinced that he's in the wrong place, our young man gets back on the train and returns to Vilna. He looks up the *shadchen* and lets him have both barrels.

"You have some nerve to send me on such a fool's errand. What kind of a *shadchen* are you, anyway? Everyone is going to know about this. Setting me up with that girl. Everyone in town knows that she's carrying on with the officers, the policemen, even the doctors. How did you dare to present me such a *shid-dach*?"

The *shadchen* looks at him and replies: "Listen to him! What's all the excitement about? *All* the officers, *all* the police-men, *all* the doctors. A person could think that Kutne is a big city. How many officers, policemen, and doctors do you think there are there?"

Now, of course, this story has a distinct Jewish flavor, but it's easy to see a non-Jewish story of pretty much the same sort. What's the big deal, the girl's just been running around with five or ten fellows before you?

These jokes, as you can see, are not the coarse stories that one sometimes finds in non-Jewish jokelore, but they do deal with sexual behavior. One of my favorites is this one, which may or may not be an Old World Yiddish story.

The rabbi of the town, a man in his forties, dies suddenly and leaves a wife, a young woman, only recently married and still in full bloom. She is despondent, will not go out of the house, wears black—a case of severe grief.

After a month, the town butcher approaches her. "You cannot go on like this. You must put your grief behind you, come out of your shell and start to mingle with people again. I will do all I can to help you. Count on me."

Well, the butcher begins to call on her and finally after several months, he says to her: "I realize that you have been a *rebbitzin* (rabbi's wife). But what was can never be repeated. You are a charming woman. I like you very much. I would like you to consider becoming my wife. I realize that I am only a butcher. I will promise to take care of you and not to bother you with any intimate advances."

After several proposals of this sort, the ex-*rebbitzin* agrees, but she makes it clear that sex is not to be thought of. She confides to a friend that the butcher for all his good heart is not at all like the rabbi and she would not think of going to bed with him.

Several weeks after the wedding, the husband, who has not touched her heretofore, informs her that he has just had word that his great uncle has died. That night, he comes to her and says: "You know, when someone in a family dies, it is a *mitzveh* (a good deed as prescribed by Judaic Law) to have intimate relations. So, would you please oblige me in memory of my uncle." Under the circumstances, she does so.

A few weeks later the husband again approaches her. "A cousin of mine has died." Again she obliges.

Two weeks later the same story, with an aunt.

Several days later, she meets her good friend, who looks at her and asks: "You know, you're looking much better. Life must be treating you right?"

"Oh, things could be better, they could be worse; with God's help, I am managing."

"Tell me, we have always been close; is your life with the butcher satisfactory? And can you bring yourself to have sexual relations with such a man after having been married to the rabbi?"

"Of course," the ex-*rebbitzin* answers, "he is not the rabbi. He is a butcher, basically a very coarse man without much learning to grace his life. And I really do not get much out of living with him. But from his family, from them I get real pleasure."

So we must conclude that sex was not unknown in Old World Jewish humor.

And how about scatology, the jokes about excrement? Jewish humor does not neglect this, either. To wit:

A *shnorrer* comes to his patron, a wealthy Jew in the town. The front gate is locked and he gets no answer to his banging on the gate. He looks for the back door. It, too, is locked.

So the *shnorrer* goes to the front of the house and shouts: "The owner of this house will not live more than three days!"

Suddenly, the door opens and the householder charges out. "What are you talking about?" he exclaims. "How can you bring yourself to utter a curse like that?"

"It is not a curse," the *shnorrer* says. "Everyone knows that if one is plugged up in the front and in the back, you cannot live for more than three days."

Another aspect of "coarse" humor can be seen in the following:

A Jew makes a loan to another Jew, supposedly for two weeks. Two weeks pass. No repayment. The lender is told that next week the debt will be repaid. As you can guess, it doesn't happen. Several more weeks drag on, filled with requests and promises.

Now the lender learns that the borrower has declared bankruptcy. He rushes to the borrower. "You are bankrupt, may God help you. But don't you think you have a moral obligation to pay me?"

The bankrupt looks at him scornfully and observes: "What kind of fool are you? To repay your loan, I would need cash. And that exactly what I don't have. So you can kiss my navel."

"How can you talk like that to me? What kind of reply is that?" asks the unhappy lender.

"Well, would you rather I told you to kiss my ass? Forget it. There's a long line there already."

Here's one with a little different emphasis.

A Chasid is sitting and talking to another Chasid about the wonders of the *Reboineh Shel Oilem*.

"Consider," he says, "consider the birds and the cows. The bird is small, and its needs are modest. And yet, the Lord gave it wings and it has access to the sky as well as the earth.

"Now, on the other hand, the cow is large and its needs are greater. So, tell me, why didn't God, in his infinite wisdom, permit the cow to fly?"

And before his partner can even answer, a bird flies overhead and lets go and the stuff falls right on the Chasid's head.

"Aha," he exclaims, "now I have my answer."

I'll See You and Raise You

Yes, dear reader, gambling was not unknown among Jews in the old country. Remember the joke about the rabbi who played poker with his wife? Well, that one is doubtful, but the following are authentic.

The bunch are playing cards, and right in the middle of the game, Goldman drops dead!

So Shloime Honig raises the question, "How are we going to tell Raizel, his wife, such terible news?"

After a couple of minute, Moishe Ingber volunteers. "I won't blurt it out all at once," he says. "I'll get her ready before I spring the bad news."

So he goes to Goldman's home. Raizel lets him in, and she asks, "Where is my Nachmen?"

He says, "You know, we were playing cards and Nachmen lost 500 groshen!"

She blows her stack: "That stinking dog, that no good. Here we need the money so desperately and he goes and loses. He should only drop dead!"

At this point, Ingber breaks in: "From your mouth to God's ear. He did drop dead."

That's what I call diplomacy! Another old timer goes like this.

Kalmen tells his friend: "Levine, I wish my son would learn how to play cards. That would make me happy."

"Kalmen, what sort of a wish is that? I could understand your wishing him to be a scholar or a doctor. But why would you want your son to learn how to play cards?"

"Because he does play and he doesn't know how! That's why!"

Not So Golden—Mean

Earlier we mentioned humor that is "sick." Remember, for example, the horrifying story about the Challenger astronauts spending their vacation all over Florida? You may wonder whether Jews have their sick humor too. I don't think Eastern European Jews had this in large quantity, but we do find it. An example:

A woman goes to the cemetery to pay her respects to her dead husband. But it is winter and the cemetery is covered with a deep blanket of snow, to the point that she cannot find her husband's grave. So she calls the caretaker, gives him five kopecks, and asks him to locate the grave. And, she instructs:

"Tell my husband that when I was here several months ago, things were going not too badly for us. But now our condition has become very bad. I married off our two daughters and now the sons-in-law are also living with us as guests (a Jewish tradition), and with more mouths we do not even have enough to eat. Explain it all to him, will you?"

Well, the caretaker supposedly carries out the instructions and comes back. The woman is still waiting. "Did you find the grave?" she asks.

"Yes."

"And did you explain everything as I requested?"

"Yes, I did," is the answer.

"So what did my husband tell you?" the woman inquires.

"He asked that you keep the children at home until Passover. After Passover, he will take them from you," is the reply.

Pretty grim sense of humor. The caretaker is probably fairly feeble-minded and is simply repeating some trite sentence. But it's sick humor any way you look at it.

No doubt, I could offer you illlustrations of other subjects that show the Jews joked about the same things as do other people. The jokes in this section, while they come out of Jewish jokelore, are universal enough that we might meet something like them in some other culture. They deal with matters that could be identified as general, if the narrator did not choose to place Jewish actors into the scene.

Epilogue

You cannot really *understand* Jewish humor without some understanding of Jewish history. Of course, if you only want to *read* jokes, you can skip this section. But if you want *background* for understanding where Jewish jokes come from, you will find it here.

Ashkenazim

Jewish humor seems to be principally the product of that segment of the Jewish people called the Ashkenazim. So let's take a few minutes and look at what that means.

The word *Ashkenazi* itself presents a puzzle. In the Bible, it refers to an area near present-day Armenia. Yet in the Middle Ages the word *Ashkenaz* came to refer to the Jews of Germany, particularly those in the Rhine Valley. So how did the Biblical Ashkenaz become the German Ashkenaz of medieval times? No one seems to know for sure, although there are a lot of theories. (If you're interested in exploring the matter further, see Volume 3 of the *Encyclopaedia Judaica*.)

In any event, the area of the Rhineland became known as Ashkenaz. What does this have to do with Jewish jokes? Read on.

Judisch

What language did the Jewish immigrants to the Rhineland speak? No, it wasn't Hebrew. Remember that when Jews move into an area, they have to communicate with the people who already live there, so they begin to acquire the language of their environment. When they were exiled to Babylonia in 586 B.C.E., they picked up the language spoken there, which was Aramaic. Under Hellenistic rule, Jews adopted Greek, or maybe adapted would be a better word. In ancient Rome they used the popular Latin. But in doing so they merged portions of their original Hebrew and Aramaic into the local language and shaped their own vocabulary and usage. Max Weinreich, noted scholar in this field, refers to the adapted Latin as *Loez*, and this is most likely the language that the Jews migrating into the Rhine Valley carried with them.

Jews already had settled in this area by the time of Charlemagne, late in the eighth century. By the year 1000, according to many scholars, "Judeo-German" was probably a mixture of Hebrew, Aramaic, Loez, and Middle German.

In the eleventh century, the great Bible commentator Rashi, who lived in what the Jews called Zarfat (present-day France), and probably spoke a form of Loez, referred in his writings to *Loshen Ashkenaz*, the tongue of the Jews of the Rhineland, where he had studied—proof that the language was already established by that time.

So far as I can find, the first conscious use of the word "Judisch" (Yiddish) in print occurred in 1478. A document describes a Christian missionary *"der kund ebraisch, Judisch redn,"* that is, he can speak Hebrew and Yiddish. Certainly the language had become the tool of the great mass of Ashkenazi Jews before this date.

Humor Born of Misery

The reason for telling you all this will be clear shortly. First, a few more facts about Jewish history.

The life of the European Jews during the Middle Ages was not always grim, but in general their story is not a pretty one. We're not sure how many Jews lived in the original Ashkenazi areas, but we do know that the First Crusade was a watershed for them. In November 1095 the Pope raised the issue of re-conquering the Holy Land. The first army to embark on this mission, the so-called People's Crusade, attacked the Jewish communities in the Rhineland, and, despite fierce resistance, and protection from some bishops and lords, the Jews were overwhelmed.

These were the first pogroms. They were followed by centuries of persecution and a great deal of animosity from the Church. The Jews suffered massacres, murders, tortures, rapes, forced conversions, legal and physical restrictions, and endless humiliations in Christian Europe.

How does one adapt to such misery? One gets accustomed to being fearful, wary, ready to move, if necessary, and, of course when things are so difficult, *one may find some refuge in humor*. But the jest was bitter. Remember the story about the ghetto cemetery? Unable to get additional space, Jews asked for an anti-dying ordinance!!

So humor can be a defense against oppression. Even the Hitler phenomenon found humor at work. Example:

> Two German police officers grab a Jew in a street in Munich and beat him up. Then one screams, "Jude, who was responsible for the humiliating defeat of the Reich in the First World War?"
> Immediately the Jew responds: "I know. It was the Jews and the pretzel makers."

The German scratches his head. "The pretzel makers? Why the pretzel makers?"

The answer comes back at once: "Why the Jews?"

Apparent stupidity at work to make a fool of the more powerful enemy—humor, the only weapon.

Much of Jewish humor deals with such negative facets of Jewish experience. Therefore it is wry, bitter, ironic. A common Yiddish phrase identifies it as *lachen mit yashtsherkes*, which means literally "laughing with lizards" but is best translated as "laughing through tears."

Ashkenazi Jewry survived despite this history of adversities. And during this time they were carrying on everyday activities: they worked, had children, suffered disease and loss, had religious holidays, celebrated personal events such as bar mitzvahs and marriages, prayed in their synagogues, and so on.

Bitter trials notwithstanding, Ashkenazi life contained joys as well as sorrows. If some of their humor was like acid, other parts were playful. As was mentioned earlier, there is one Jewish holiday, Purim, when Jews are virtually required to forget their normal problems and literally make fools of themselves. So you should understand that Jewish jokes do not represent only laughter through tears.

Go East, Young Man, Go East

In Western Europe, the Jews had been forced from agriculture and also had never been permitted to enter the craft guilds, even though they had always been competent artisans. Their specialties were mainly commerce, money lending (which was taboo for Christians), and tailoring. As life in Western Europe became more and more difficult, Ashkenazim drifted towards the East. Poland and Lithuania were just becoming established nations; they were largely agricultural with little or no developed middle class.

The trickle of emigrants became a flood as Western European countries began to expel Jews around 1300. They settled in Poland, in the Grand Duchy of Lithuania, and in the emerging Russian area. Here they were welcomed because of their competence in finance and commerce. By the end of the fifteenth century there were some sixty Jewish communities in the Poland/Lithuania area. In the next two centuries the tide became stronger. One expert in this field has noted that this "was the first time that Ashkenazi Jewry achieved a large population in any European state." For instance, it is estimated that by the middle of the seventeenth century there were over 50,000 Jews in the Ukraine in as many as 115 settlements.

Linguistic Luggage

Along with the other prized possessions that the Jews carried with them to Eastern Europe was their developed language, Yiddish or Judisch. Two puzzling questions come up here.

First, why didn't the Jews drop their Yiddish and pick up a Judeo-Slavic language? They had apparently had no difficulty losing their Judeo-Latin Loez. One possible reason was that they had to keep in contact with their kin who stayed behind. Also, if they settled in large groups in towns, Judeo-German was the most natural means of communication, as it would later be for their descendants who settled in New York. Maybe, too, German was regarded as the language of a more developed people, in contrast to Slavic languages.

Whatever the reason, Yiddish continued to develop as the language of the Ashkenazim. In the words of the *Encyclopaedia Judaica*, "In the Slavonic territories their use of the Judeo-German language became a prominent distinguishing feature of Ashkenazi Jewry."

The second puzzler has to do with Jews who were already living in Eastern Europe. They had drifted there from Byzantium, Greece, and perhaps the Middle Eastern countries, where there were plenty of Jews. According to Weinreich, they spoke Knaanic, a sort of Judeo-Slavic tongue. Now why did these

Jews lose their patois and ultimately adopt Yiddish, rather than the other way around?

The answer isn't yet clear. Weinreich does note: "We do not know how long after the arrival of the Ashkenazim, Knaanic and Yiddish existed beside each other. . . . By the middle of the fifteenth century, however, Yiddish was already victorious." Possibly the number of speakers of Knaanic was much smaller than that of the newly arriving Yiddish speakers. The reasons given above may also have played a part.

In any case, it was Yiddish that survived and became the dominant language of the Jews settling in the territories of Eastern Europe. However, the language did undergo some changes, absorbing a fair number of Slavic words and expressions. It is estimated that about 20 percent of Yiddish comes from Slavic. (This is not so different from the formation of English–Celtic overlaid with Anglo-Saxon, Church Latin, and Nordic vocabulary and topped off with Norman. The result is a vocabulary rich in synonyms and also in many nuances and shades of meaning.)

In about 1300 there were approximately half a million Ashkenazim compared with about one and a half million other Jews—including the Sephardim of Spain, the Jews of the Middle East, those in northern Africa, and sprinklings elsewhere. Over the next 600 years the Ashkenazim continued to increase while the other Jews decreased. By 1700, there were about a million of each. But in the eighteenth and nineteenth centuries, the East European Ashkenazic population surged.

At the beginning of World War II there were almost 16 million Ashkenazim versus about a million and a half other Jews. Moreover, the Ashkenazim had been migrating from Eastern Europe to Western Europe and North and South America. It is claimed that 85 to 95 percent of the Jews in the United States are descendants of Eastern European Ashkenazim. Clearly, Yiddish-speaking Jews were the culturally dominant segment of the Jewish people. In fact, British historian Toynbee, tells us that when people think of Jews, they virtually always are thinking of these Ashkenazim.

The point of this little historical excursion should be becoming clear: *The roots of what we usually think of as Jewish humor are found in the experiences of these Ashkenazi Jews and in their folk language, Yiddish.* Most modern Jewish humor began as Yiddish humor. The stories in Jewish joke manuals are based in Yiddish, and also many of the stories used by Jewish-American comics have their origin in that language and that experience. (Note I am talking about Jewish humor, not humor *about* Jews, such as some of the derisive anti-Jewish humor created by non-Jews.)

The Jewish Jokers

The preceding sections help to explain why Jews have such a great sense of humor. In regard to Jewish jokes before the development of Yiddish, we have few records. As far as I know, there are no jokes in the Bible. Sarcasm, yes. Elijah taunts the followers of Baal, telling them to call to their god in a louder voice, because maybe he is asleep or deaf. Or, the Israelites, watching the Egyptian army approaching to force them back to slavery, needle Moses: Why did you take us out of Egypt; weren't there any graves for us there? That sort of sarcasm you will see from time to time. But not jokes. Evidently, God didn't think in funny terms when he handed down the Torah.

Still it's possible that people told jokes in ancient Judah. People seem to have done that everywhere. I can imagine one member of King David's court asking another, "Did you see that lady with the king last night?" and getting the answer, "That was no lady. That was my wife!" And in rural areas I can picture a farmer praying for rain to save his crop only to have the Lord provide him with a deluge, to which he may have responded: "God, I asked for help, but not that much!"

These are only guesses, of course. We have no real evidence.

There are, however, several factors that pushed the Jews in the direction of such humor. For example, in the thirteenth century Jews in Italy were compelled to participate in the carnival buffooneries. Let's call it coerced comedy, the comedy of derision. They were forced to make fools of themselves both in what they said and what they did (for example, to be ridden by soldiers). Similarly, many noblemen in the Middle Ages apparently compelled Jews to be court clowns and buffoons. In later centuries, Muslim potentates, such as the sultan in Constantinople, did the same thing.

If Jews could clown for the Christians and Muslims, why not for themselves? The Purim holiday, during which Jews read the story of Esther and the deliverance from Haman, provided a great occasion for this kind of fun. Purim *shpielers* (players) appeared, mainly itinerants, who made fools of themselves, clowning and jesting for Jewish audiences. Rabbis decreed that on this day not only was it permissible to do this but it was obligatory for Jews to have a good time and even to get drunk—the only exception to the rule dictating sobriety for Jews.

Thus, by the fourteenth century a sort of professional class of jokers had appeared, *lezim* (mockers) and *marshaliks* (buffoons). What jokes they told, no one knows.

Later on there appeared the *badchonim* (fools), who were present at Jewish weddings in Eastern Europe, kidding the bride, the groom, and the parents, and providing entertainment for the guests in jokes and songs, many in the form of rhymes, similar to what calypso singers do.

Another strand in this development in the Ukraine and Poland followed a rash of massacres in the seventeenth century. Jewish life then reached a low point of despair and poverty, when a Jewish teacher appeared, a man who came to be known as the *Baal Shem Tov*, the Master of the Good Name. A charismatic figure, though not a great scholar, he taught that prayer did not demand the profound logical display of the Talmudic scholars of the time, but could be accomplished by simple people in simple ways, that singing and dancing and joy of all kinds constituted the touchstone of piety. An anecdote illustrates this perfectly.

A young shepherd, untutored in the Hebrew prayers, comes to the house of prayer. He knows little of what is going on but is deeply impressed by the ritual. How to participate? He pulls out his pipe and starts to play right in the middle of the service, accompanying the prayers as well as he can.

The congregants are aghast. "Stop him, stop him," someone shouts. "He is blaspheming against the Torah reading."

But the Baal Shem Tov quiets everyone. "To the contrary," he announces, "this fellow is probably reaching the Lord better than any of us."

His teachings, given the name of Chasidism (pious action), spread like wildfire throughout the Jewish communities in Eastern Europe, bringing comfort in a time of psychic need. It is reported that one of his disciples, a rabbi, actually felt that it was important to tell jokes at the Sabbath morning services.

The Baal Shem Tov inspired the kind of sentiment that gives us the following story about one of his Chasidic followers.

A Chasid is talking to a *balagolleh* (a wagoner). The latter tells him: "You know, sometimes I feel terrible. Why did God make me a wagoner, without education in our Torah and prayer? I can't even find the time to go to shul regularly."

So the Chasid asks, "If you know a person is poor, do you charge him for riding on your wagon?"

"Many times I let them ride for nothing."

"So don't worry. It is a good deed and a way of serving the *Reboineh Shel Oilem* (the Master of the Universe)!"

So Jewish American comedians did not suddenly appear from nowhere. There is a long Jewish tradition stretching behind them from which they have drawn. The late Harry Golden said: "I heard . . . [stories] as a boy on the Lower East Side of New York. I heard them in Yiddish. But I also heard many of them in English in the American theatre told by comedians who changed the locale and the . . . characters."

Most authentically Jewish jokes, then, are rooted in the language of the Ashkenazim, in Yiddish, and in the thousand-year history of that segment of Jewry. As to whether other segments of the Jewish people have different humor, it's not easy to say. Jewish historian and anthropologist Raphael Patai has said that the humor of Sephardic and Oriental Jews has been greatly neglected. In recent years, Israeli scholars have been digging out their stories. But so far they have not really entered the mainstream of Jewish humor.

And that's the background for understanding Jewish humor.

And in Conclusion

Just a few words before we go our separate ways.

Someone has said that Jews are like everyone else—only more so! I think this book has proved that. It must be clear by now that their joking includes the things other people joke about—and more, for behind the Jewish joke one can see vistas of Jewish life and Jewish history.

I hope that while you were reading, you found yourself smiling, or chuckling, or laughing outright from time to time. The fact is that living in our so-called civilized society demands that we be able to laugh. It's been said that people nowadays are so tense that they can't even fall asleep in church, or, I suppose, in the synagogue.

Jews learned that lesson long ago. And so I leave you with an old Yiddish saying: *Lach! Lach! Duktoirim zugen ahz lachen iz gezunt!* Which means, "Laugh! Laugh! The doctors say that laughing is healthy." Amen!

Index

ABOUT THE AUTHOR

Henry Eilbirt received his B.S. in economics and social sciences and his master's degree in educational psychology from City College of New York. He earned his doctorate in personnel administration from New York University. Dr. Eilbirt has held teaching and administrative positions and was Dean of the School of Business and Public Administration at Baruch College, City University of New York. Now retired and living in California, Dr. Eilbirt considers himself a humorologist and is a popular speaker and storyteller.